As I Saw It

Reviewing over 30 Years
of Fianna Fáil and Irish Politics

Pádraig Faulkner

WOLFHOUND PRESS

First published in 2005 by
Wolfhound Press
An imprint of Merlin Publishing
16 Upper Pembroke Street
Dublin 2, Ireland
Tel: +353 1 676 4373
Fax: +353 1 676 4368
publishing@merlin.ie
www.merlinwolfhound.com

ISBN 0-86327-909-0

A CIP catalogue record for this book is available from the British
Library.

5 4 3 2 1

*The publishers have made every reasonable effort to contact the
copyright holders of photographs reproduced in this book. If any
involuntary infringement of copyright has occurred, sincere
apologies are offered and the owner of such copyright is requested
to contact the publisher.*

Typeset by Gough Typesetting Services
Cover design by Merlin Publishing
Printed and bound by J H Haynes Ltd, Britain

Grá agus Buíochas

Dom' Bheanchéile

Kitty

Agus d'ár gclann

Tomás, Parthalán, Máire agus Pádraig

Contents

Preface

For some years, as the humour took me, I wrote, and rewrote, recollections of my time in Dáil Éireann. I hoped that the presentation of the facts, as I saw them, would help to provide historians with a balanced view of the events which occurred during my time there.

One major event was the great upheaval of 1969/70 and the fallout of the Arms Trial. I deal with this at length as I believe that, after Charlie Haughey and Neil Blaney were dismissed, a flood of propaganda emanated from people within the parliamentary party, and from outside it, against Jack Lynch. We refrained from replying in kind at the time, in the interests of maintaining party unity. This was not a planned policy but a natural reaction by us.

I have no doubt that the stand adopted was the correct one, at the time; reducing as it did internecine wrangling and strife and holding intact the fabric of the State. In the long term, however, permitting inaccurate and distorted accounts of events to go unchallenged over many years often results in the creation of a mythology, which is accepted as fact even by many eminent commentators. I now hope to redress that situation.

Many books, articles and features, dealing with crucial periods of our recent history, including the start of the Troubles and Charlie Haughey's period as leader of Fianna Fáil and Ireland, have been published in recent years. Having given some thought to the matter, I came to the conclusion that it was now time to publish memories of events as I saw them.

One

My Early Years

My grandfather, Pat Faulkner, was born in 1845. When he left the family home in Ballymagera, he rented a derelict building in the village of Dunleer and built a house on the site. He worked as a postman, transporting the mail from Dunleer to Ardee by horse and car and also maintained a horse and sidecar for hire. Later on he set up a fowl and egg business in a store attached to his house. This is the period in which I remember him best – a tall bearded man, wearing a hard hat, whose eye I was most anxious to catch on my way home from school, because, once I had his attention, I became one penny richer.

Pat Faulkner married Mary Daly and they had three sons, James, Patrick and Thomas, the last named being my father. My grandfather purchased a farm at the townlands of Trean and Slieveboy, about 30 statute acres in all, but continued to live at Dunleer. My grandmother died at a relatively early age from goitre. Tradition has it that she sang the Benediction hymns on her deathbed. When she died her family was young and her brother and sisters, who had emigrated to Liverpool, took the eldest boy, James, to live with them. Except for holidays, Jimmy never returned to Ireland. Patrick followed in his father's footsteps and became a postman.

I have heard it said that my father Tommy was also invited to live in Liverpool, but for one reason or another didn't go. He lived with my grandfather and step-grandmother, Mary Anne Torris, at Dunleer. For some time he served as a monitor in Dromin National School, assisting the teacher. Apparently he didn't like teaching and one day, when a man passed by the school driving an ass and cart towards Dunleer, he slipped out the door and onto the cart, never to return. From then on he helped run the farm at the Trean, while continuing to live at Dunleer.

My father was an avid reader. He had a particular interest in politics and actively supported the Irish Parliamentary Party, which supported Home Rule and was led by John Redmond, MP. He was a fine public speaker and addressed public meetings on behalf of Dick Hazelton, the Irish Parliamentary Party candidate. In the early twentieth century Dick Hazelton and Tim Healy, an anti-Parnellite, contested the Louth seat with varying success. My father became a member of the Ancient Order of Hibernians (AOH) and later became County President of the Order.

He once told me about a meeting in Dunleer where young men were being encouraged to join the British army to fight in World War I. He went along with his friend Séamus Laing, a national schoolteacher and ardent Republican. They were both opposed to conscription and Séamus Laing became incensed. As there were many police around, my father advised him not to intervene, pointing out that he would be knocking his head against a stone wall. Laing, however, jumped onto a windowsill facing the platform and called to the Chairman of the meeting to send his own sons to the Front. The enthusiasm of the platform members quickly evaporated.

Thomas married my mother, Elizabeth Casey, in St Patrick's Cathedral, Dundalk, in 1917. They met when she came to Dunleer to work as book-keeper and shorthand typist in Bertie Gannon's garage and shop. She was also interested in politics. My maternal grandfather, John Casey, was, for years, secretary of the Irish National Foresters' Society in Dundalk and served on the Dundalk Urban District Council. The Casey family supported Tim Healy, the anti-Parnellite at this time. I don't know why, but it may have been related to the Catholic Church's attitude *vis-à-vis* Parnell and the divorce case. Later they supported Sinn Féin.

When my father and mother married, two opposing political traditions came together, with my mother supporting an independent Ireland and my father supporting the Home Rule party. A year later, in 1918, a general election was declared. Sinn Féin secured a significant election victory in Ireland but refused to take their seats in the British House of Commons. As the War of Independence continued Sinn Féin successfully took control of some British government powers, especially at local level.

My mother and one of her sisters, Letitia, became very active members of Sinn Féin joining Cumann na mBan, the women's branch. She ran functions to raise funds for the White Cross, an organisation that gave financial assistance to the wives of Republican prisoners in British jails and to the widows of Republicans killed in the struggle for Irish freedom. She also helped to provide safe houses for members of the IRA. I remember one particular story about Paddy Hughes, a Dundalk man and a member of the IRA. During the War of Independence he was on the run and for some time my mother kept him hidden in a room in Gannon's house. As Bertie Gannon, a well-off businessman, was known to have no sympathy with the Republican cause, the police didn't raid his house. The local RIC sergeant, however, knowing my mother's views, was suspicious. He called in on her on a number of occasions, in a futile attempt to get information. Bertie Gannon, who knew what was happening, kept mute at my mother's request. After some time she smuggled Paddy Hughes to Clogherhead, dressed as a priest. Paddy Hughes was a brother of Peter Hughes, later Minister for Defence in the Free State Government.

The Government of Ireland Act 1920 partitioned Ireland between the Irish Free State and a Statelet made up of six counties to be known as Northern Ireland. A truce was arranged in July 1921 between the British Army and the Irish Republican Army and preliminary negotiations were held between Éamon de Valera and Lloyd George, the British Prime Minister.

In December 1921, a negotiating team, headed by Arthur Griffith and Michael Collins, was sent to London to discuss a treaty. The Treaty offered the Irish delegation much less than a Republic and retained partition. The Treaty was signed, but de Valera, amongst others, was not prepared to accept it.

The provisions of the Treaty were discussed in the Dáil in December 1921/January 1922. Lloyd George had promised to set up a Commission to examine the partition question and all sides in the Dáil were led to believe that large areas with Nationalist majorities in Northern Ireland would be transferred to the Free State, thus making Northern Ireland non-viable. With this in mind the partition question was sidelined in the debate and the question of monarchy took centre stage. After much discussion the Treaty was approved on January 7, 1922, by 64 votes to 57 votes. Éamon de Valera resigned the presidency, which was taken over by Arthur Griffith.

Civil War broke out between the pro-Treaty side, led by Michael Collins, and the anti-Treaty forces led by Liam Lynch and later by Frank Aiken. Both Michael Collins and Liam Lynch were killed in the fighting and Arthur Griffith died of a heart attack. While my Aunt Letitia continued to be active on the anti-Treaty side during the Civil War, the presence of a very young family restricted my mother's involvement. She was little more than an observer, though there was never any doubt as to where her sympathies lay. The Irish Free State forces arrested Letitia and she served a period of imprisonment in Kilmainham jail. Paddy Lalor's mother Frances Kelly was with her in prison. Many years later I served in the Dáil with Paddy Lalor, TD Laois/Offaly.

The pro-Treaty forces won the Civil War and they formed a political party, Cumann na nGael, later Fine Gael, under W T Cosgrave. Anti-Treaty Sinn Féin continued in existence, but its TDs refused to take their seats in Leinster House. Éamon de Valera formed a new party, Fianna Fáil, in 1926, taking many of the Sinn Féin TDs with him. They entered the Dáil in 1927.

With the establishment of the Irish Free State in 1922, my father, like the majority of the Parliamentary Party supporters and the members of the AOH in Louth, lent his support to the Cumann na nGael party led by W T Cosgrave. My mother continued to support Sinn Féin and later Fianna Fáil. Throughout the upheavals of the Civil War period, and throughout their lives, my parents both clung tenaciously to their own political philosophies. This was unusual in rural Ireland as, at the time, the wife usually adopted the husband's political views, but they respected one another's viewpoint. I cannot recall that either allowed the slightest degree of bitterness to intrude on family life, even in periods when political tensions were high. There were, of course, many minor incidents. My father had a bust of John Redmond of which he was particularly proud and he never tired of showing it off to visitors. As my mother then taught me to say 'Up de Valera' every time the bust was exhibited, my father became somewhat circumspect about displaying it in our presence.

On one occasion our house was raided by the Black and Tans. My mother later told me that as I sat on her knee during the raid, she pinched me to make me cry. She was afraid I would mention the names of IRA members whom she knew. Peculiarly enough, I have a faint memory of that raid. In my mind's eye I can see strangely garbed men stretching up their arms to see if there was anything on top of the dresser that would connect us with the IRA.

Shortly before my birth my mother returned to her mother's home at Seatown, Dundalk, and I first saw the light of day there on March 12, 1918. I was baptised in St Patrick's Cathedral and we remained in Dundalk for a short time. We then went back to live with my father, my grandfather and my step-grandmother at Dunleer. My mother had very fond memories of my step-grandmother, who died shortly afterwards.

Some time later we moved to the farmhouse at the Trean, Dunleer. The farmhouse was a rather long building built with a mixture of stones, lime and yellow clay, with a thatched roof. The outer walls were whitewashed and when newly thatched and painted looked very well indeed. It had the advantage of being cool in summer and warm in winter. As the family grew, a new room was needed, which was built with the aid of a £40 grant from Louth County Council.

Our house was built on a height, facing south. From the rear, on a bright day, there was a marvellous view of the Cooley and Mourne Mountains. When I was quite young I read Standish O'Grady's books on Cúchulann, *The Coming of Cúchulann*, *The Gates of the North* and *The Triumph and Passing of Cúchulann*. As much of Cúchulann's activities were reputed to have taken place around my home I found myself, in my imagination, playing hurling with him, or, indeed, rushing around with him in his chariot as he defended Ulster against the men of Connacht. I became so imbued with the Cúchulann saga that, many years later, when I was a student in St Patrick's Teacher Training College and a professor asked me from which province I had come I replied, 'Ulster'. I was quickly brought down to earth when the student who sat next to me, said: 'Louth is not in Ulster.' The Cúchulann saga developed in me a love of history, which ultimately, I feel, led me into political life. In a sense it encouraged me to play a role in what will eventually become history.

My father continued to work the farm for his father and was paid ten shillings a week, on which our family was expected to live. Life was tough on a small farm at the time, and later on, the provision of the necessities of life for a family of six children, four girls and two boys, Clementine, Maura, Nuala, Theresa and Sean, was a struggle. Owning a small farm ensured that we, at least, had enough to eat and while luxuries were in very short supply, what we never had we didn't miss. Basic foodstuffs at the time were porridge meal, home-baked bread, homemade butter, home-cured bacon, eggs, milk and potatoes, and to that extent there was self-sufficiency. Eggs and homemade butter were exchanged with the bread man for baked bread and similarly exchanged with the grocer to pay his bill. Money, however, was needed for other necessities such as clothes, coal, furniture, schoolbooks and the all-important tea. The availability of ready cash depended on the sale of cattle, calves, bonhams, fat pigs and corn in the harvest time. Should the crops and livestock do well, then purchases could be made, but should crops fail, much-needed purchases were put off until the following year. Small farmers, a sturdy and independent people, could not afford to fall into debt.

Mixed farming was the norm in our district. We grew small amounts of a variety of crops, kept two horses for ploughing, tilling and carting, four cows, which, judged by today's standards, were of doubtful value, cattle, pigs and poultry. In the haggard were ricks of hay and straw. Fat pigs were in demand then and I can remember that the buyer invariably began negotiating the price by saying, 'Aw, they are narra'. At Christmas time my mother reared turkeys, one for ourselves and the remainder for sale.

Cattle were sold at fairs held on the main street in Dunleer once a month. Haggling over the price went on for hours. When agreement was finally reached it was sealed by each man slapping the other's hand. We younger folk were much more concerned with the stall owners who attended each fair with stalls laden with a wide variety of sweets and other goodies. The big fair day was held on May 14, a date beloved by all Dunleer schoolchildren, as the national school closed. Our theme song was:

> *The fourteenth of May*
> *The big fair day*
> *If we don't get a holiday*
> *We'll all run away.*

When I was young basic foodstuffs were relatively cheap, and farm workers' wages, especially when the worker lived in, were low, so most small farmers kept a workman. He usually slept in the loft and dined with the family. As a boy I remember once stooking barley with our workman. When the bell tolled for six o'clock I told him that I was going home. He pointed to the sheaves still lying on the ground to be stooked before nightfall but I persisted and left. When he arrived home, much later in the evening, he told my father he could make what he liked of me, but he certainly wouldn't make a farmer of me.

As our family grew larger and economic circumstances worsened, we could no longer afford a hired help and the children took over the chores. During the very busy farming seasons, haymaking and harvesting, neighbours co-operated with one another to ensure that the crops were saved. We enjoyed haymaking and harvesting, especially jaunting on the hayslide.

Clocks, and more particularly watches, were rare in those days. When working in the fields the church bell tolling told us when twelve noon and six o'clock in the evening had arrived. In our district we could see the trains passing by and these were also our timekeepers. When thinning turnips, we were always particularly happy to see the goods train pass by at 5.20 pm – only 40 minutes to go to stopping time. Dinnertime in our house, and indeed in all the houses in the district, was at 12 noon and work commenced again at one o'clock.

My father was responsible for farming generally. Even though not reared in a farming tradition he made a reasonable success of it. In the depths of the Economic War with Britain, when farm produce and particularly cattle were at a disastrously low price, we survived. His life was a very arduous one as almost all work was done manually. He tilled the land, sowed the seeds and cared for his crops. I played my own part in this work. I well remember one occasion when I was raking hay, the horse stopped unexpectedly and an iron prong cut into my leg. I unyoked the horse and ran home to be treated by my mother with iodine and ointment and was none the worse for it, but the mark is still there to this day. I can also still recall my grand-uncle teaching me a certain way of making a tying, to tie up the sheaves of corn after the mowing machine had cut them, so it must have impressed me. As children our job was to gather up the pieces of straw scattered around. We called this work tacaring, from the Irish *ag tacar*, meaning gathering or gleaning. When the threshing mill arrived we followed it from haggard to haggard because we invariably were given bread and tea at each house. It wasn't any different from what we got at home but the plus factor was that it was in somebody else's house and the sweeter for that.

When working in the fields the tea was invariably taken there in a tin can with enormous amounts of bread and butter. Everybody sat down and, as the tea and bread was consumed, the workers smoked their pipes and chatted for a good while on a variety of topics. If I had been told then that a machine called a combine would harvest a big field in a very short space of time my reaction would have been that it would give farmers and their workers more time for chatting. Unfortunately the opposite is the case.

My father also milked the cows by hand and a small bit of the milk was used at mealtime. The rest was kept in large crocks where it became sour and was then churned into butter. We regarded it as a great scientific development when we got a separator machine, which separated the cream from the milk. In summer the cows were milked in the field and I often did this job. I had to be careful because, as happened to me once, if a cow became fractious she might knock over the bucket and spill all the milk.

My mother, a townswoman, took to country life like a born rural dweller. She looked after the family, the household chores and the fowl. My mother was, in fact, the general manager, taking control of what little money was available, thus ensuring that our heads remained above water. She was small in stature, but so far as we children were concerned, she was the authority. Nobody dared disobey her commands. She was basically a kind and gentle person, always at the beck and call of neighbours who needed assistance, but we all knew where we stood. My father rarely took us to task.

On occasion, when called on by my mother he went through the motions of taking his belt off to punish the offender, but we all soon learned that the belt would never actually come off. My mother's commands were far more significant, so far as we were concerned, than twenty paternal belts.

My mother was a far-seeing woman in another sense. Coming from a town where post-primary education was available, she saw to it that her family was well-educated. This was very much the exception for a small farmer's family in rural Ireland at the time. It is true to say that I, as the eldest son, benefited most from this approach. Traditionally in rural Ireland, the eldest son inherited the farm and from an early age was kept at home to work on it. He usually remained unmarried until the younger members of the family had left home. Since my mother was determined to see to it that I received an education, my life took a different route.

The pleasures, the escapades and the general happiness of my youth are clearly etched on my mind to this day. Thankfully, the sadness, the pain and the suffering are effaced and all but forgotten. My parents worked well as a team. They did their best to ensure that we were well-reared, and so far as they could manage it, happy as well. We all had a deep affection and respect for our parents. They worked extremely hard, in difficult times, to feed and clothe us. They attended Mass each Sunday, said their prayers each day and by precept and example taught us to use our best endeavours to be faithful to God's law and to respect and help our neighbour. In the process our characters and our attitudes developed, resulting, I think I can say, in smoothing the rugged path of life for others as well as for members of our own family. I owe my parents a debt of gratitude for their loving care and for the cultural heritage they passed on to me.

It was an era when everyday living was also influenced in many ways by religious beliefs. A large majority of the population in my area was made up of Catholics but sectarianism, as such, did not exist in Dunleer. Farmers, especially, assisted one another whenever the need arose, regardless of their religious persuasion. However, although we learned our lessons and played together, the fact that some of the children did not attend the religious classes at school, gave us the feeling that there was something strange about them. I remember a woodwork class in which a large number of boys, including two Protestants, participated. Apart from the name of a boy who lived close to me, I can now only remember the names of the two Protestant boys, which exemplifies the same attitude. I cannot remember being explicitly told to keep away from Protestant churches, but there was a general feeling that they should be avoided. As I grew up attitudes were changing. Today cordial relations exist between people of all faiths in Louth.

Incidentally, from my earliest days, I never felt repressed by my church. Some people, who pride themselves on being Liberals, now spend a considerable amount of energy endeavouring to convince us that such was the case. I, however, tend to agree with Liam de Paor's comment about Woodrow Wilson, the President of the United States during World War I. De Paor commented that like all true Liberals, Wilson believed that people should be allowed to believe what they liked, so long as it was something in which he believed. Many of those who attack the church in modern times are guilty of the type of intolerance and intransigence of which they accuse the church. Missionaries preached Hellfire sermons in my young days, supposedly to frighten the wits out of us and to keep us in a subservient condition.

The reality was that if such sermons were not preached the general consensus was that the mission had been an unmitigated failure. I have long been convinced that my firm belief in my own faith helped me, as I grew older, to appreciate and respect the sincerity of those who professed a different faith and helped me to be much more tolerant than I might otherwise have been.

At the time, the Catholic Church not only provided religious ceremonies but its religious orders provided services such as health, education and social welfare. Father Thomas Magee PP, for example built Dunleer National School in 1836 at an estimated cost of £180 18 shillings. This was the same schoolhouse that I entered, as a pupil, in the early 1920s. It was divided into two rooms, one for the boys and one for the girls. There were still the same small paned windows, the same long, rough and heavy desks, the same official notices on the walls, except that some of these soon appeared in the Irish language, as the new Saorstát Éireann Government policy developed.

I was taken to Dunleer Boys' National School for the first time by my aunt, Peg Casey, who taught in the Girls' National School and who lived with us in the Trean. In my early school days quite a number of us went off to school in a large group each day and we soon became known as 'the Trean Boys and Girls'. In summer some boys went to school in their bare feet, which they hugely enjoyed. Even where boys began the journey with boots on they tended to take them off and hang them around their necks by the laces before reaching the school building.

The playground at the back of the school was divided in two by sheets of galvanise. The girls occupied one side and the boys the other. Another playground at the front was for the boys' use only. School medical services were non-existent and toilet facilities were primitive. A pump near the road supplied water for the district and we sometimes used it to get a drink. There were two single sex schools in Dunleer, while there were also two mixed schools in the parish. The church and the education authorities regarded single sex schools as the ideal and mixed schools were accepted out of necessity. Today the reverse is often the norm.

Looking back on my national school days I remember such games as marbles, skipping, catch, tig, skittles and button pitching. To own a ball was the exception. In my later days at Dunleer NS we went down to the ball alley at lunchtime to play handball, which was the 'in thing' at the time, rather than football.

Louth County Council offered six post-primary scholarships each year. When my parents found me reading Canon Sheehan's *Lisheen* at nine years of age, they evidently felt that I could win a scholarship. In 1932 I succeeded in winning one worth £20 a year for five years. As large bullocks were being sold at the time for £6 or £7 each, I was now, in terms of small farmer finance, a wealthy young man. My mother chose the Christian Brothers' School, Dundalk, rather than Drogheda, which was closer to home, because I could have a mid-day meal in my grandmother's house in Dundalk each day.

I started my new school life in September 1932, catching the bus at 8.20 am and arriving home at about 5 pm. I can remember running the mile from my home to Dunleer, each morning, hampered by a can of milk for my grandmother and thoroughly enjoying the bus ride. I travelled on the GNR bus. At the time HMS Catherwood Ltd, based in Northern Ireland, provided another bus service. There was an intense rivalry between the bus companies, in which we young people participated. We took great pleasure in recounting the story that Catherwood wouldn't purchase as much as a tyre in the Free State. To us the initials HMS must surely stand for His Majesty's Service. At a time when the new Irish Government in the early 1930s, was in the process of abolishing the Oath of Allegiance to the King of England, we felt very patriotic indeed travelling on the GNR bus. There was, however, a fly in the ointment. Our very old and much loved parish priest always travelled on the Catherwood bus, where we noted that he was treated with great courtesy by the bus conductor. We may have felt that the parish priest was letting the side down, but I'm certain we didn't express such a view in public.

As a result of the extra distance to Dundalk few local boys travelled with me. Dundalk CBS was an 'A' school, where all subjects, except English, were taught through the Irish language. The staff was small, consisting of a couple of Christian Brothers and a few lay teachers. Their commitment to their pupils was of a very high order. The teachers, both religious and lay, were nationally minded, with a particular interest in the Irish language, which they regarded as a major symbol of nationhood.

Our maths teacher, Joe Tallon, a brilliant mathematician, compiled a geometry textbook in the Irish language for use in post-primary schools. He had taken part, with his brother Séamas, in the Easter Rising in the GPO in 1916. I already followed my mother's political philosophy and these beliefs were strengthened during my secondary school career by the atmosphere that prevailed in the school.

For a short time during my early days in the CBS I had some difficulty in adjusting to being taught in Irish. I still remember being asked in Irish for an answer to an algebra problem. I replied in English, 'seven'. The question was repeated several times with the same result and I was wondering why my fellow pupils were grinning at me. I was beginning to think I had the wrong answer when I finally tumbled to the fact that 'seacht' was the right one. I don't think I had any difficulty with it from then on.

Brother Kennedy, a man of outstanding ability and character, was the Superior. He was an excellent teacher with a great love of the Irish language. He left an indelible imprint on generations of young men in Dundalk and district. He was a disciplinarian, who very rarely used the leather; nevertheless his word was law and nobody even thought of disobeying him. In all my years at the school I saw him use the strap only once. It was on a boy who had 'mitched' from school for some time and successfully cloaked his absence from his parents by collecting letters sent home from the school before his parents saw them.

I can well recall the day when Brother Kennedy asked me my age and when I said that I was over 16 years he produced a Pioneer pin and stuck it in the lapel of my coat. At the time it would hardly have been regarded as a momentous occasion, but I have long appreciated its worth in helping to shape my lifestyle. That same year our old-fashioned desks were replaced by dual desks and George McAdam and I were placed in the same one. From that simple beginning a lifelong friendship evolved.

* * * *

I sat the Leaving Certificate Examination in 1936, and as a result I went to St Patrick's Teacher Training College, Drumcondra, Dublin, to train as a national schoolteacher. The transition from CBS Dundalk to St Pats was a traumatic one. The majority of the college students had come from preparatory colleges; they knew one another and were used to institutional life. The small number of us who arrived through open competition had rarely been away from home before. I soon settled down, however, and when, some months later, I was offered a place in the Civil Service, having consulted with Brother Kennedy, I turned it down. This decision, although I didn't know it at the time, had major implications for my future career.

Life in St Pats was very confined in those days. We were only allowed to leave the college grounds for a few hours, a couple of days each week, and on Sunday morning. Apart from that our time was spent praying, attending lectures, studying, playing games and dancing. It was an all-male environment, within the confines of the high walls, encircling the College grounds. Pocket money, for most of us, was scarce and walking into the city and window gazing provided our chief entertainment, except for an odd visit to matinées in the Drumcondra Grand Cinema. When Mussolini, then at the height of his power in Italy, appeared on newsreels, the children invariably booed him. To add to the atmosphere, we embryo teachers clapped him, with the expected consequences.

One incident that occurred during my time at St Pats illustrates the awe in which the new field of broadcasting was held at the time. Gus Redmond, Professor of Music, was an exceptionally able choirmaster and conductor. In 1937/38 his student choir was of a high quality and were invited to give a performance on Radio Éireann. We arrived at the GPO in O'Connell St, Dublin, then the headquarters of Radio Éireann, and we were conducted upstairs to the broadcasting studio. The studio was a large room with little more equipment than a microphone hanging from the ceiling and a red bulb on the wall, which would light up to indicate that the performance should begin. Gus Redmond was a tough little man who, apparently, feared nothing. However, when he took his place in front of the choir, with one eye on the choir and the other on the red bulb, he suddenly said: 'If I should collapse, continue singing.' We were surprised to say the least. The performance, however, was excellent and Mr Redmond was still on his feet when it was over.

On very rare occasions students were granted what was known as a 'free' night when they could remain abroad until the unearthly hour of 11.30 pm. On such occasions most of us attended a dance in the Teachers' Club in Parnell Square, and, for a few brief hours, we were in contact with the great wide world.

Authoritarianism was in full flow at the time, and was experienced even in the students' own regulations, passed down from generation to generation. The second year students, or seniors, were known as 'Most Pure Gents'. They occupied the rear of the large study and had their own dormitory. All of these were out of bounds for first year or junior students, known as 'Most Vile Hedgers', and any infringement of the rules was punished, sometimes physically, by the seniors. When our junior final examination was completed, we juniors congregated beneath a fountain in the enclosure and as the water drops fell on us were transformed into 'Most Pure Gents', provided of course that we passed the exam.

My scholarship had paid most of my college fee of £22.10s. for the first year. My parents had to borrow the £22.10s to pay for my second year. It was, however, only when I joined a branch of the St Vincent de Paul Society in the college that I realised what real poverty meant. Social welfare payments were almost non-existent at that time and in one house 17 families lived there, each occupying a single room. I used to visit a family every Sunday morning and present them with dockets for food and clothing. They lived and slept in a basement room and none of the family was employed. We had the greatest sympathy for them, living in circumstances where the putrid air made it very difficult to even pass over the threshold. Thankfully, new housing schemes were helping to eliminate overcrowding, but we thought the process was much too slow.

The nation was, however, developing. The college professors deserve great credit for the successful manner in which, with scarce resources, they provided the country with large numbers of qualified national schoolteachers who contributed in a significant way to the development of the Irish Republic. I only discovered, many years later, that these professors had, then, neither pension rights nor security of tenure.

The two year teacher-training course finally came to an end. The familiar sound of the Dean's voice as he entered the dormitory at 7 am, calling out *Benedictamus Domino* followed by a sleepy *Deo Gratias* from us, would be no more. With the final exams completed and, hopefully, successfully passed we were no longer 'Most Pure Gents' but, at long last were fully qualified national teachers. As we made our farewells and passed through the college gates for the last time I was only too well aware, as were my friends, that teaching posts were scarce and that quite a number of our predecessors had not got permanent posts. So it was with more hope than expectation that we faced our new world.

I was lucky – I found out that a teacher was about to retire from a school just six miles from my home. I applied for the position and was fortunate enough to get it. I spent a carefree summer awaiting my first job, which would begin in October 1938.

Two

The Teaching Years

I began my teaching career on October 3, 1938, starting as an assistant teacher in Clogherhead National School, Co Louth. I could not help but feel a certain satisfaction that for the first time in my life I was not a pupil or a student, but a teacher doing an important job and getting paid for it. An added bonus was that as my new job was close to home, I was able to make the journey by bicycle each day.

I had responsibility for infants, first and second classes. Shortly after I started I was worried when the school manager told me that the Department had refused to sanction my appointment. I had fallen foul of Rule 127(b). For a male teacher to be officially recognised as an assistant teacher in a boys' school, the school had to have a certain average attendance. The problem was that the infant boys I was teaching were officially in the girls' school. Without these infants, the school did not have the numbers to employ a male teacher. In the meantime, the manager of Blackpitts NS in Dublin had written to St Pats looking for a newly trained teacher. When I was offered the Dublin post I told the school manager that while I was most anxious to remain in Clogherhead, the matter of sanction would need to be cleared up quickly or I would have to go to Dublin. A sense of urgency, missing up to that point, took over and thankfully the Department sanctioned my appointment. I received the three months salary, £36 15s, due to me and the sun shone more brightly than ever before.

After that somewhat uncertain start I quickly settled into my first job as a teacher. My education both at secondary school and at college had been conducted through Irish. I had acquired a good speaking knowledge of the language, but when I left St Pats in 1938 I had no particular interest in Irish as such. I simply regarded it as a part of our culture that had almost disappeared and as a subject to be taught. Strangely enough my real interest in the language stemmed from my early teaching days. I realised that in the circumstances of the time a high standard of Irish would be required of any young teacher so I set to work to try to achieve this.

From the outset I used Irish as the language of the classroom. At first this method proved to be a frustrating task, as the children had no idea what I was saying. Persistence, however, won out. Repetition ensured that the children picked up and understood a word here and a phrase there. Eventually they spoke a somewhat garbled version of the language, for which they received due praise. A penny prize to the child who spoke most Irish in the playground heightened their interest, particularly as I unashamedly chose a different pupil each time. When a little fellow named Joey used the word *gheobhfaidh* correctly, I remember saying to the class: '*Dúirt Joey gheobhfaidh agus gheobhfaidh Joey pingin.*' The word *gheobhfaidh* was firmly implanted in the children's vocabulary ever after. When I saw how quickly the children picked up the language and how fluent they had become in a relatively short space of time I became an enthusiast. I was convinced that if this important facet of our national culture could be revived we could become a bilingual people.

There were times in my early days as a teacher, however, when the bureaucratic approach of officialdom almost drove me to despair. I will always remember one particular incident. An English reading lesson, 'The Crow and the Pitcher', was in progress in the presence of the school inspector. In English he asked the children to tell him the crow's colour and a pupil replied '*dubh*'. I was very pleased but the inspector was not. After he left the Inspector's Observation Book informed me that when questioned in English the child should reply in English. I simply couldn't believe it. Of course I knew the reply should have been in English but I thought that the child's reply in Irish was something of an achievement and merited, at least, a kindly word.

Despite these ups and downs, I continued to awaken an interest in the Irish language among my pupils. This was highlighted by a number of incidents. Every year, the Railway Cup competition was broadcast in Irish on St Patrick's Day. It was, then, an important feature in the GAA calendar, and one year, as quite a number of Louth players were on the Leinster team, there was tremendous interest in our district. Few people could understand the Irish language and so one pupil proudly acted as interpreter. On another occasion, a group of pupils employed thinning turnips spoke Irish so that the farmer could not understand their conversation. He told me that it reminded him of his young days, when old women in the district spoke Irish to one another so that the children could not understand what was being said.

Episodes such as these, simple in themselves, underscored the point that the Irish language was no longer simply a school subject to these young people but was a useful means of communication. I was greatly encouraged. It is interesting to note that despite the fact that the Normans had conquered my area of County Louth before 1200 AD, introducing their language, the Irish language had endured. It continued to be spoken by some of the older generation within living memory. I once asked an old Republican in mid-Louth if he thought the Irish language would have been completely saved if we had obtained our freedom 100 years earlier. He doubted it as he feared that if we had achieved freedom then it would not have been Gaelic orientated.

I persevered and my pupils' Irish came on by leaps and bounds. I quickly settled into the day to day routine of my life but I will always remember one day during that first year when, standing at a school door facing the sea, I saw a large vessel appear on the horizon. I later learned it was a German warship. The ship was soon surrounded by three British destroyers and they all disappeared from view. World War II was about to break out and this was a sign of things to come.

When my first year ended I was glad to have the summer holidays to look forward to. In August 1939 I spent a holiday in my Uncle Jimmy's house in Liverpool. Many of the people there had been involved with, or at least remembered, World War I and they were depressed and fearful. The hope that Chamberlain's peace pact with Hitler had brought them was fading fast. I left Liverpool for home on the last night before the 'blackout' and I still have a vivid memory of having camouflaged ships pointed out to me, as they lay lined up at the dock, on the opposite side of the Mersey. I would never have been aware of them otherwise. It was to be many years before I visited Liverpool again.

On reaching Dublin I was on my way to Amien Street station when I read in a newspaper that German troops had invaded Poland. On September 3, 1939, as I went to Mass, I learned of Chamberlain's broadcast to the British people. He had declared that Britain was now at war with Germany. The world was never to be the same again.

The Irish Government, under Éamon de Valera, adopted a policy of neutrality, and throughout the war, despite threats and scares from powerful sources, that policy remained intact. Ireland was now faced with a wide variety of problems and difficulties. Without a merchant navy many necessities could not be imported, including wheat. Farming, always of great importance in the Irish economy, was now a vital element in ensuring our very existence. Compulsory tillage was introduced. Home-grown wheat replaced the foreign variety even though farmers complained about the damage they claimed wheat growing was causing their land. Consumers, for a time, resented the brown/black bread made from Irish wheat, which replaced the white bread, but they soon got used to it. Fertilisers were in short supply but farmers co-operated with one another and achieved miracles. Cattle, sheep, pigs and other types of food were exported to Britain. Tea was rationed to a half ounce per person per week. Sugar was scarce. I can well remember a parody on an English dance tune *Bless 'em all* which went: 'Bless de Valera and

Seán McEntee/For the loaf of black bread and the half ounce of tea.'

Raw materials for many of our industries were virtually non-existent. Some of these industries closed down, while others changed products. A local factory at Dunleer, for example, that normally produced electrical goods changed over to making wooden toys. Thousands of people became unemployed, many of them joining the rapidly expanding Irish army, while others emigrated to England. Petrol and oil stocks were severely depleted, so private cars vanished from our roads. Most cars had their wheels removed while the body was placed on cement blocks in a shed, there to remain until the end of the war.

Clothes were rationed and coupons, as well as cash, were needed to purchase them. When rationing was introduced it took some time to have coupons issued. One draper in my area lost out by selling garments before the coupons were available. He had serious difficulty replenishing his stocks.

Bus and train services were few during the war. The bicycle and the pony and trap were the principal means of transport, so movement was limited. For entertainment and sporting activities we were thrown back on our own resources. Our minds were fully occupied in planning what to do next and, interestingly enough the word 'bored' was never heard. A group of us got together in Dunleer and we established a new Gaelic football team, named Lannléire, the ancient name of Dunleer. Later, when I taught at Phillipstown NS, Dunleer, I helped a number of local people to establish another Gaelic football team called St Kevin's. From the ranks of the newly formed Local Defence Force (LDF) an athletic club was formed, mainly for young men but including young women. They competed in running and bicycle races at sports' meetings. Both the football team and the athletic club events attracted large crowds of spectators. Louth GAA teams had a relatively high standard at the time, and large numbers of people travelled to Croke Park. These games, especially when Louth was victorious, were a topic of conversation for weeks on end.

St Brigid's Hall, Dunleer, had a large room with a billiard table, a smaller room where cards were played and another room where the older members sat listening to a radio, a scarce commodity at the time. The hall had achieved some notoriety when the Black and Tans raided it and stole the pipe bands' musical instruments. St Brigid's was for the use of men and boys only. In the era before the acceptance of equality, women's rights were not heeded. The attendance each evening was excellent and the age mixture greatly assisted discipline. Unfortunately, as the war continued and fuel became scarce, the hall was closed.

Another local hall was used for drama presentations and ceilithe and other forms of dancing. It was packed to capacity when the local drama group or travelling players performed there. A local curate, a beautiful singer himself, organised a number of talent competitions, and some artists, who later became famous, cut their teeth on the Dunleer stage. In the early 1940s large numbers of young people were taught Irish dancing there. Later, when a Céilí Mór was held, with the seven McCusker brothers from South Armagh providing the music, the demand was so great that you had to arrive early to ensure admission. A variety of clubs also organised dances. These were well attended, especially when the Carlton Band or Jackson's Band from Drogheda or the Regal Band from Castleblaney, was booked. Films were also shown in the hall.

So while there were problems and difficulties and shortages affecting our lives during the war, we managed to bring a little balance into the equation. However, when bombs destroyed the house of my uncle in Liverpool our family quickly returned to the real world. During the war I remember seeing a German fighter plane closely followed by an English fighter plane, fly low at great speed over the schoolhouse at Clogherhead. We were also constantly reminded that war was in progress when the bodies of airmen and seamen were washed ashore.

In our locality and, I believe, throughout the State, Irish people had an ambivalent attitude towards the combatants. They didn't mind seeing the pride of Britain and its Empire getting a bit of a knocking. They listened regularly, and with some pleasure, to *Lord Haw Haw* and commented caustically on British pronouncements on strategic withdrawals when it was obvious that they had been forced to retreat. Nevertheless, except for a few extremists, they did not want Germany to win the war. Despite the age long fight for Irish freedom, the Irish people were closely associated with Britain. Numerous Irish relatives and friends lived there, and there were close commercial and economic ties. While there might be conflicting thoughts in many minds on the subject, the heads rather than the hearts ruled the day.

In 1944, as the war continued, I was appointed Principal teacher at Phillipstown National School, Dunleer, with responsibility for third, fourth, fifth and sixth classes. Phillipstown was a mixed school with a large number of boys and girls on the roll. It was my first time teaching in a mixed school and I wondered how I would manage. I discovered in a very short time that I saw the boys and girls simply as pupils.

When I arrived at the school my predecessor, John J O'Neill, whom I had known for some time awaited me. We shook hands; he welcomed me and wished me well in my future endeavours.

The school building had been built in 1862. Vere Foster, the well-known philanthropist, had prevailed on his older brother to provide a

site from his estate for a new school. Over 80 years later the school was now in rather poor condition. There were three short desks in the junior room and when the number on the rolls reached 85, I had great sympathy for the assistant teacher, because the children were forced to sit all over the place, including the floor. When I went into the room each day to call the roll, I had to step very gingerly indeed. However, we managed as well as we could until a new school was built in 1954.

As in Clogherhead, I found the children in Phillipstown pleasant and co-operative. I also discovered that teaching senior pupils was more congenial and I would not have wished to go back to teaching the junior classes.

World War II was moving towards a climax with the invasion of France by June 1944. As we had been on the periphery of the conflict there were no dramatic changes in our circumstances but the shortages and other restrictions continued as the years passed.

On September 14, 1948, I married Kitty Landy, who, like myself, was a native of Dunleer parish and came from a large family with a farming background. I had known Kitty and her family for quite some time but as we lived some distance apart on either side of Dunleer, we rarely met. However, when I produced a play for the local community, *The Money Doesn't Matter* by Louis Dalton, in which Kitty had a part, we started to meet regularly at rehearsals. The only thing I can remember about the play, apart from the fact that I met Kitty, was a conversation between a farmer and his farmworker about money. The workman said to the farmer that he couldn't understand why people were so concerned about money because, after all, what more could anybody want but enough and a little over, to which the farmer replied: 'Yes, but it is the little over that is the problem!' Human nature changes little.

Kitty and I had met regularly after the play and a couple of years later we decided to get married. We had set the date of 15 September 1948, but as the day approached we were reminded that it was one of the Ember days, a day of abstinence, and as no exemptions were allowed at the time, we brought the wedding forward to the 14th. It was 1948 and Ireland had not yet recovered from the war shortages so we had to supply the hotel hosting the wedding reception with some of the food and drink. I also remember that we had only one film for our camera. Despite these minor problems, the marriage took place and, thank God, we have had a long and a happy life together.

We were fortunate that a teacher's residence was available at Phillipstown, so we didn't have to look for a place to live. It was a single-storey house, which had a further storey added to it and we were very glad to have it. Vere Foster also helped to finance the residence. Foster spent much of his fortune financing the development of education, and when the Irish National Teachers' Organisation (INTO) was established, he was elected its first president, even though he was never a teacher. All four of our children, Tom, Bartle, Mary and Pat were born while we lived in the Phillipstown house.

It was shortly after my marriage that the rural electrification scheme was introduced. It did wonders to assist the development of facilities in rural Ireland. Not only did we have the prospect of light being available at the touch of a switch but more important still it would be possible to pipe water into the houses. In a district where we all carried cans of fresh water to our homes from a well half a mile away, this would make a great difference. With a neighbour I canvassed the people of the area, asking them to join the scheme and in the main we were successful.

As their houses were being connected the children were delighted and fascinated. They quickly adjusted to the facility that meant there was no more need for oil lamps or candles. As a new school had been proposed for Phillipstown the existing building was not connected. We had to wait until the new school was built in 1954. In the meantime I found having electricity at home particularly helpful in preparing class materials.

I had been the Principal at Phillipstown for six years when, in 1950, I was co-opted onto Coiste na Coláiste (The College Committee) of the Irish college in Rann na Feirste, Co Donegal and appointed treasurer of the college. I was pleased in view of my interest in the language and because I would be in regular touch with native Irish speakers for at least one month of my summer holidays for some time to come. An tAthair Lorcáin Ó Muirigh, a noted Gaelic scholar and GAA activist, had founded an Irish college in Omeath, Co Louth, where native Irish speakers were still to be found at the time. But by the early 1920s he recognised that Irish as a spoken language was in decline in Omeath. I knew the last native speaker, Mrs O'Hanlon, who spoke the language beautifully, interspersing her conversation with poetry and song. An tAthair Ó Muirigh set out to establish a new college in a district where the language was in full bloom. He finally decided on the beautiful area of Rann na Feirste, Co Donegal, and the first group of students arrived there in 1926. The college, which was built of flimsy material, was blown down in the winter but a much more solid structure replaced it. Large numbers of students attended the college each summer, many of them returning year after year. By 1950 about 500 students attended the college each year.

An tAthair Ó Muirigh had laid down the college rules, most of which, were concerned with the students' safety. Students were boarded out in houses in the Rannafast Gaeltacht. The secretary of Coláiste

Bhríde, Seán Mac Duinneacha, and I helped students with travel arrangements, in the allocation of houses and were in charge of the general operations of the college. In a relatively short time my own fluency in Irish improved significantly.

Incidentally I first met Jack Lynch when, as a parliamentary secretary, he accompanied the Taoiseach, Éamon de Valera, to Rannafast to join in the Silver Jubilee Celebrations of Coláiste Bhríde, in 1951. I found him to be a kindly and courteous person and one incident stands out in my memory. Jack attended a drama presented by the local people but without the Donegal Gaeltacht *blas*, he found it difficult to follow. When the Taoiseach asked him what he thought of it, Jack was in a quandary. He was much relieved when the Taoiseach added, 'Oiread agus focal amháin níor thuig mé.', (I didn't understand one word).

Getting involved in different societies and activities, like the Irish colleges, was something I always enjoyed and found very rewarding. While I was teaching at Clogherhead I had got involved in the life of the Dunleer community, becoming Group Leader of the LDF, helping found the Gaelic Football Club, Lannléire, and becoming an active member of the GAA County Board. I was interested in the Fianna Fáil party at Government level, but I was not actively associated with it at local level. The party was poorly organised in mid-Louth and south Louth and the Fianna Fáil Cumann in Dunleer had gone out of existence. Consequently in the early 1940s Joe Sharkey, another supporter, and I had decided to reform it. We approached a number of people and requested them to join up. One Fianna Fáil supporter asked me to which party I was referring, evidently expecting me to favour my father's party, Fine Gael.

While teaching in Phillipstown NS I became a member of the South Louth Comhairle Ceantair representing the Dunleer Cumann. I held a number of officer posts over the years as I continued to teach in the district. I was, later, a member of the Comhairle Dáil Ceantair, the constituency governing body. For a time the Dunleer Cumann provided personnel to cover quite a number of polling stations at general elections. This was found to be less than satisfactory and I proceeded to re-organise the whole area until we had an excellent network of cumainn set up.

Little did I know that after 12 years as both a teacher and a school principal, my burgeoning interest in politics was about to lead my life in a new direction.

Three

The Political Scene

Frank Aiken was elected to Dáil Éireann for the three-seat constituency of Louth in 1923. He remained the only Fianna Fáil deputy for Louth until 1937 when a second candidate, Laurence J Walsh, was elected. I was still a student in St Pats at the time and I saw Walsh's election as a major breakthrough for the party. The same result was repeated in the General Election of 1938. Nevertheless, Louth remained a marginal constituency with Fianna Fáil holding the second seat only after every second election, from 1938 until 1957.

It is possible that, over the years as I worked within the party in Louth, the thought of becoming a TD had entered my mind but I never regarded it as a real possibility. I lived in a small rural area, miles from Dundalk and Drogheda, which were the centres of population in the constituency. In the past candidates from rural areas, including Dunleer, had contested general elections for Fianna Fáil but with poor results.

With the death of James Coburn, the long-standing and popular Fine Gael TD for Louth, in 1954, the situation changed. My friend, Joe Sharkey, urged me to let my name go before the bye-election convention for selection. I felt it would be a waste of time. I was also considering Kitty's feelings. When the possibility of my becoming a candidate was first mooted she had not been keen on the idea. We had been married for about six years, had two very young children and had settled into the quiet life of a national schoolteacher at Philipstown, which suited her rather quiet disposition. Having discussed the bye-election for some time she eventually said she would not stand in my way. A groundswell of favourable opinion was also noticeable in party circles. With all this in mind I decided to enter the contest. I was delighted when I was selected at the convention.

The 1954 bye-election was a difficult one for Fianna Fáil. George Coburn, the Fine Gael candidate, was James Coburn's son and a sympathy vote could be expected. Fianna Fáil had also already got two seats in the three-seat Louth constituency but perhaps the greatest obstacle of all was a Fianna Fáil budget that had reduced food subsidies, causing, for example, the price of the loaf to increase by 50%.

During the bye-election campaign I occasionally travelled throughout the constituency with Éamon de Valera. He was an awesome figure in his long, dark cloak and black hat. There was little small talk. The Taoiseach sat in his car thinking about his speech for the next public meeting and, because of his poor eyesight, requesting his aide de camp, Colonel Brennan, to read short passages from the printed copy. After each passage was read de Valera continued to think and he finally delivered a word perfect speech. Exceptionally large crowds attended his meetings. At the Dundalk meeting, not only was the large square packed to capacity, but people also hung out of hotel and house windows to catch a glimpse of the charismatic figure.

In my own speech in Dundalk, I declared that I was not a 'runner'. I knew that many native-born Dundalk people had an aversion to people who came to work in the town and called them 'runners'. I had been born in Dundalk, simply because my mother had returned from Dunleer to her mother's house to await my birth. During my subsequent canvas of the town I later discovered that there were a considerable number of 'runners' living in Dundalk who were far from impressed by my speech. I had learned my first lesson about my dealings with people. One can be much too clever at times.

I passed through Dundalk a couple of days after the monster meeting and I saw a tiny meeting being addressed by Fine Gael spokesmen James Dillon and Patrick McGilligan. My confidence received a boost but I was soon to learn that huge public meetings were not synonymous with electoral success. An era was ending.

While I had built up a good organisation in Louth, I had not experienced the time-consuming nature of electioneering as a candidate. I soon became torn between my responsibilities to my pupils and the need to win the election. To the annoyance of the headquarters in Dublin I continued to teach as regularly as I could while the bye-election was in progress. I also wasted quite an amount of time canvassing in local rural areas, instead of fully concentrating my energies on the populous urban areas. However, I also arranged to speak at as many after Mass meetings on Sundays as possible. In 1954 almost the entire congregation remained to listen to the speakers. Interruptions from the audience were rare in County Louth. When the meeting ended a polite applause followed and the people returned to their homes. I doubt if many converts were made at such meetings but at least the public saw me in person and my own supporters were encouraged to come out and vote on polling day.

In the event George Coburn won the election but, in the circumstances, my vote of over 12,000 first preferences was regarded as respectable. Stephen Barrett, a Fine Gael candidate, won a Cork City bye-election on the same day and Éamon de Valera called a general election shortly afterwards. Even though I succeeded, relatively quickly, in putting the defeat at the polls behind me, the memory of it remained with me when many of my later successes had faded into oblivion. The encouraging sounds during the counting of votes and the tumult and the shouting when the result was declared all belonged to the other side. The candidate holds centre stage for the weeks before any election campaign. Then suddenly, with defeat, he or she feels rejected, isolated and alone. While a member of Dáil Éireann I have always had an appreciation of the feelings of those who, by losing their seats, went through a much more severe ordeal than I did in 1954, and, deep down, I could genuinely sympathise – even with my opponents.

Bye-election conventions can be acrimonious affairs. A number of candidates go forward for selection but only one can be chosen. Some of the other candidates and their supporters can feel aggrieved. When the selected candidate then fails to be elected moves are sometimes made to isolate him. We already had two Fianna Fáil TDs in our three-seat constituency. With this attitude in mind I decided not to allow my name to go forward to contest the upcoming General Election. I hadn't given any forewarning of my intention and when the convention opened I found a group had already decided to block my nomination. Among the accusations made against me, the one that stung me most was that my father was a Fine Gael supporter. It was my pleasant duty to let the members concerned know what I thought of them with the support of the convention chairman, Tomás Deirg, TD.

In the subsequent election Larry Walsh lost his seat to Paddy Donegan and for the first time in many years Fine Gael held two seats in Louth. A coalition government was formed, supported by the Clann na Poblachta party, led by Seán McBride, which held the balance of power.

By 1957 Clann na Poblachta put down a motion of no confidence in the Government and it was clear that a general election would ensue. I was pressurised to have my name put forward on the grounds that Larry Walsh was old and new blood was needed. In 1954 I had allowed my name to go forward for the bye-election without giving much thought to the consequences. Now I had had the time to seriously consider the matter. I considered how my wife and three young children would fare should I be regularly away from home. My teaching career had been very satisfying up to this point but I wondered if I would continue to find it so if I spent one term in the Dáil and was then defeated in the following election. This was the pattern in respect of the third seat in County Louth at the time. I was also conscious of my good relationship with Larry Walsh, whose thriving business had declined because of his public service commitments and who was anxious to contest the election so I refused to let my name go forward for selection.

The pressure continued. Seán Lemass asked me to go to see him in Dublin but, because I guessed he would ask me to contest the election, I did not go. Subsequently, at a Comhairle Dáil Ceantair meeting, I stated publicly that I proposed to support Larry. Nevertheless the pressure still continued. I finally told Frank Aiken that if Éamon de Valera, as Taoiseach, should nominate Larry for the Senate, and if Larry would agree to take a Senate seat rather than trying for a Dáil seat, I would let my name go forward. I had decided that I would overcome the home problem by returning to Louth after the Dáil each night.

I understand that when Éamon de Valera made the offer Larry replied, 'Whatever you say, Chief,' to which de Valera replied that it was not what he said that mattered but what Larry, himself, said. Larry accepted the offer but apparently he was not entirely satisfied with the situation. It was only after a further discussion with Seán Lemass, on the morning of the convention, that he finally agreed to withdraw his name. Consequently he had not informed any of the other delegates. When the convention opened he publicly withdrew his name. There was consternation, principally among some of the Drogheda delegates. When Frank Aiken and I were selected as candidates, a number of the Drogheda delegates left the convention, informing me on their way out that I wouldn't get a vote in Drogheda. Hardly an auspicious start to my campaign! Those delegates from Drogheda who did not leave, among them Jimmy Whelan, were left high and dry, without transport, and I later drove them home.

An effort was made by the dissident group to have Larry repudiate the convention decision and to stand for election. He consulted with Jimmy Whelan, who had been his right-hand man for many years. Jimmy told him that as the official Fianna Fáil candidate I would have his support. He then pointed to a large ledger and a small ledger on his desk. 'The large ledger is the Dáil seat, of which you have no hope,' he said to Larry. 'The small ledger is the Seanad seat and you are proposing to throw it away.' Larry agreed with him and my election campaign got under way.

I had a difficult task facing me. Frank Aiken's territory was in the northern end of the county, while mine was at the southern end. Apart from Fianna Fáil and GAA County Board circles and my brief appearance in the 1954 bye-election, I was virtually unknown outside my own locality. How would the people of Drogheda and Ardee take to me, a new and untried candidate? How would I fare against Paddy Donegan, a hard-working and popular deputy? What effect would the dissatisfied Fianna Fáil people in Drogheda have on the result? These were just some of the questions to be answered.

In my favour was the public opposition to tough measures taken by Gerry Sweetman, Coalition Minister for Finance, in an attempt to correct the economy. The fact that the Government had been forced to go to the country and thereby couldn't choose the timing of the election was also a plus factor. As for Drogheda, once the drum beat for battle commenced the adverse comments made at the highly emotional convention were forgotten and all but a tiny few worked with a will. Some time after the election was over there was a total reconciliation.

On election day nobody could be certain how the seats would go until all the boxes and the counting of the votes were over, but our expert tallymen were claiming victory long before the end of the count. When the official results were announced I was overjoyed to hear that I had won the second Fianna Fáil seat. I had displaced Paddy Donegan, who was later elected to the Senate and re-elected to the Dáil in 1961. Paddy Donegan and I were political opponents who actually lived within a few short miles of each other, but our personal relations were good. Strangely enough, the fact that the mid-Louth area in which I lived was predominantly Fine Gael in outlook had worked to my advantage. I had received quite a number of Fine Gael votes, on a personal basis, which reduced the Fine Gael candidate's prospects of election.

The electrical factory in Dunleer, AÉT, had also played its part. Big farmers in County Louth were almost entirely supporters of Fine Gael and there was a tradition that most of those who worked for them voted as their employers did. However, as large numbers of young people now worked in the AÉT factory, the tradition had been broken.

When I was elected there was tremendous joy and jubilation for my wife and family, my father and mother, and my supporters. My father had given me his fullest support in my efforts to become a Teachta Dála and was very proud when I was elected. Unfortunately he lived only about a year and a half after that. For my mother to have a son become a member of the parliamentary party led by Éamon de Valera was really something. Kitty was also naturally very pleased with my success, but she was primarily a homemaker. While taking a full and effective part in public functions at national and at local level, she attended them largely out of a sense of duty. Kitty never really involved herself in the party political side of my life, neither canvassing nor working on polling day, nor attending political meetings. I was happy with this attitude, because after a long day at my office or meeting with constituents we could close the door and become a private family, discussing the children's needs and let the world of politics pass us by – if only for a short time.

Our supporters made their way to our headquarters in the Gaelic League rooms and lined up for a march through the town, giving the usual thumbs down sign as they passed the Ancient Order of Hibernians hall. A cavalcade of cars moved out on the main road to Drogheda. As we passed through villages, throngs of supporters greeted us, many of them joining the cavalcade. When we reached the railway bridge at Dunleer a tremendous group awaited us, headed by pipers Paig Stanley and Peter Curran, who piped us into the square. As I stood on the stand there, thanking the people of my own parish for their support, I found it difficult to absorb what was going on. On the one hand I felt that I must be the same person who had spent his life there, but on the other it was obvious that something new had happened and much would be expected of me. I hoped I would be able to live up to expectations.

We reached Drogheda, the second largest town in Ireland, where a similar parade started out. When we reached the Tholsel, I thanked the people for their support. As I had lived at Phillipstown, Dunleer, and had gone to a secondary school in Dundalk, I knew little about Drogheda and the people of the town knew less of me. In a few short years, I would personally know thousands of Drogheda people and every nook and cranny of the town.

Four

Entering the Dáil

During the 1954 bye-election campaign, Neil Blaney had spoken on my behalf at a meeting in Dundalk. At the time the poet and writer Patrick Kavanagh had recently taken a legal action against a local paper, winning a one-shilling award. Much to his own discomfiture, and to the huge amusement of his audience, Neil ended his speech by calling on the electorate to give their number one vote to Patrick Kavanagh. Three years later, as I entered Leinster House for the first time as a deputy, Neil Blaney, who was standing in the doorway, put out his hand and said: 'You're welcome, Patrick Kavanagh.'

I had now entered a new world. Deputies, who had been but a name to me because of their part in the fight for Irish freedom were now my colleagues. I was getting to know government ministers who had previously been aloof and shadowy figures. I particularly remember deputies whose idiosyncrasies made them a people apart. Most of all, perhaps, I was now one of a large group of deputies, from varying backgrounds and occupations, with a wealth of experience in their own fields, who were trying to achieve a new Ireland.

I took my seat on the back row of the Opposition benches beside Kevin Boland, also newly elected in 1957. We carried on a desultory conversation. Little did I know that he was about to be appointed to the Cabinet that same day. The story goes that Séan Lemass told Éamon de Valera that he would not serve in the Cabinet if Gerry Boland was appointed to it and that de Valera, hoping to placate Gerry, appointed his son instead. I don't think Gerry was particularly pleased. I had a good relationship with Kevin Boland for years, both of us being keenly interested in the Irish language. He was a good minister, an excellent organiser and very approachable, but with a stubborn streak, which, to quite an extent, was his undoing in later years. Being thrown in at the deep end to a position of power on his first day in the Dáil made it difficult for him to adjust. With politics, as in other walks of life, serving an apprenticeship is helpful in the long term.

Leinster House in 1957 showed little change since 1922. The Seanad was housed in a room with an exquisite ceiling, in the former residence of the Fitzgerald family. The Dáil was situated in an extension, built originally as a lecture room and concert hall. Facilities for deputies were primitive. A small number of telephone booths were placed around the House, from which deputies could telephone departments in Dublin only. There were a tiny number of typists available, so most deputies wrote letters in longhand. Free postage was not available and the cost of stamps was a heavy drain on each deputy's allowance. On any one day many of us sat around a very large table, in our party room, writing letters. We were, regularly and, I might add, pleasantly distracted by older deputies regaling us with past exploits.

Interestingly enough those deputies who had been deeply involved in the War of Independence and in the Civil War never spoke about their activities during those periods. There was, however, one humourous story about events at that time that I have always remembered. A retired RIC officer owned an outlying farm some distance from his house. He heard rumours that the IRA was using it, so he sent his son to stay there each night. What the father didn't know was that his son was actually a member of the IRA. One night the father decided he would visit the farm to see how his son was faring. The mother, who knew about her son's activities, tipped him off about the visit. As the father approached in the dusk, the son fired a couple of bullets over his head. A second attempt to approach brought the same result. The father gave up the attempt and returned home, satisfied that his son was very alert in protecting their property. The son was a member of Dáil Eireann when I arrived there.

Éamon de Valera was proposed and seconded for Taoiseach. As I moved up the centre steps in the Dáil Chamber to record my first vote, I saw Michael Hilliard standing at a table where votes were recorded. As I knew him, I walked in his direction, only to be told in no uncertain terms to quickly get back to the other side. I was unaware then that as voting was taking place on the nomination of Éamon de Valera for Taoiseach, the Fianna Fáil Chief Whip took his place on the Tá (yes) side while the Assistant Whip took his place on the Níl (no) side. They checked on deputies as they passed through to vote. A similar arrangement operated for the opposition. It would scarcely have been an auspicious start to my career had I voted Níl (no) to de Valera's nomination!

When the Taoiseach announced his new government, which included my colleague, Frank Aiken, as Minister for External Affairs, one vacancy, Minister for the Gaeltacht, remained. To the chagrin of deputies from the West of Ireland, no minister had been appointed from there. They were adamant that at least one minister must come from the West. The Taoiseach appointed Mícheál Ó Móráin, a TD from Mayo. As Mícheál was missing from Leinster House for a while it appeared that he had been instructed to spend time in the Gaeltacht to improve his expertise in the Irish language. When he returned he was appointed Aire na Gaeltachta.

Shortly afterwards Seán Lemass addressed a gathering of new Fianna Fáil deputies of which there were quite a number at the time. I expect we were told to conduct ourselves properly and to be present for all divisions. The only instruction I can clearly remember was a warning never to go guarantor for anybody, as this could lead to personal bankruptcy, with the loss of the Dáil seat. Other than that we were left to our own devices to find out for ourselves how the Dáil functioned, what the Order Paper was about and how to deal with other important aspects of Dáil business. I quickly discovered that the Dáil Chamber was usually well attended for Question Time but it was some time before I had occasion to have a question for a minister printed on the front page of the Order Paper. So there we were in the middle of the twentieth century, with no research facilities, few telephones, little or no typing facilities and with no expert advice to aid us in our efforts to help govern the country.

The House itself was intimidating to a newcomer up from the country. Sitting high up on the backbenches, the Dáil Chamber appeared immense. To rise to one's feet to speak required a considerable degree of courage. Particularly when we were aware that across the floor of the House were ranged a number of seasoned deputies, ready, willing and anxious, to pounce on any error made or to interject a 'one-liner' capable of leaving one dazed, if not out for the count. At first I let opportunities to speak slip by. In fact I should have spoken but I found it easy enough to mentally excuse myself. An old cliché that did the rounds, that more people talked themselves out of the House than ever talked themselves into it, was a comforting one. I was well aware, however, that, clichés or no, I had been sent to Dáil Éireann to represent the interests and the needs of the people of Louth and that I was unlikely to achieve that objective by remaining silent. I began to research subjects in which I was interested and the implementation of which I believed would benefit my constituents. I finally got to my feet. I don't know how well I performed, but I do know I felt very good indeed when I sat down. I could now well appreciate the story about an astute old deputy who was said to make it his business to congratulate new members on their maiden speeches. He would tell them that, in all his experience, he had never heard a better one, thus ensuring a friend for life or at least a glass of whiskey. The ice was broken and I never found speaking in the Dáil quite so difficult afterwards.

The discipline of a teacher's life ensured that I prepared carefully for the Dáil, particularly for what I regarded as important issues. In those days only ministers were allowed to read from scripts, and, should a deputy do so, the attention of the Ceann Comhairle was drawn to the fact, and he was ordered to desist. Nowadays it appears to be the norm for all deputies to read from typed scripts. This may be quite businesslike and satisfactory but to the television viewer it appears somewhat stilted.

Fianna Fáil parliamentary party meetings were held regularly each week in the large party room and Éamon de Valera attended each meeting, without fail. Forthcoming legislation was discussed, followed by consideration of motions submitted by deputies. There was a public perception of Dev as an autocrat but my experience of parliamentary party meetings certainly failed to confirm this. Deputies were free to express their views, as they thought fit, without prior approval or hindrance, and they did so. I remember John Moher, an eloquent deputy from County Cork, making a slashing attack on the Irish language. This was a subject very dear to Dev's heart but Moher's right to express his view was never questioned. Of course, when the Taoiseach was opposed to a motion or to an amendment, its chance of success was minimal, but such applied to all Taoisigh and ministers. This was largely because all deputies were rarely committed to any one matter and those not deeply concerned supported the establishment. Dev dealt with motions and speakers in a kindly fashion, even when opposed to the views expressed. He usually spoke at the end of a debate, his thumbs and forefingers placed in his waistcoat pockets, commenting on the speeches, praising the various speakers who had contributed and ending by saying, 'But I think… ', and that was that. Few were offended in the process and the party room was always filled to capacity at those meetings.

The older members of the Fianna Fáil parliamentary party adored the Chief. He had led many of them through the War of Independence, through the devastating Civil War, through the political impotence of the 1920s and on to victory at the polls. To them, he could do no wrong. I had the greatest respect and admiration for Dev, but my mixed political background did not allow for the same level of adulation as that felt by those who had passed through fire and water with him. Backbench deputies rarely saw the Taoiseach except when he attended a Dáil session or at the parliamentary party meetings. When not in the Dáil Chamber he remained in his office. Usually only those deputies who consistently caused problems were admitted, and then to be reprimanded. I met him only twice in his office. The first time he asked me to deliver a letter to a Franciscan priest in Drogheda whose letter to the Taoiseach had been mislaid with no reply, an omission that troubled Dev. On the second occasion, he asked me to bring flowers to Dorothy Macardle, author of *The Irish Republic*, who was a patient at Our Lady of Lourdes Hospital in Drogheda. Other than that I don't think I ever spoke to him, on a personal basis, while he remained in the Dáil. I got to know him much better in later years when I became parliamentary secretary to the Minister for the Gaeltacht.

In 1957 Dáil deputies were paid £12 a week and had no pension rights. Details of severe hardships suffered by deputies who had served for many years and been defeated began to surface. In some instances businesses and farms they owned had gone out of existence. Jim Ryan, Minister for Finance, decided it was time something was done to help. A proposal for a contributory pension scheme for deputies came before the parliamentary party for discussion. One condition that caused debate was that where former deputies drew £1000 per year from public funds they would not be entitled to a pension. At that time the prospect of a teacher, for example, drawing a £1000 salary per annum was so remote as to appear laughable. However, I objected strongly to the condition on principle, pointing out that if a deputy had paid their pension contributions and fulfilled the other conditions it would be unjust to deny him or her the pension. The Minister then changed £1000 salary to £1000 pension from public funds, but as the principle was the same I continued to object. Finally the Minister withdrew the condition. Today such a condition would likely prove to be unconstitutional.

While I was involving myself in the business of the Dáil and getting to know my colleagues I also realised that I needed to pay close attention to the fact that the third seat in the Louth constituency was by no means secure. I believed that a good constituency organisation was the secret and, fortunately, I liked organising. Before my election I had spent much of my spare time re-organising the Fianna Fáil party in south Louth. After I took my seat I set about strengthening it further, recruiting new members into existing Cumainn and founding new Cumainn. My purpose was to have a Cumann situated in the district of every polling station. There is no substitute for men and women actively supporting the party in their own locality. They know the party supporters and they see to it that, as far as possible, they all vote on election day. An election machine second to none was welded together, which played no small part in securing the majority of the seats in County Louth for Fianna Fáil in subsequent years.

The Cumann is the heart and the nerve centre of the organisation. It consists of a group of dedicated people who give their time, voluntarily, to promote the party and its policies. Such people are real patriots, whatever their political allegiance, men and women who dedicate themselves to an ideal – the improvement of living conditions for the people of Ireland – with, for the vast majority, no material benefit to themselves. They simply have the feeling of fulfilment that goes with a job well done. Over many years I have seen these men and women striving away, year after year. They would be working at elections, taking up the National Collection and, perhaps most important of all, effectively defending party policy. Many of them grew old in the service of the party, happy with the contribution they had made. Most were also involved in parish work, in promoting games and in local activity generally. They prove the truth of the old saying that busy people can always make time to do more. People so wrapped up in themselves that they have no time for their neighbours' problems find it difficult to understand the enthusiasm of the voluntary workers in the Fianna Fáil organisation, often attempting to attribute it, without foundation, to material gain.

I had a very close affinity with the Cumann members and I had no doubt that when the drum beat for battle they would man the polling stations, ferry the voters to the polls where necessary and ensure the return of their two Teachtaí Dála. In retrospect, I was fortunate to have had the task of developing the Fianna Fáil organisation in south Louth, as the majority of the members were about my own age or younger. They were not only organisation stalwarts but many became personal friends as well. Friendship and mutual trust grew up between us, which held firm to the end of my career in public life. I am deeply grateful to all of them.

Each year I attended the annual general meetings of all the Cumainn in south Louth and some of those in north Louth also. The meetings were held in winter and early spring and were onerous, in the sense that the nights were dark, the weather was cold and damp and more conducive to sitting by the fire than going out to meetings. They gave me the opportunity to meet all the Cumann members, however, and to discuss local and national problems and difficulties, as well as having a friendly chat on all kinds of topics. Over the years I came to know what to expect at each individual Cumann meeting. A very few had formal agendas but most meetings were informal occasions, where we chatted about the most recent political highlights or indeed about matters not even remotely related to politics. At one particular Cumann, apart from electing a committee for the following year, we invariably spent the night discussing football and the relative merits of the local teams. Some Cumainn had complaints, which arose year after year, such as the rock that hadn't been removed from the centre of a stream. It is now part of the folklore of the district that at a subsequent Árd Fheis Donogh O'Malley promised the Cumann members that he'd come down and blow the rock out of the river himself, should his Department, the Board of Works, not do so. The rock is still there.

For electoral purposes the Fianna Fáil party divided the three-seat County Louth constituency in two. The north Louth Comhairle Ceantair

(CC) stretched from Castlebellingham to Omeath and the south Louth Comhairle Ceantair (CC) ranged from Castlebellingham to Drogheda. Three delegates from each Cumann, in each area, formed the Comhairle Ceantair. North Louth CC held its meetings monthly in Dundalk on the first Sunday of each month at 12 noon while the south Louth CC held its meetings at Dunleer on the second Sunday again at 12 noon. Many deputies expressed surprise and, on occasion, envy when they learned that we could muster a full complement of members for a mid-day meeting on a Sunday. The tradition became so strong that if a meeting had to be postponed all members had to be notified – otherwise they would all turn up.

There was no fixed agenda for the Comhairle Ceantair meetings. Delegates proposed motions, on the day, which were thoroughly discussed. Some meetings could be tense, but rarely if ever, descended to personalities. Patience was a very real virtue at Comhairle Ceantair meetings. I learned to take cognisance of the other person's point of view, even where it differed radically from my own. I had been Group Leader of the Dunleer LDF for most of the war years and afterwards a lieutenant of An Fórsa Cosanta Aitiuil (FCA). My experiences there helped me to relate to the various individuals in my political organisation and did much, I believe, to keep it intact and very active during the course of my career. I learned to differentiate between the person with a chip on their shoulder, and the solid individual, who, while they rarely spoke, contributed in a very worthwhile fashion to the debate whenever they did speak.

The Comhairle Dáil Ceantair (CDC) is the governing body for the constituency. At the time it was made up of three delegates from each of the Comhairli Ceantair plus three co-opted members, the Dáil deputies and the constituency delegate. Thus, in my early days, the Louth CDC had 12 members. It was a compact and very effective body that met before an election to appoint a Director of Elections and to co-ordinate the election work. It met after elections to deal with finances and to scrutinise results.

While we needed money for election purposes, Frank Aiken, Joe Farrell, Secretary of the Louth Comhairle Dáil Ceanntair and Director of Elections, and I were careful about the source from which it came and the possible strings attached. In my early days in the Dáil we received a cheque, through a supporter, from an exporter outside the constituency. The amount, though small by today's standards, would, at the time, have been sufficient to cover most of the election expenses. We considered the matter and decided against accepting it. This was no reflection on the donor personally, as none of us knew him, nor, indeed had ever heard of him before. We simply preferred to follow our usual procedures. We continued to win two seats out of three.

During my time in the Dáil, Taca, a new fundraising scheme involving meetings between businessmen and prominent Fianna Fáil people, was announced. When opposition to the scheme was apparent at the subsequent Árd Fheis, Neil Blaney, one of its authors, made a powerful speech in its favour and it was accepted. In those days in County Louth, we relied almost entirely on the voluntary efforts of our organisation, and relatively small amounts of money were spent on elections. We were almost always in the black due, largely, to the efforts of Joe Farrell, who kept a tight grip on the purse strings.

We were unhappy with the new fundraising scheme in Louth. Joe received a letter from headquarters outlining how the Taca scheme should be put into effect. At the following north Louth Comhairle Ceantair meeting, Joe presented Frank Aiken with the letter. Frank read it, then removed the lid of the solid fuel heater, in the meeting room, and dropped the letter into it. Thus Taca died in the Louth constituency.

With the party organisation in Louth runing smoothly I settled down into public life. Rather then an official 9.30 am to 3 pm position my working day extended from early morning until late at night, which took some getting used to. I was now dealing with problems at national level in the Dáil while the Cumainn in my constituency kept me abreast of affairs at local level. I became keenly interested in what I was doing. Whatever misgivings I might have had before the General Election now faded into oblivion. I was enjoying my work as Dáil deputy for Louth, both in Dáil Eireann and in my constituency, and I hoped to be able to continue with it.

Five

Deputy for Louth

When I was elected to Dáil Éireann in 1957 the 'clinic' system now prevailing was virtually unknown. Those in need of help or guidance called at the deputy's home, wrote a letter to him, met him at meetings or at fairs and markets. The majority of the electorate supported a particular political party and usually remained firm in their convictions throughout their lives. The floating vote, always important, was relatively small, but growing, at the time. In most instances people only called on their party deputy when the need arose.

My Fine Gael opponent in the area, Paddy Donegan, lived some miles from Drogheda, so he established what would now be called a clinic in Drogheda. When I was elected, my Drogheda supporters urged me to do likewise. I established a clinic in the Foresters' Hall, and every Monday evening I saw constituents there. Constituents were also welcome to call at my home on any day and at all hours. I made no change in this pattern during my whole political career.

A small ripple on the surface occurred later on when Paddy Donegan, then Minister for Defence, advertised 'clinics' in all the towns and villages of the constituency of Louth. I was in a quandary whether to follow suit or not. The people of Louth are independent-minded and I was aware that, especially in rural areas, they would not wish to be seen approaching political clinics. My belief was verified by reports from my organisation, so I decided to continue as I was. As I had foreseen, the scheme collapsed and we both continued as before.

I was fortunate in having an innate and genuine sympathy for people in trouble. I never grew tired or resentful of the large number of people who called at my home. Problems varied from the near tragic to the relatively simple. I always kept in mind that what might be small to me could be of very real importance to the individual concerned. The spectrum ranged from those who knew already that the desired solution to their problem was an impossibility and who simply needed somebody to listen and to share their burden, in the knowledge that their secrets were inviolable, to a group of people one might term the chronics, who returned on a regular basis with a new item each time.

From a psychological point of view, I was particularly interested in a tiny group whose objective apparently was to move the burden of guilt for any wrongdoing from themselves to their TD. When they first outlined their case it seemed straightforward and I had little difficulty in predicting a favourable outcome. Then, at the last moment, usually when they were just walking out the door, and in passing, a vital piece of information was volunteered. This information would alter the whole complexion of the case. Their reasoning appeared to be that having now told me everything, if they got outside the door without more questions, and then got what they wanted but were not entitled to, they could accept it with a clear conscience. As they had fully informed me about the matter they seemed to believe that the responsibility was now mine. In these cases I invariably asked them to sit back down to discuss the matter further. I would explain my own attitude and tell them that if they were not entitled to something neither a TD nor a Minister could get it for them. On the other hand, it was possible to guide people towards getting their entitlements when, because of bureaucratic red tape, they were at a loss how to proceed. Strangely enough, thanks and appreciation were expressed much more often for help in minor matters than for success in major ones.

In my early days in the Dáil, when some people requested my help, or after I had successfully assisted them, they offered payment in cash or in kind. I invariably refused, and the practice ended. I was glad when it came to an end, because it embarrassed me. I knew that refusal could be misunderstood and could cause offence. In those days too, I remember at my clinic in Drogheda some people I didn't know asked me for loans. For a short time, being a new deputy, I felt under pressure and gave tiny amounts on a couple of occasions. I felt unhappy about the matter and I decided to end it. When the next man approached me, with a friend, he named a sum and the purpose for which he needed it. In reply I told him that I was willing to help him or, indeed, any of my constituents to the best of my ability, but that loans were out. He then proceeded to reduce the amount several times. It finally reached a level far below the amount required to achieve his objective. I held firm in my decision. I can only assume that the two men made disparaging remarks about me, as requests for loans ended. The loans, as I expected, were never repaid.

In contrast, I remember a man in dire circumstances calling on me. He didn't ask for money but simply asked if I could do anything to help him. As it would take a good bit of time to deal with the matter and knowing his plight, I made an exception and helped him financially. Years later he returned to me with the money. As it had not been a loan I felt like telling him to keep it but my instinct told me he would be offended and I accepted it.

The numbers attending my clinic in Drogheda increased rapidly.

Through them I soon learned of the very serious unemployment problems in the town and the dire consequences arising from it. I have a clear recollection of those early days, sitting in my room in the Foresters' Hall after my clinic had ended, discussing the problems and possible remedies with members of my organisation. Coupled with attempts to encourage local industry to develop and expand, I made constant efforts to encourage foreign industrialists to set up in Drogheda. In co-operation with the Drogheda Chamber of Commerce and the Drogheda Trades Council, I drafted literature setting out the very considerable economic, social, cultural and educational amenities available in the town, the port facilities and the proximity of Dublin airport. Most important of all, I stressed the large, skilful and experienced workforce available who were anxious to obtain stable employment. The document was translated into a number of languages and circulated in Western Europe and the United States.

Unemployment continued to be a big issue and during my first Dáil term the major problem facing the Government in Louth was the pending closure of Dundalk Railway Works. As closure would have had catastrophic consequences for the town Frank Aiken and I were constantly in touch with management, unions and individual workers. We brought pressure to bear on Seán Lemass, then Minister for Industry and Commerce, to quickly provide a replacement capable of using the skills of the Railway Works' employees. He eventually came up with a package of new industries to be called the Dundalk Engineering Works, or DEW. Despite some hiccups, the DEW successfully fulfilled its role and tided Dundalk over a very difficult time.

Around the same time Clarks' shoe factory, another large employer in Dundalk, claimed that their premises were unsuitable for expansion. They proposed to buy the Dundalk Athletic Grounds, which were privately owned. If they failed to acquire the grounds they would close down the Dundalk factory and build a new one at Dublin airport. The grounds were in the centre of town and the people were deeply divided on the issue. There was a storm of protest from GAA and other sporting bodies, while company employees and many unemployed people supported Clarks. In view of the unemployment problem and against my personal feelings, I supported the company and the grounds were sold. Years later when the economic climate improved, and I noted the total lack of playing facilities in the town centre and when Clarks, eventually, closed down their Dundalk factory, I doubted the wisdom of my earlier stance but it was a difficult time for everybody concerned.

Another major difficulty that had to be faced at the time was that when it became known that an industry was interested in coming to Ireland quite a number of towns began competing for it. Secrecy, therefore, was vital, should I be on the trail of an industry not yet in the public domain. In one such case I approached the *Drogheda Independent* and explained that I had an industry in mind. I requested them not to publish any stories they might hear about it and in return I would give them an exclusive on the full details as soon as it was secured. They agreed and I fulfilled my part of the bargain. On another occasion the Department of Industry and Commerce endeavoured to have an industry with whom we were negotiating go elsewhere. We persisted in our efforts and finally persuaded the owner to state publicly that his preferred site was Drogheda. The owner did so, and as it was the publicly proclaimed policy of the IDA to allow industrialists to choose their own venue, the industry came to Drogheda.

I can remember another case where a prospective industrialist asked me for information, including the numbers on the live register in Drogheda. He wanted to ensure that sufficient workers would be available. The number on the live register was high at the time and he decided to come but, at a later date, said that he was far from happy because few of the workers on the list were suitable for his industry. We had, however, convinced him of the attractiveness of Drogheda generally, and he sent an instructor to the Drogheda Technical School who began by training three people. From this small beginning a large industry evolved. He told me afterwards that he was glad he had been forced to start his project this way because while training is a costly affair initially it is the soundest basis for ensuring a satisfactory workforce.

When I was elected to Dáil Éireann in 1957 the electrical industry was going through difficult times. I was especially interested in the local factory in Dunleer, Aibhléisí Éireannacha Teoranta (AÉT). The Managing Director, Martin McCourt, told me that levies were having a detrimental effect on the industry so I approached Seán Lemass and asked him to consider their removal. He agreed and the numbers employed at AÉT rose. I continued my support for the factory at Dunleer during good times and bad. Later on I used what influence I had to prevent GEC from transferring it to Dundalk. When the industry closed down a few years later I tried to have the factory taken over as a going concern. While it was closed I continued to impress on the Government the urgent need to have an industry established at Dunleer. The IDA board finally accepted that Dunleer should be treated as a priority for new industry. At the time Westinghouse Corporation was considering establishing an industry in Ireland and a Vice-President of the American parent company was in Dublin to meet with the IDA. The IDA had tried to persuade him to establish the factory at Dunleer, but without success so I agreed to meet him. As we were discussing the proposal he told me that he had operated in parts of the world where one could only move around in relative safety in an armoured car. Fearing a similar situation he said that he didn't feel that he could recommend to his company that they should locate the factory so close to the border. I countered this argument by pointing out that I was a Cabinet minister, living only a few 100 yards from the site, that I didn't even have a guard at the gate. I said that there was no basis for the fearsome scenario he had painted. I suggested that he consult with the Managing Director of a large American company, ECCO, in Dundalk, who would assure him that there was nothing to fear.

The Vice-president finally agreed to visit Dunleer, accompanied by his advisors, examined the site and consulted with a number of industrialists in the area. He pronounced himself satisfied and he recommended Dunleer to his board.

In the meantime I continued my efforts to interest some firm in taking over the Dunleer electrical industry. Finally Martin Naughton Chief Executive of Glen Electric decided to take it over, with great benefit to the people of Dunleer and Louth.

Westinghouse continued to operate in Dunleer for some time, but difficulties with the parent firm in the US led to its closure. Again Martin Naughton, came to the rescue, and established a new industry, Chilton Electric, there. I was delighted with the outcome.

I also took a particular interest in helping to build up and develop the Drogheda Industrial Estate. As the economy improved there was an increase in industrial employment and my quest for industry continued. When some industries eventually failed, the buildings remained and other industries replaced them. As the need for more housing arose, extra employment became available in the building industry, which in turn created an extra demand for cement and increased employment in places like the Drogheda Cement Factory.

I continued to look after the interests of the people of Drogheda throughout my career. In later years, the Drogheda Harbour Quays were in poor structural condition and in serious need of repair. Eventually some of the quays cracked up and partly fell into the Boyne. I succeeded in prevailing on the Government to provide very large sums of money to renovate and reconstruct the quays. Understandably, my efforts were much appreciated by the dockers in Drogheda.

As I worked to provide my constituency with new jobs and to help people with their day-to-day problems, an era was coming to a close. Éamon de Valera who had played a major role, not only in the foundation of the State but in the governing of it, was about to hand over the reins of power to his successor.

Six
Political Changes

A presidential election was due to take place in 1959 and the Fianna Fáil party decided to nominate Éamon de Valera as its candidate. Having successfully brought Fianna Fáil back into government in 1957 it was an appropriate time for Éamon de Valera, now aged 77, to hand over the leadership to a younger man. Seán Lemass had served a long apprenticeship and was his obvious successor. In the years ahead Seán would use his great abilities to continue to transform a rural economy into a modern industrial one. The young boy who fought with Pearse in the GPO could hardly have imagined he would one day appear on the cover of *Time* magazine, cited as a miracle worker who had industrialised Ireland.

In an era when it was accepted that the ideal occupant of Áras an Uachtaráin should be an elder statesman, experienced in the ways of government, nobody was more qualified than Éamon de Valera. There could be no doubting his determination and ability to jealously guard the freedoms he had fought so long to establish. Who better to act as guardian over the Constitution than its principal architect? He was the only surviving Commandant of the 1916 Rising and although he rejected the Treaty, he eventually led the vast majority of the Republican movement back into the Dáil, under the banner of Fianna Fáil. Once there they achieved many of their objectives, such as the abolition of the Oath of Allegiance, and the return of 'the Ports' through peaceful means. By declaring our neutrality in World War II and holding firmly to this policy, despite pressures and blandishments, he saved Ireland from the horrors of war.

I gave Éamon de Valera my full support in the presidential election. As soon as he was declared as a candidate the whole organisation in Louth went to work with a will. Every one of us wanted to see 'the Chief' continue to represent his country. The entire constituency was canvassed and reports of widespread support were very reassuring.

As election day approached, the party decided to hold a referendum on the same day to ask the people to vote for the abolition of Proportional Representation (PR). They wanted to replace it with the British-style, straight vote system. Proponents of the PR system argued that it catered for minority representation in parliament and that the system had worked well here and, also, in various countries in Europe. Opponents claimed that it was well nigh impossible to form stable governments under PR. They pointed to Italy, where governments only continued in office for short periods, leaving the real government of the country to the bureaucrats.

Feelings were very mixed in the party on the issue. Many of those elected under the PR system felt that the devil they knew was safer than the devil they didn't. Their support and effort during the campaign was, at best, half-hearted. As a new deputy, and a believer in stable government, I felt it was my duty to work hard to achieve change. I was under no illusion, however, about the difficulty I would experience in winning a seat in mid-Louth if it succeeded. As it happened, on the day, Éamon de Valera was successfully elected President but the PR referendum was defeated, so the problem did not arise.

The next issue on the political agenda was constituencies. The Constitution states that the ratio between the number of members to be elected at any time for each constituency and the population of each constituency, as ascertained at the last preceding census, shall, as far as is practicable, be the same throughout the country. The Government of the day decided on the constituency boundaries and tried to avoid breaching county lines. This method resulted, however, in considerable discrepancies in the population numbers deputies were representing. For example, in 1959 each deputy in Monaghan represented 10,540 voters, whereas in Louth each deputy represented 13,938 voters.

John O'Donovan, a parliamentary secretary in the 1954/57 Coalition Government, had lost his seat in the General Election of 1957, but succeeded in winning a seat in Seánad Éireann. Apparently without consulting his own party, he petitioned the High Court to decide whether the manner in which constituency boundaries were decided was constitutional. I attended the court hearing as a witness on behalf of Fianna Fáil. My case was that a deputy in my constituency represented the second highest population figure in the country, but because County Louth was small in area, constituents from any part of it could reach their TD without any difficulty. This contrasted with the very large west Cork constituency, for example, where some people rarely, if ever, saw their deputy. I pointed out that if O'Donovan's case succeeded, my constituency would be reduced in size while the west Cork constituency would be further enlarged to increase the population figures the deputies represented.

Mr Justice Budd heard the case and the decision would rest on his interpretation of the words 'as far as is practicable' in the Constitution. Liam O'Buachalla, Cathaoirleach of An Seanad, told me he believed O'Donovan would be successful, as Justice Budd had been appointed to the Bench because of his expertise in company law. Two and two would make four and no extraneous matters would enter into his decision. Liam O'Buachalla's assessment was correct.

Justice Budd's decision had an immediate effect in my constituency. A large slice of territory was cut off the Louth constituency and added to the Monaghan constituency. Far the greater area, including Ardee and its hinterland, were hived off my particular end of the constituency, but I did not seek a revision of the way Fianna Fáil divided our constituency between candidates. The people of Ardee were particularly annoyed and frustrated by the change. They felt isolated and their enthusiasm for participation in elections waned.

As Seán Lemass called a general election, soon afterwards, in 1961, I was understandably uneasy. Aside from my reduced constituency, no political party had held two seats in my area, after two consecutive elections since 1938. I threw myself into campaigning with the tireless support of the party faithful. Whatever each of us thought, the word 'defeat' was never part of our vocabulary.

On the day of the vote I will never forget the sense of tension I felt when, during the count, 500 of my votes went missing. Understandably, I was very relieved when they were found. I was delighted when the final results were tallied and I had retained my seat. I had a much-reduced first preference vote but the vital hurdle was crossed. Peculiarly enough my final vote, after transfers, gave me roughly the same majority as in the 1957 election, where my first preference vote had been much larger.

I returned to the Dáil a somewhat chastened deputy because of the fall in my first preference vote, but of course, I very much appreciated being re-elected at all. A few of my colleagues had lost their seats and I knew I had to accept that this was a factor of public life whatever I might personally feel. I met up with a number of my colleagues, all naturally pleased to be re-elected, and after greetings had been completed it was back to work again. We were soon immersed in affairs of the nation and of the constituencies, as if we had never been away. Fianna Fáil had returned 70 deputies, the rest 72. Frank Sherwin, a Dublin deputy, and Joe Lenaghan of Mayo, a former Fine Gael supporter who had failed to secure a nomination at their convention and who then took the seat as an Independent, supported Fianna Fáil. Seán Lemass was elected Taoiseach for a second term.

The greatest test of the loyalty of the two Independents came with the introduction of the 2½% turnover tax, which was fiercely opposed by the public, particularly in Dublin. Day after day there was a spate of letters in the *Evening Herald* attacking Frank Sherwin for his stance and demanding that he oppose the tax. Brian Lenihan added further confusion and spice to the debate by publicly stating that he didn't know why ordinary people should concern themselves about the tax as it applied only to 'fur coats and *Jaguar* cars'. The two Independent deputies stood firm.

During the debate Frank Sherwin went home to tea, on a bicycle, each evening. His fellow Independents, apart from Joe Lenaghan, of whom there were many, enjoyed the luxury of voting against the tax on a regular basis, without endangering the Government. They awaited Frank's return each evening in fear and trepidation, fearful that a vote would be called in his absence. Jim Carroll, another Independent, was on the horns of a dilemma, anxious to be seen to vote against the tax but fearing a Government defeat. Sherwin told me that on one occasion Carroll actually upbraided him for tarrying on his way back to the Dáil.

The tax debate brought home the fact that we were now a minority Government with its obvious problems. However we had approved the first Programme of Economic Expansion in 1958 and our new leader, Seán Lemass, pressed forward with its implementation with all the energy and enthusiasm for which he was renowned. He was determined to achieve an increased annual growth rate, to encourage investment, to increase employment and to reduce emigration. The programme was a great success and this term of office proved to be an exhilarating time to be in government.

Seven

An Ghaeltacht

Seán Lemass called his second General Election in 1965. I could sense an approval of government policy in my constituency and I felt more confident of re-election than I had done in 1961. My confidence was justified as my first preference vote increased by 2,500 votes.

Lemass was elected for a third term as Taoiseach and Frank Aiken was appointed Tánaiste and Minister for External Affairs. When we returned to the Dáil the usual discussion among deputies on possible appointments took place. I would, of course, have been pleased if I was promoted, but as Louth was a small constituency and with Frank Aiken as Tánaiste, I felt that the prospect for me was non-existent.

At the parliamentary party meeting, as the Taoiseach moved to his place, he informed some deputies that he proposed to appoint them as parliamentary secretaries or junior ministers, but I was not aware of this at the time. When the meeting ended, my friend Paddy Lalor informed me that the Taoiseach wished to speak to me. As it was quite common after an election for deputies to jokingly make such comments, I ignored him. I went off and telephoned a department on constituency business. As Paddy persisted, I agreed to go to see the Taoiseach on condition that he would accompany me to the door of the office to prove that the request was genuine.

When we arrived Paddy opened the door and told the Taoiseach that he had had great problems persuading me to come and speak with him. As the Taoiseach invited me into his office he smiled and pointed to a chair telling me to sit down. Not a man to waste much time on small talk he simply told me that he proposed to appoint me Parliamentary Secretary to the Minister for Lands and the Gaeltacht, Mícheál Ó Móráin. I was particularly pleased when he informed me that my specific responsibility would be the Gaeltacht. I thanked him and hurried to the car where Kitty was waiting for me. I wanted to give her the good news but found that Paddy Lalor, under the impression that I had already told Kitty, had already congratulated her on my promotion. She was delighted for me, as she knew my feelings about the importance of the Irish language and that I had acquired a pretty thorough knowledge of the Gaeltacht and of its people and a deep interest in the Irish language, through my earlier activities at Rann na

Feirste (Rannafast). I now felt that I could put that information to practical use.

Mícheál Ó Móráin had the reputation of being difficult to work with and of not co-operating with parliamentary secretaries. My experience of him was quite different. I found him to be very helpful. My one problem was how to get hold of him when I needed to have matters brought to Cabinet. His attendance in his office prior to Cabinet meetings was erratic, so I devised a system. As soon as he arrived his private secretary rang my office. I then raced down the stairs, into a waiting car, rushed from Earlsfort Terrace to Merrion Street and, with luck, got hold of him before he left for the Government meeting.

Ó Móráin had a superb knowledge of land tenure and particularly of the highly complicated system of land ownership in the West of Ireland. This was a knowledge he used to good effect in the Department of Lands. He was highly regarded as a solicitor and there were many stories going the rounds of his exploits in this field. I remember one story he told me about his successful defence of two old brothers. They were owners of a public house that was rarely open during the daytime when they farmed, but was usually open from nightfall until the early hours of the morning. A high wall surrounded the yard at the rear of the pub, and placed against the wall was a huge manure heap. When the Gardaí knocked on the door at night, the customers' practice was to rush out the back door, climb the manure heap, cross the wall and disappear. Finally the pub owners were caught for after-hours' trading and, with their customers, ordered to appear in court. They asked Mícháel Ó Móráin to defend them. He immediately told them to remove the manure heap. The prosecution's case was that although this was the first time the defendants had actually been in court they had been involved in after-hours' trading for quite a long time. The prosecution maintained that when the Gardaí arrived the customers always escaped over the wall. Ó Móráin's case was that no human being could cross the wall and he requested the Justice to come and view it which he agreed to do. The Justice apparently looked at the very high wall and agreed, possibly with tongue in cheek, with Ó Móráin. He dismissed the case with a caution. The manure heap was returned to its original location a few nights later.

When I took over at the Department of the Gaeltacht I was aware that the future of the Gaeltacht was entering a critical phase. For generations migration had been the lot of the physically fit people. They worked in Scotland and England from spring to autumn and returned home for the winter, but migration was rapidly turning to emigration. Many people were now marrying abroad and only returning for a couple of weeks' holiday in the summer. The most serious aspect of the situation was the pernicious belief in the minds of the Gaeltacht people that those who remained at home were weaklings.

After becoming familiar with the Gaeltacht in Rannafast I knew that steady and worthwhile employment all year round was the key to stemming the flow of emigrants but the question was how to achieve it. In the Rannafast Gaeltacht I had grown to know and love, there were a large number of people owning tiny pieces of land, which they worked to the best of their ability but with little return. Some owned a cow and perhaps a calf and maybe a small portion of bog on which they cut turf for winter use. Many people were in receipt of social welfare. A few tradesmen and handymen eked out an existence and a small number of people, mostly women, worked in minor industrial projects. A couple of businessmen made up the total. There were special facilities available to native speakers living in the Gaeltacht, such as housing grants, grants for children whose home language was Irish and so on, but these had only a peripheral effect on the standard of living. Generating employment would be no easy task and I realised that I needed to get to know, at first hand, the problems and the requirements of the Gaeltacht as a whole before I could start to implement any type of plan.

I travelled far and wide throughout the Gaeltacht, addressing groups of people. I listened to the views of farmers, fishermen, housewives, road-workers, small shopkeepers, people involved with small industries and anybody else who wished to contribute, learning, in the process, of their hopes, their desires and their fears. I used the knowledge to help formulate policies which I believed would not only stem emigration but which would also restore to the people of the Gaeltacht a belief in themselves – a belief that was essential to success.

To begin with, I felt that attitudes in the English-speaking areas of Ireland towards people living in the Gaeltacht had to change. It was relatively easy to refute the arguments that Gaeltacht people had no right to special facilities. Interestingly enough, when attempting to put radical proposals into effect I often had the most difficulty with some of the Irish language enthusiasts living outside the Gaeltacht. These people were almost invariably of a strong Nationalist outlook, consistently bought Irish-made goods and supported all kinds of Gaelic cultural activities. Some of them appeared to assume that because their own patriotic activities evolved from speaking Irish therefore all Gaeltacht residents were patriots by nature. The idea seemed to be that however low their standard of living, Gaeltacht people would be happy living there, to ensure that the Irish language survived. This assumption could also be detected from the portrayal in English, and Irish, novels of the blissful, idyllic lives enjoyed by people in the Gaeltacht. The reality, of course, was quite different.

To the vast majority of the people in the Gaeltacht the Irish language was simply their ordinary means of communication. Contrary to popular belief elsewhere in Ireland, and because of migration to Scotland, the latest fashions often appeared on the streets of the Donegal Gaeltacht before they were ever heard of on the East coast. In Rannafast the sales of Irish national papers were low and a framed photograph of the Glasgow Celtic soccer club featured in some of the homes. People living in the Gaeltacht varied as much in their views and aspirations as the population throughout the rest of the country. They wanted jobs, education for their children, well-appointed houses, water and sewerage schemes, good roads and proper recreational facilities, and they were not prepared to remain at home without them. A satisfying Gaeltacht lifestyle had to be provided for the people living there or the Gaeltacht would die a certain, though perhaps slow, death.

To achieve this better lifestyle I was convinced that the development of larger industrial projects would solve the chronic unemployment. The problems involved, however, were immense. Generally speaking the Gaeltacht areas are in remote parts of the country. Raw materials for industrial purposes were few and bringing them to factories and then conveying the finished goods to market would add to the price of the product and reduce competitiveness. The difficulties appeared insurmountable. Nonetheless, industry had provided employment for a large number of my constituents in Louth and I took courage from this success. I believed that what had been accomplished there could be achieved in the Gaeltacht.

Gaeltarra Éireann, a semi-state body, was the Industrial Development Authority for the Gaeltacht. The Board was made up of enthusiastic supporters of the Irish language. They were very hard-working people who did all they could to provide employment there. It was felt, however, that they did not have the industrial expertise nor the business experience to achieve the radical changes necessary. Mícheál Ó Móráin raised the matter with me, and Gaeltarra Éireann was reorganised. People were appointed to the Board who were mainly involved with industry, could speak the language and were well disposed towards it. Colm Barnes, owner of Glen Abbey, became chairman. The new Board appointed Cathal MacGabhann Chief Executive and the drive was on.

The language purists were not happy with my ideas. They claimed that industrialisation would introduce English to the Gaeltacht to the detriment of the Irish language. The Gaeltacht, as I saw it, was being bled white by emigration. If we did not introduce industrialisation there would be nobody left to speak any language. Nonetheless, I considered the points made and I introduced Irish language courses for middle management.

Attitudes of workers in the Gaeltacht itself also had to change. Some of the workers in the small existing Gaeltacht industries owned farms and turf banks. When the time of year arrived for saving the crops or cutting the turf, the workers simply stayed away, and production fell. New industries would not tolerate this approach but it took quite some time to convince the workers that this was the case.

Perhaps because I was personally involved in the project, I have particularly happy memories of the establishment of the Gaothdobhair (Gweedore) Industrial Estate. It started when a number of businessmen purchased a tract of land at Bunbeg, to create an industrial estate. The attempt failed but the purchasers deserve great credit for their initiative. We were told about the situation and I decided that my Department would take over. Shortly after the property was purchased I received a telephone call from Charlie Haughey, then Minister for Finance. He asked me what the dickens I was doing, purchasing land without either his own or his Department's permission. Frankly, I had been so taken up with the project that I hadn't thought of asking anybody's permission. We had a few brief, though somewhat heated words on the subject, and finally permission was granted. I had, in a sense, the upper hand in the argument, as the land had already been bought. Much later I learned that at the time I was entitled to go ahead with the purchase without Finance's permission.

We all worked hard to secure industries for the estate. I especially remember GT Carpets, an industry that provided good employment for many years. As it was an industry of considerable consequence, other companies followed. I had been familiar with Gaothdobhair over many years and was delighted to see its people flooding back from abroad to work at home. The unemployment trend was reversed. I subsequently stayed in a hotel in the West of Ireland where Údarás na Gaeltachta, the successor of Gaeltarra Éireann, were holding a meeting. I asked how the industrial estate was faring and it gave me great pleasure to learn that there were a 1,000 people employed there. The effort and the risk taken, many years before, had been well worth it.

Another area that played an important economic role in the Gaeltacht were the Irish language colleges. Courtesy of my involvement with Rann na Feirste I was aware of the proliferation of colleges throughout the Gaeltacht and I was in an excellent position to suggest changes in the system, where appropriate, to ensure their continued success.

I also took a special interest in the islands while I was in charge of the Gaeltacht. I visited Oileán Cléire (Clear Island) a number of times.

I spoke the Donegal dialect but I had no difficulty in understanding southern and western Irish dialects, nor had the people a problem with me. I had much more difficulty understanding a Cork boatman's accent on my way to Oileán Cléire, when we were both speaking English. On several occasions I had to ask him to repeat himself.

My visit to Toraigh (Tory Island), off the coast of Donegal, was unforgettable. It was the first time a Minister had visited the island and, as I approached, a large crowd waited at the quayside. Flags and bunting of every description bedecked the quays and I was warmly welcomed. A tractor and a trailer, on which a large armchair was placed, awaited me. I was invited to sit on the armchair and was driven on a tour of the island as if I were a king. I had a long discussion with the people and I must admit, in this case, that I was fortunate to have spent a long time at Rann na Feirste, as otherwise I would have had difficulty understanding them. They were very proud of their island and regarded it as a separate entity from the mainland. If they left the island they invariably spoke of going to Ireland.

I also paid an official visit to Oileáin Árann (Aran Islands), off the coast of Galway. The trawler was unable to approach the quay at Rosamhil so a rowboat was sent over. When the Secretary of the Department, Liam Tóibin, the boatman and I, settled into the boat the water reached the gunwale and almost spilled over it. A photographer from a local paper standing on the quay shouted: 'They'll do for your obituary, anyway!'

We reached the trawler safely and off we went to Inis Mór. Large crowds awaited me and I was given a conducted tour of the island. After discussing their problems we went on to Inis Oirr (Inisheer). I was particularly impressed by the beautiful strand and thought the texture of the sand was the finest I had ever seen. A storm arose and I feared we would be unable to travel to Inis Meáin but the captain of the trawler agreed to try it. This was fortunate as the people were expecting us and had the whole place decorated with flags in our honour. We got an exceptional welcome and I'm sure the islanders would have been deeply offended if we had not arrived.

Éamon de Valera, a fluent Irish speaker, showed a great interest in the islands. He believed that the Irish language was the heritage of all the people of Ireland, North and South, and felt that it could be the catalyst that would bind them all together. The islanders could particularly identify with him, which, in turn, raised their morale and heightened their pride in their mother tongue. Having a Head of State, Uachtarán na hÉireann, who took a particular interest in Gaeltacht affairs was a valuable asset and I came to know the Chief much better at this time. We had a number of telephone conversations on the

Gaeltacht and on the Irish language, all initiated by him. He was punctilious in observing the proprieties and never commented directly on policy. I found him to be a very human person, with a good sense of humour, who laughed heartily at simple jokes. He was quite a different person from the one symbolised by his ordinarily austere appearance and from my earlier experiences with him in 1954.

I met Sinéad, Bean de Valera, on a few occasions and found her a charming, kindly person, as the following incident portrays. Kitty and I were invited to a dinner at Áras an Uachtaráin. The invitation said 7.50 pm for 8 pm, but being unfamiliar with the terminology, and being a stickler for punctuality, I decided to arrive at 7.45 pm. We entered to find the President, Sinéad de Valera, their son Vivion and daughter Maureen, preparing to receive the guests, none of whom had yet arrived. It was our first official function of this nature and we were embarrassed to find ourselves alone in such august company, Kitty more than I, as I at least knew Vivion personally. Bean de Valera quickly sized up the situation and taking Kitty by the hand led her to a sofa, saying: 'We women will sit here and have a chat.' In my mind the formality of the Áras disappeared and I saw a gracious old Irish countrywoman courteously leading a guest by the hand to a chair by the fireside.

Some years later I was seated beside Bean de Valera at a dinner in honour of the King and Queen of the Belgians and I remarked to her that she had something in common with the Queen, as both of them wrote stories for children. She agreed, but added that she had little time for writing fairy tales when her family was young, her husband often being absent from home, in prison or on the run. She added jokingly: 'Indeed I had grounds for divorce.' She was about 90 years of age at the time but her sense of humour was as keen as ever.

Seán Ó Riada and his wife were also very friendly, welcoming people who had a deep interest in preserving the Irish language. When I visited the small Gaeltacht of Cúl Aodha in County Cork where Seán Ó Riada lived with his family we were invited into his house. While I was there their door was always open and the local people walked in and out as if they owned the place. The people of Cúl Aodha deserve great credit for preserving the Irish language surrounded as they were by a veritable sea of English speakers. The local people were particularly proud of Seán Ó Riada. They knew he was special long before he became world famous for his music. His death was a grievous loss to Ireland and to the world of music.

As I travelled throughout the Gaeltacht areas I continued to discuss matters with the people. I spent some time in the Connemara and the Mayo Gaeltachtaí discussing their problems and also in An Rinn (Ring), Co Waterford. In every instance the natural beauty of the scenery was breathtaking. Previously my only knowledge of the Kerry Gaeltacht had been gleaned from books, such as Tomás Ó Criomhthain's *An t'Oileánach*. Through my talks with the people there I considerably added to my book knowledge.

Travelling around the Gaeltacht it also became clear that the development of the natural resources in each area – farming, fishing, tourism and so on – had to continue apace. Special Gaeltacht schemes had been put in place to encourage this development. In one instance, some years earlier, land in the Rath Chairn area in Co Meath had been taken over, divided into Land Commission farms and allocated to families from the Galway Gaeltacht in an attempt to create a new Gaeltacht area. Taoiseach de Valera had taken a personal interest in the project and the transfer took place successfully. I felt that the people deserved great credit for continuing to speak Irish under difficult circumstances. For some years they had been unable to qualify for entitlements under all Gaeltacht schemes because the land and facilities in Meath were better than in other Gaeltacht areas. I was not happy with this limitation and I gave the Rath Chairn people the right to benefit under all schemes.

It took some time before people in Meath accepted the new families. I remember when I paid a visit to Rath Chairn, Meath and Galway were about to play in the All-Ireland football final in Croke Park. I spoke to a young man of about 17 years of age, who had come from Galway to Rath Cairn when he was a baby. I asked him which team he supported. 'Galway,' he replied. 'That's strange,' I said to him, 'after all you have lived in County Meath almost all of your life, so why not support them?' 'They won't let me,' he said. 'Every time I meet a Meath man he tells me that they are going to beat us in Croke Park on Sunday!'

There were many outstanding organisations including Conradh na Gaeilge, Gael Linn and Comhaltás Uladh, involved with the Gaeltacht. They all recognised the vital importance of the Gaeltacht in relation to the revival of the language and they constantly spurred me on to greater efforts. These organisations did Trojan work to stimulate interest in the language and the culture among Irish people everywhere. Many of them were voluntary organisations and their work was a labour of love. Ireland owes a deep debt of gratitude to them.

There were also many zealous individuals living in the Gaeltacht constantly endeavouring to improve the standard of living there. I once met with Father McDyer in County Donegal who told me that he didn't wish to be too be hard on me and would ask only that a bridge be built in a particular spot that I would see on my way home. As my Department provided grants for building bridges over small streams I said I would look into the matter. I later discovered that what he wanted was a bridge over an inlet of the sea, which would probably cost more than all the money given to my Department by the Dáil. That is not to say that people like Father McDyer do not deserve the highest praise for their achievements. He awakened courage in the people of congested areas and inspired them to greater efforts.

At one stage Goronwyn Roberts, Minister of State for Wales paid me a visit. He was interested in the use of Irish in our legal system in the Gaeltacht areas. We visited the courts in the Galway Gaeltacht areas and talked to the legal profession there. I was subsequently invited to Wales, to see how the Welsh language was faring and what government support was available to it. I also proposed to study the development of industrial projects in rural areas. I was welcomed at a formal banquet and, accompanied by a Minister from the Welsh Office, we travelled throughout the Welsh-speaking parts of Wales, flying the Irish flag. At one dinner, the council members burst into song in Welsh, of which they were justifiably proud. Even then, Welsh speakers recognised the dangers of the English language. As a rule they continued to speak in Welsh, even when a number of non-Welsh speakers were present. In contrast, Irish speakers with one English speaker in their midst would change to speaking English. I think perhaps the Welsh had got their priorities right.

I was deeply absorbed in my work in the Gaeltacht Department and the first year and few months flew by. It had been a busy time – travelling throughout the Gaeltacht, discussing its future with its own people and later, drawing the strings together in discussions with my officials. I had learned much of the lifestyle of Gaeltacht people and now had a clear knowledge of the difficulties involved. I was still anxiously trying to increase the number employed in industrial projects. My experience with industry in Louth stood me in good stead. I feel, without especially thinking of it at the time, that I was following Seán Lemass' lead, though on a much smaller scale.

As I began my second year as parliamentary secretary, I had no idea that Seán Lemass was about to make an announcement that would change the future of the party.

Eight

Party Leadership

Seán Lemass announced his intention to resign as Taoiseach and leader
of Fianna Fáil in November 1966. I was dismayed and disappointed.
As far as I was concerned the announcement was totally unexpected. I
realised we were losing a leader of great ability, vision and determination
and I didn't know what the future held for us. Unlike 1959, when Lemass
succeeded de Valera, there was no one obvious successor in 1966. When
it became known that the Taoiseach had told George Colley, who was
in America on official business, of his impending resignation and
advised his immediate return home, it appeared that he favoured Colley.
However, he also notified other possible contenders. Seán's son-in-
law, Charles J Haughey, Minster for Agriculture and Fisheries,
announced his candidature shortly afterwards. For a time it appeared
that only those two ministers would be in contention.

Shortly afterwards Kevin Boland, then Minister for Social Welfare,
telephoned my Dáil office asking me to call into his office to discuss
the leadership issue. Since the first day we'd started together Kevin
and I had been on friendly terms; we still shared similar views,
particularly on the importance of the Irish language. When I arrived he
asked me what I thought of the position and whom I proposed to support.
I told him I had decided to support Frank Aiken, Tánaiste and Minister
for Foreign Affairs, if he was willing to allow his name to go forward.
My decision was based firstly on my high regard for Frank and secondly,
I felt that if he did not wish to enter the contest it would give me more
time to assess the merits of the various candidates. Kevin was satisfied
to support Frank, adding that Haughey and Colley had to be stopped at
all costs. He was bitterly opposed to both men and let me know this in
no uncertain terms.

Frank Aiken was attending a meeting at the United Nations in
New York so we rang Mrs Aiken and asked her opinion. She replied
that only her husband could decide and that we could telephone him in
America, which we did. Frank turned down the proposal on the grounds
that he was too old, but he recommended George Colley, whom he
proposed to support. Frank's suggestion was anathema to Kevin and
so far as I can remember he indicated that he would seek another
candidate. I returned to my office to think things over.

Later on I heard that Kevin had announced Neil Blaney's candidacy. I went to his office and asked if this was true. He confirmed that Blaney had agreed to enter the contest. In case there should be any misunderstanding, in view of our earlier agreement to co-operate on the Aiken candidacy, I informed him that I did not propose to support Blaney.

There were now three candidates for the leadership, Blaney, Colley, and Haughey. I had been friendly, on a personal basis, with George Colley since he was elected in 1961 and I decided to support him. By this stage quite a number of the older Fianna Fáil deputies had become uneasy. These deputies were, in the main, Old IRA veterans who had served under Éamon de Valera and had witnessed the smooth transition of leadership from the Chief to Seán Lemass. They now feared that a contest between the three candidates would create divisions and dissension in the party – no matter who won it. Seán Lemass apparently had similar thoughts. He had approached Jack Lynch on the subject of the leadership but Jack told him that he wasn't interested. The older deputies, among whom were Tom McEllistrum and Eugene Gilbride, voiced their fears to Lemass and eventually Jack Lynch was persuaded to become a candidate. Neil Blaney and Charles Haughey subsequently withdrew their names but George Colley remained in the race.

I discussed the forthcoming contest with Frank Aiken. He said he didn't think Jack Lynch was decisive enough to be Taoiseach and expressed the view that Colley would win. I was much closer to the rank and file of the parliamentary party than Frank and I told him that my best estimate was that George would only receive 19 votes. My estimate was to prove remarkably accurate.

The vote took place in the Fianna Fáil parliamentary party room. The ballot was secret in the sense that each deputy received a piece of paper on which to write the name of the candidate he or she supported, but there were no polling booths in which to vote. Each voter marked the paper where they happened to be sitting. A number of those who voted for Jack Lynch did so ostentatiously, letting everyone around them see their vote. I remember, particularly, Donogh O'Malley holding aloft his voting paper with the name Lynch clearly visible on it. Most deputies were well aware that Jack Lynch would win the contest, so I wondered if the show of ostentation was for the purpose of annoying the Colley supporters or perhaps with an eye to future prospects, ensuring that Jack knew who had voted for him. Strangely enough, I never felt that my position as Parliamentary Secretary would be endangered because I voted for the loser. In view of the procedures adopted at a later date, this says much for the new leader and the times that were in it. Jack Lynch retained Paddy Lalor, Jim Gibbons and

myself as parliamentary secretaries even though it was widely known
that we had voted for Colley.

Some years later Paddy Lalor and I, then Cabinet Ministers, met
the Taoiseach in his Dáil office to discuss an item of government
business. In the course of a chat after business had been completed,
Jack Lynch told us he had come under considerable pressure not to re-
appoint us because we had not voted for him. I pointed out that he had
always been a very private person and that by 1966, even though I had
been in the Dáil with him for over nine years, I scarcely knew him. I
was friendly with George Colley, respected his ability, believed he would
make a good Taoiseach and party leader and, accordingly, voted for
him. I added that none of the deputies who voted for Colley thought he
would win and, therefore, probably voted for the same reasons as I did.
Jack Lynch appeared to accept what I said. I continued that the majority
of those who had voted for him did so because they were equally
convinced that he would make the best leader and Taoiseach. The
conversation ended soon afterwards but on my way out I wondered
which ministers had been anxious to prevent us from having a role in
the Government.

Jack Lynch was fully accepted as leader by the vast majority of the
parliamentary party. There was a vague underlying feeling, however,
that some senior ministers, who had declared their intention of seeking
the leadership, could be biding their time. My theory was that there
was a small group who voted for Jack largely because they believed he
was too soft to continue for long in the position. They believed that
their opportunity would come sooner rather than later. The next general
election would do much to determine the future.

Not long after the party settled down again under the new leadership
I received some sad news. I was engaged in a bye-election campaign in
Wicklow in 1968 when I found out about the sudden death of Donogh
O'Malley, the Minister for Education. We were shocked as he had, to
all appearances, been in good health and in very good form. O'Malley
was a flamboyant and colourful character. He was a larger than life
figure in Irish political folklore because of his introduction of free post-
primary education and indeed for his many real and imaginary exploits.
The fact that there had been no government decision to provide free
education and that, apparently, nobody except O'Malley himself and
the then Taoiseach, Seán Lemass, knew of the announcement, was
irrelevant to a large section of the Irish people who were now visualising
their children gaining a full education. O'Malley, as I saw him, was a
man who psychologically reached the heights and plumbed the depths.
I visited him in his Dáil office, which was close to mine, on many
occasions. At times he was in an exuberant mood, detailing with great

élan how he proposed to develop post-primary education or to merge the universities or whatever. At other times he was sitting silently in an armchair, a leg thrown over one of its arms, replying to questions in monosyllables, if at all. There was rarely a middle of the road approach. He was very much influenced by the media and it was rumoured that he often stayed up at night waiting for the morning newspapers.

O'Malley's death brought the usual spate of media speculation on a new Cabinet appointment. There were six parliamentary secretaries, any one of whom could be a possible choice. Mícheál Ó Móraín and Seán Flanagan, represented the same county, Mayo, and were both Cabinet Ministers, so I suppose I was entitled to wonder if a similar situation could arise in Louth with Frank Aiken and myself.

Meanwhile my work in the Department continued. When not in the Gaeltacht I was usually in my departmental office but on a particular Friday after Donogh O'Malley's death I had to deal with some very important constituency business and travelled to Dundalk instead. As my business would take some time my driver parked the car in the County Council office yard.

When I returned home around six o'clock Kitty, told me Frank Aiken had telephoned asking to speak with me. When she told him that I was in Dundalk he said he would ring the Garda Barracks there and ask the Gardaí to contact me. The Garda car searched the town but failed to find me or my car. I telephoned Frank's office, but as it was now late in the evening he had gone home. He had left a message saying he would like to see me in Iveagh House on Monday morning. By this time I had guessed what was in the air, but in political life nothing can be taken for granted. The seconds ticked away rather slowly over the weekend.

On Monday morning I duly called at Iveagh House and Frank told me that Jack Lynch wished to contact me. He rang the Taoiseach who informed me that there would be a Cabinet reshuffle and he proposed to appoint me Minister for Lands and the Gaeltacht. He told me to remain silent on the matter until after the official announcement in the Dáil the following day. It is a measure of the man that Frank Aiken, Tánaiste, did not himself tell me what the Taoiseach had in mind. This was the prerogative of the Taoiseach and Frank wouldn't undermine it, even by a whisper.

From Tuesday morning to Tuesday afternoon was one of the longest periods of time I have ever experienced. Paddy Lalor and Jim Gibbons, who were also parliamentary secretaries, were close friends of mine and we lunched together regularly. The conversation was naturally devoted to the Cabinet vacancy and in the circumstances all I could do was try to talk as naturally as possible.

On Tuesday afternoon I came down in the lift with James Dillon of Fine Gael, who asked if it were in order to congratulate me. I muttered something unintelligible in reply. As we gathered in the ministers' waiting room before entering the Dáil for Question Time, there were many comments on how happy some aspirants appeared to be and how well-dressed others were.

Paddy Lalor sat next to me in the Dáil Chamber, as usual. As Question Time was drawing to a close he scanned the visitors' gallery and seeing Kitty sitting there exclaimed that the cat was now out of the bag. The announcement was soon made, Ó Móráin to Justice, Lenihan to Education and Faulkner to Lands and the Gaeltacht.

My family were delighted to learn of my promotion, as indeed were my constituents. I was now a member of Cabinet with two departments, Lands and the Gaeltacht, and I could express my point of view and put my proposals forward without the need of a go-between. Having been responsible for the Gaeltacht for some years, I had already received an excellent training there, which I knew would stand me in good stead.

Decentralisation of government departments had been on the agenda for some time, as indeed it still is today. However no Cabinet decision had been taken on the matter, nor had there been any consultation with the civil servants, when, out of the blue, during his term as Minister for Lands and the Gaeltacht, Mícheál Ó Móráin had announced his intention of transferring sections of the Department to Castlebar. There was a tremendous furore among the civil servants, furious at the lack of consultation and thoroughly despondent at the idea of being transferred. Few wished to leave Dublin and morale had reached rock bottom when I assumed office.

My appointment gave some hope, for, as somebody quipped, the farthest the Department was now likely to go was to Drogheda or Dundalk. I immediately initiated talks and an agreement was reached that civil servants below a certain grade would not be compulsorily required to transfer. Morale rose somewhat but I felt that something more was needed. Legislation provided for four Land Commissioners and there were two vacancies. It was customary for governments to fill these vacancies with suitably qualified, loyal party activists. On this occasion I felt that appointments from within the Department, resulting in promotions down the line, would boost morale. I decided to recommend to Government that these appointments be made, but some members of the Cabinet treated my proposal with disbelief. I persisted and was eventually successful but it was a very real baptism of fire for me.

Having come to grips with my duties as Minister for Lands and with discussions on decentralisation proceeding in a much calmer atmosphere, I turned my attention to the issue of land division. Changes had been proposed which might benefit the lives of farmers and their families. As more Irish people were employed in industry and enjoying a half-day Saturday and a free day on Sunday, the major complaint among the farming community was that the farmer and his wife worked a seven-day week, with little or no free time. In an attempt to overcome the problem I tried an experiment. An estate was about to be divided into four farms. Rather than building a house and a farmyard on each individual farm it was decided to build the four houses in close proximity to one another. The idea was that the whole estate would be worked as a unit, with each farmer in charge of what he did best. One farmer and his wife would be in charge each weekend, giving the other three families a weekend off. I'm afraid Irish farmers proved much too individualistic for this style of farming and the project failed to get off the ground.

The Department of Lands was also concerned with wild life. As a boy, like most children of my generation, I got great pleasure from the wide variety of wild flowers I passed each day and the wild animals I saw, but more especially from watching wild birds. As I walked to school each morning during the nesting season, I peered into hedges hoping to find a bird's nest. When I found one I boasted of my success and gave the number of eggs but its situation was my secret. Like every other rural child I knew that if a person so much as touched an egg the parent birds would forsake the nest. With this background it is no surprise that when the Department was considering the Wild Life Bill I took a particular interest in it. Naturists and rural dwellers were becoming very perturbed about the detrimental effect new farming methods were having on wild life. New pesticides, destruction of natural habitats and the wanton killing of species of birds and animals were all cause for concern. I fully supported the Bill as it was designed not only to protect wild life, but also to develop what is one of Ireland's greatest assets – the countryside.

Forestry was another area that required attention. We were planting 25,000 acres each year but at times it was quite difficult to acquire enough suitable land. When the price of mountain sheep was high, little land was available; when sheep prices were low more land came on the market. Other initiatives were also in place. In 1968, President Éamon de Valera opened the John F Kennedy Arboretum, where rare trees and shrubs are cultivated, in Wexford. This was a landmark in the history of the Department of Lands, which had carried out the development of this magnificent park. The late President's sister, Eunice Shriver, and his sister-in-law attended the ceremony.

I had spent over a year in my first ministerial position when a general election was called in June 1969. The media, and the pundits generally, expressed the view that Fianna Fáil would fail in its attempt to remain in power. In my view this was a vital election. I felt that Jack Lynch's tenure as leader could well depend on a successful result. I plunged into the election with all the energy I could muster. Once again our local organisation campaigned strongly and I urged all our workers and supporters to ensure that the Government was re-elected.

Lynch confounded his critics by winning an overall majority. He had proved himself. He formed a new Government and all seemed set fair for a relatively peaceful four or five years in office. Little did we know, however, that fate had decided otherwise.

Nine

Minister for Education

The Taoiseach, Jack Lynch rang me at my office in Lands soon after the General Election victory and asked me if I thought a former teacher would be a suitable choice for the new Minister for Education. I said I believed so and reminded him that teachers had already held the position. He listened to what I had to say but the conversation ended there and I still didn't know his decision. I waited for another call from him but none came. It was getting late in the evening and rather than go home in a state of uncertainty I decided to ring Jack and ask him if he had made a decision. He replied 'yes' to the appointment. I thanked him and that was that.

While I was waiting for the official announcement an assistant secretary called into my office and I asked him to get me a copy of the Wild Life Bill, which we were still working on at the time. When he arrived outside my door again he met the Secretary of the Department and I heard him say: 'It's alright. He's not leaving. He asked for the Wild Life Bill.' Clearly they were anxious that I should remain on in Lands and I was naturally pleased to discover this. I would miss my time working in the Gaeltacht but I was happy to change over to a vibrant department that I felt would have more immediate relevance to the development of the Irish nation. I also knew that the major functions of the once powerful Department of Lands, the break up of large estates and land distribution, was coming to an end. A few years later the Department no longer existed.

I returned home that evening elated with my new appointment. I had been involved with education all my life – as a pupil, a student, a teacher and a parent. I was now being given the opportunity to make a contribution to the development of Irish education at the highest level. It was the norm at the time to keep Cabinet appointments secret until they were officially announced in the Dáil but I naturally gave Kitty the good news. With, I must admit some trepidation, I also told my mother, warning her that if she mentioned it to anybody before the official announcement she would jeopardise my position. I later learned that as soon as my brother Seán walked into the house she couldn't resist telling him! When the news became public I was inundated with congratulations.

Being a teacher and a very active member of the Irish National Teachers' Organisation (INTO), I was au fait with many of the problems and difficulties parents, pupils and teachers, faced. When I left St Pats in June 1938, unemployment was widespread and I knew I had been very fortunate to get my position at Clogherhead. Many teachers trained in the 1930s and early 1940s didn't secure permanent teaching posts for years. I had joined the INTO in April 1939 and had served for a time as Chairman of the Drogheda Branch. During my years in the INTO I was involved in a wide range of activities aimed at improving the educational system. These concerns helped me to quickly come to grips with reality on my appointment as Minister.

I was officially appointed Minister for Education on July 2, 1969, during one of the most exciting periods in the history of education. One report after another had made the western world conscious of the disadvantages that adversely influenced many children. In Britain the Plowden Report (1967) had advocated positive discrimination in favour of primary school children from disadvantaged areas. In the United States President Johnson introduced the 'Head Start' pre-school programme as one of the main strands in his 'War on Poverty'. In Ireland the 'Investment in Education' Report (1966), had painted a similar picture.

With all this in mind it is hardly surprising that the right of all children to equality of educational opportunity became the cornerstone of my education policy. Firstly I felt that the education of the child, the pupil, the scholar, must be relevant to his or her natural ability. Secondly I believed that the child's education must be relevant to the part he or she would play in later life. I was delighted to now be in a position to pursue these goals. To achieve equality, I knew account also had to be taken of children from deprived backgrounds, of physically handicapped and emotionally disturbed children, and of the children of travellers. I was looking forward to the challenge of working in a cauldron fired by these needs.

On the day following my appointment, I walked from the Dáil to my new department for the first time. As I had never been in the Minister's office before, I asked the girl at reception where to find it. She promptly asked me if I had an appointment. When I smilingly identified myself she quickly rang my private secretary who came down to meet me. While I was waiting for him I rambled around the large foyer, getting a feel for the place. I was pleased to see a bust of the educational philanthropist Vere Foster, the man behind the provision of the school at Phillipstown. Seán MacGearailt, the Secretary of the Department, then arrived and took me up to his office. He introduced me to the assistant secretaries and principal officers. I briefly spoke to them and explained my brevity by referring to a story I had recently read that went something like this:

> A new Minister had been appointed to a Department of State in the USA. He was very proud of his appointment and wanted to infuse the civil servants with his own enthusiasm so he gathered his staff together to give them a pep talk. As he spoke one civil servant turned to his neighbour and whispered that the new Minister hadn't yet mentioned that theirs was a wonderful country and if they worked well together their success was assured. With that the cliché came forth, and so it went on, one cliché following another and each being quietly anticipated by members of the audience.
>
> When the speech ended the Minister felt he had the civil servants in the palm of his hand and asked for questions, anticipating an outflow of high-flown inspirational remarks. Finally one civil servant rose to his feet and asked, in view of the fact that they had worked overtime for a few weeks, when could they expect days off in lieu!

Ireland was fortunate at a time of rapid change to have officials of exceptional ability and dedication in the upper echelons of the Department of Education. They had a thorough grasp of fundamentals and the foresight to ensure that Ireland kept abreast, and, hopefully, ahead, of other countries. Irish civil servants are an especially loyal people. When governments change some of the new Ministers continue to use their predecessor's private secretary, which surely underlines the integrity of the civil servants concerned. The Department officials included the Secretary, Seán MacGearailt, who had a special insight into what was involved. Seán O'Connor, assistant secretary for third-level education, Dominic O'Leary, assistant secretary for post-primary education and industrial relations and Tomás Ó Floinn, assistant secretary for the primary branch also all did Trojan work. I came to realise very quickly that they were as good a top-layer team as any Minister could wish to work with.

With so many new educational developments there was no time to waste and we got straight to work. The provision of better educational facilities was an immediate concern. At the time research showed that children in larger schools were better off than those in small ones, so I decided to secure larger school units around Ireland.

Understandably, there was opposition to the closure of some small schools, mainly centred on the importance of the national school as a focal point for the community. While I sympathised with this view, I had to provide for the best interests of the children. It was generally accepted that pupils in small schools lagged behind pupils in schools where there was a teacher for each class. Even in my own primary school days this problem was recognised and County Councils always reserved at least one scholarship for pupils attending small schools. In my training college days, we students added to *The Litany*: 'From one teacher schools, O Lord deliver us.'

The battle over the closure of the one-teacher school in Dún Chaoin, Co Kerry caused a tremendous furore and seemed to epitomise the problem. I decided to amalgamate it with a much larger school in Ballyferriter. Both schools were in the Kerry Gaeltacht and both catered for native Irish speakers. Local people were divided on the issue but there was a tremendous outcry from Irish language enthusiasts in Dublin, some of whom had holiday homes in Dún Chaoin. To those opposing closure I pointed out that I had a responsibility for the children's education in Dún Chaoin, that I was ensuring that no damage would result to the Irish language, and that I had no alternative. I wondered, indeed, if my Dublin-based opponents would send their children full-time to a school with one-teacher. Fine Gael, not noted at the time for a commitment to the Irish language, took up the cudgels on behalf of the school, with full support from the section of the media that liked to regard itself as the Liberal wing.

The school was closed.

When I left office the school was re-opened by my successor. He attempted to justify this decision by saying that in this case the cultural and social aspects of the situation should have been recognised. As the amalgamation was with another Gaeltacht school the cultural side had obviously been taken into consideration, while the social side pertained to every amalgamation. Re-opening the school was unfair to the children, and many families supported my view by continuing to send their children to Ballyferriter. Ironically the new Minister for Education then went on to refer to the educational disadvantages of small schools and stated that no more would be built. The reality is that pressure from powerful influences, which I had resisted, forced the new Minister to impose a system on the children of Dún Chaoin which, by his own words, he regarded as educationally unsound. I might add that I'd had a request from the school manager to close the school, but when the row broke out there was a deafening silence from that quarter. However, the responsibility for the school closure was mine and at no time did I mention this fact during the protracted and bitter dispute. If I'd had any illusions, the reality of life as Minister for Education was becoming crystal clear.

I had to contend with many similar school closure situations and I was anxious to deal with them as quickly as possible, as introducing the new primary school curriculum was another pressing concern. When I arrived in the Department work was already in progress on the new curriculum. Educational research had provided clear sign-posting on the need for a child-centred curriculum in primary schools. This was a significant development and I was delighted to finally introduce it in July 1971. Its introduction marked a new era in Irish education, where no major changes had taken place since 1926.

As an experienced national schoolteacher the change from a 'subject-centred' system, dictated by a rigid compulsory programme, to a more humane 'child-centred' pedagogy, had my full support. I had felt in the past that the Department had based its curriculum on the assumption that all children had the same level of ability. Children in each class had to read from the same page, learn the same poems and do the same sums, on the same day. I remember as a teacher then having to fill in the exact particulars in respect of each subject in the weekly syllabus and to state, in the monthly return, what had been achieved. In such circumstances the weaker children were unable to keep up and learned little, while the more intelligent children, who wanted to forge ahead, became frustrated and often disruptive. In the new curriculum the child was accepted as a person in his or her own right, with natural powers that had to be developed at their own rate.

I was well aware that to successfully implement the curriculum it was essential to convince teachers of the efficacy of the changes and to provide the necessary training. So side-by-side with the development of the curriculum, plans were being laid to restructure the teacher-training course. The proposed extension of the course from two to three years meant that for a few years there would be a need to counteract the loss in the output of teachers. I was anxious that these problems be tackled urgently.

During the campaign for a three-year teacher-training course I had regular pickets on my office in Marlborough Street, which was once invaded by students in my absence. Picketing was one thing but invading the Minister's office was way over the top and the protestors were quickly removed. Posters proclaimed: Faulkner out – North and South, a reference to Brian Faulkner, a government minister in Northern Ireland. The posters and slogans had absolutely no effect on me and certainly did not assist their protestors' cause.

One incident, however, portrays how isolated a minister can be when he is in difficulty. Students who had completed their teacher-training course returned to the college each autumn to be presented with their certificates by the Minister for Education. I arrived at St Pats to find students sitting on the avenue leading to the college and my car couldn't proceed. I remained there for quite some time, chatting with my driver, and not one member of the college authority came to my assistance. When I finally arrived at the door of the crowded assembly hall, the President of the College pleaded with me to cancel or postpone the ceremony. I refused. The large number of young people who had assembled there, from all parts of the country, were entitled to be presented with their certificates. It was then suggested that I enter the stage through a side door. A stubborn streak in me insisted that the usual procession of professors and other dignitaries should take place.

When I reached the stage I spoke in Irish, amid howls and disturbances. As I was coming to the conclusion I raised my hand and, strangely enough, silence fell. I said that I would proceed as rapidly as possible to deal with students' concerns, but that if they thought their conduct that day would help their cause they were sadly mistaken. The clamour died away. In the late sixties and early seventies student protests were a worldwide phenomenon. It was almost obligatory for students to protest about something. I simply returned to my office and put it from my mind.

It is interesting that students who vigorously campaigned for a three-year course with university degree qualifications for primary teachers, impressed on me that the desired change should apply to the next group of students to enter the training colleges. The main concern of existing students seemed to be to leave college as quickly as possible, human nature apparently triumphing over logic.

Another area with no shortage of protesting students was the College of Arts. It was under the direct control of the Department of Education and before I took office there were constant disruptions and demands for reform, including a protracted 'sit-in', when students barricaded the building.

When I became Minister the students continued to protest. Other students, however, being fearful of the radical students, came to see me in secret. They complained that their work was being disrupted, that they were being bullied and were unable to study. It was obvious that something had to be done and I agreed to meet a deputation of the Student Union. Seán MacGearailt was not particularly happy about the idea, as there had been a contentious meeting with my predecessor, which went on for three hours without a result.

Knowing what I was up against I decided on a plan of action. I asked Seán to bring the deputation to his room and to place them around the large table there, leaving a chair for me at the upper end and to leave us to it. As I entered the room a couple of the students began to rise to their feet, but seeing that the remainder had no intention of doing likewise they swiftly sat down again. I took my seat and remained silent for some time.

Finally I said that I understood they wished to see me. When one student broke into a propaganda tirade I stopped him and said that as I didn't have much time I wanted to hear their problems, quietly and succinctly. After listening to them for a short while I told them that I wanted to improve the situation in the College of Art. I added, however, that in view of their activities, I should advise them that anyone who thought they could climb over my back to victory should be aware that they were dealing with the wrong man. I then left the room.

In spite of the tough attitude I felt compelled to adopt with these students, it was obvious that change was necessary. Clearly a government department was totally unsuited to the management of, above all things, a College of Art. In the end I guided a Bill through the Oireachtas setting up the National College of Art and Design Board to manage college affairs.

Being in office at a time of student protests can sometimes prove uncomfortable. Nevertheless, looking back on that period, many of the students were fired by an idealism that motivated them to protest against what they believed to be injustices or shortcomings in our education system. In some ways their protests reflected an optimism that problems could be overcome. In modern times students don't seem inclined to, nor perhaps have the time for such protests, and the development of our educational system may be the worse for that.

All through this period of radical change I also felt that it was vitally important never to lose sight of the fact that another school function was to make children conscious of their cultural inheritance. This was outlined in the new curriculum and I tried to ensure that a positive attitude towards the Irish language permeated the education system. My time teaching and working in the Donegal Gaeltacht and working as a Minister in Roinn na Gaeltachta had all served to reinforce my conviction that the Irish language is a vital part of our inheritance.

A realisation of the importance of physical education had also begun to surface in Ireland's schools and the new curriculum dealt with it in detail. A scheme for providing sports' equipment for national schools was introduced and a parliamentary secretary was assigned to me for the first time to take charge of sport and of the building program that had begun in Limerick for a National College of Physical Education.

Perhaps because I had worked under the old system, I was very aware when I introduced the new curriculum that a change of immense importance was about to take place. The work of the teacher would not be easier, only different. 'At his or her own rate' was the key. There is little doubt that to quite an extent, the curriculum was a cornerstone in changing children's attitude towards school and I believe it has stood the test of time.

* * * *

The Kennedy Report

In 1967, the then Minster for Education, Donogh O'Malley, had set up a committee, under the Chairmanship of District Justice Eileen Kennedy. Its purpose was to survey reformatory and industrial schools, as well as other homes catering for children in care, and to make a report with recommendations to the Minister. I received the final report in 1970. It was an excellent report, highlighting as it did the serious deficiencies in the service, which I accepted. It gave my Department a base on which to build for the future.

The Kennedy committee met formally on 69 occasions. All industrial schools and reformatories in the State were visited by members of the committee, some more than once. They also visited a number of voluntary homes, foster homes and other institutions and took the opportunity to speak with the children. I remember being pleased that in reference to religious institutions the committee stated: 'We are very much aware that if it were not for the dedicated work of many of our religious bodies the position would be a great deal worse.'

There were many recommendations in the report, two of the more important ones being that St Conleth's in Daingean should be closed as soon as possible and that Marlborough House should be closed immediately.

When I was appointed Minister for Education one of my first official visits had been to St Conleth's. It catered for an older age group, referred there for serious offences. I had spent the day speaking with managers, teachers and pupils, discussing their problems. I remember visiting a metalwork class and asking the children which they preferred, woodwork or metalwork. A substantial majority favoured metalwork. When I asked the school manager why, he'd replied simply: 'Keys are made from metal.'

As I had moved through the class I saw a pupil filing a large penny. When asked what he was doing he'd replied, 'Nothing'. After further questioning the pupil had explained that if he placed the filed penny into a telephone coin box he could phone someone, talk to them for as long as he wished and then retrieve the penny for further use. The boy asked the officer if he wanted the coin and the reply being yes, handed it over. The official told me later that on his way home he decided to test the coin. He told his wife what he proposed to do so that she could explain what was involved if he had a problem with the law. He went to a nearby telephone booth, inserted the coin, rang his wife, had a few words with her and then retrieved the coin – it had worked perfectly.

It was obvious to me after that visit that there were many young people there with excellent capabilities if we could find a way to cater for them. I could also see that the buildings were in very poor condition and that educational facilities were poor, through no fault of management or teachers. I had realised then that drastic action was needed and I was pleased when the Kennedy Report backed me up. Having discussed the matter with my officials, I decided to close Daingean as soon as a replacement was built. A site was acquired at Oberstown, North County Dublin, and a new modern complex, to be conducted on open lines, was in the course of construction when I left office in 1973. In the meantime I improved education facilities at Daingean.

We had anticipated the recommendation regarding Marlborough House and when I received the report St Laurence's Training Centre at Finglas was already being built to replace it. In the Education Estimate, 1971/72, I proposed that the money for reformatories and industrial schools be increased by 40%, most of which was to be allocated to Marlborough House.

The original purpose of Marlborough House had been to serve as a remand and detention centre for young offenders. It was intended for the boy whose offence the Court did not consider merited committment to a reformatory school for more than one month. In reality the one month detention system was a failure. The boys being sent to Marlborough House at this stage were, in general, those whom other reformatories couldn't cope with. The centre was completely unsuitable for this purpose. It was run by a staff who had no special training in childcare. This omission may have arisen from a belief that the training wasn't necessary as the children were expected to be in Marlborough for on average a few days or a month at the most.

St Laurence's on the other hand would be well provided with trained professional staff, psychological and psychiatric services with occupational and recreational facilities. Courts might refer first and second time offenders there but not those guilty of serious crimes. There were many specialist teachers for subjects such as woodwork, physical education and music and drama. A remand assessment unit, with full medical, educational, psychological and, where necessary, psychiatric examination facilities, was also provided.

St. Laurence's opened its doors on January 14, 1972 and most of the young people in Marlborough House were transferred there. Marlborough House was closed down completely in August 1972.

Other recommendations from the Kennedy Report were also put in place. The amount per pupil paid by the State and by the health boards towards the upkeep of children in care had doubled by the end of 1969. During the subsequent Dáil debate, Garret Fitzgerald, Fine Gael's spokesman on education, stated that his party was pleased that, at last, the sum of money provided had been greatly increased. He congratulated me for doing something about it. Barry Desmond, spokesman for Labour, commented that he appreciated the attention the deprived child was getting. To double a grant is very unusual but the fact that the proposal passed the stringent scrutiny of the Department of Finance and the Opposition parties in Dáil Éireann proves the necessity and urgency of my action. It also lends credence to the argument that for quite a considerable time the various religious orders used their own resources to make up the difference.

I was glad to be in a position to help. I was learning more about the needs of children in care and now that something had been achieved I was anxious to do more. I wanted to change their living conditions, to introduce a more homelike atmosphere with smaller self-contained units. New group home units were provided and many children attended local schools. Parents were invited to visit their children as often as possible and to facilitate this I introduced a scheme of free travel for them in September 1971. In some circumstances children were allowed home on weekends.

I felt that moves to new well-equipped buildings and staff training would help to raise morale. Schools with modern facilities were established and special in-service training courses for staff were organized. An intensive course in childcare was held in July 1971 for senior members of reformatories and industrial schools. From then on it was necessary for managers of remand and training centres to have suitable academic qualifications and experience before they could be appointed.

I was also anxious to provide a soundly based education programme geared towards rehabilitating children in care to give them a fresh start in school. The hope was that they would be motivated to continue their education when they returned home, or that they would be prepared for employment.

I was able to achieve much of my programme because of an improving economic climate and the guidelines in the Kennedy Report. When it was published the report helped to greatly increase public interest in the welfare of children in care and I welcomed this. In a relatively short space of time great strides were made towards implementing its recommendations.

It was to be quite some time after I left the Department of Education that I first heard the word 'paedophile'. During my time as Minster I hadn't an inkling that child sex abuse existed. When I published the Kennedy Report in 1970 Dáil questions on a variety of aspects of it came thick and fast. Some deputies praised the diligence and selflessness of the religious orders in caring for children in care. Nobody raised the question of abuse. Dr Noel Browne and Dr John O'Connell were among my most persistent questioners and nobody doubts that if these two deputies had heard so much as a whisper about abuse they would immediately have raised the matter in the Dáil.

I suppose in a way, like most people, I was living in an age of innocence when nobody believed that people in authority, be they religious or lay, could commit such heinous crimes. None of us was then aware that perpetrators of child sex abuse are very devious people. We did not know that they were often able to deceive the public about their nefarious conduct, for years on end. When I introduced training courses for child carers I established a screening system to ensure that only genuinely caring people would get places. Years later I read about a man who had been held in very high esteem for a long period of time, for his work in child-care. He had just been brought to court and charged with child abuse. From the dates given I was horrified to realise that he had passed through the tests and the courses. He would have passed through an interview board at the top of his group. We know that now; we didn't know it then. The difficulty of detecting an abuser when we knew nothing about paedophilia and could therefore not ask the right questions is now obvious.

When *States of Fear* was first shown on television I was shocked and saddened by its contents. On one of the few occasions since my retirement I agreed to give an interview to talk about child-care at the time and my involvement in it. I welcomed the proposal to set up a Commission to assist those who had been abused. I hoped that treatment and counselling would help the victims and that the perpetrators would face the rigours of the law. I also expressed my sympathy for the plight of the large number of nuns, priests and brothers, who had dedicated their lives to bringing love, affection and the benefits of education to thousands of children in care. They did this for no personal gain and were now being held up to public scorn. They had been found guilty by association because of the shocking activities of the few within their communities who seriously betrayed their trust. *States of Fear* performed an important service in bringing the plight of people who were abused to public attention. I feel, however, that it was a pity that a more balanced documentary was not presented, so that, while emphasising the shocking crimes committed, many innocent people would have been spared considerable anguish.

* * * *

Providing for children in care was not my only concern. I was also anxious that the children of the travelling community and the children of the settled community should learn about each other's way of life.

To achieve this the ideal solution was to have travelling children attend ordinary national schools. However, in one instance, because of a large number of travellers' children in one Dublin area it was necessary to build a school solely for them.

I can still clearly remember the official opening of the school. Beautifully clad little children formed a guard of honour for the Archbishop of Dublin, Dr McQuaid, and for me as Minister for Education. Press photographers were present and as I moved through the ranks I asked the children if they liked being photographed. They all happily replied that they did. I said that their photographs might appear in the newspapers, thinking that they would be delighted but they immediately covered their faces and started to hang their heads. I was surprised and asked the social worker why they disliked something that settled children would be excited by. She said that travellers' photographs and names rarely appeared in the media except when they were in trouble with the law.

I walked around the classrooms and stopped to speak to six little children, sitting around a table in one room. When I asked them what class they were in, they pointed at the table and said, 'this class'. The literal truth of the answer brought back memories of my days teaching in Clogherhead. I was determined that these children and others like them would be treated the same as all the children in the nation. Unfortunately, despite all efforts, problems in this area continue to exist today.

Around the same period my attention was drawn to the needs of children, then known as mentally handicapped. At the time these children were rarely seen in public and lived at home, where their parents coped as best they could. I was fortunate enough to know something about their needs. When I first became a TD I regularly called into St Mary's, a home for mentally handicapped children with learning difficulties that was established near my house by the St John of God Brothers. When the Brothers then decided to establish a school at St Mary's I was delighted. A fully qualified teacher from the local national school offered to teach there and applied to the Department of Education for permission to do so. She was told that she could but that the Department would not pay her salary. As she had decided to go to St Mary's in any case, she had then come to me as her newly elected TD. I had battled with the Department to have her recognised and was subsequently successful. In my role as Minister I continued to pursue a campaign on the children's behalf. In no area has so much been achieved, in a relatively short space of time. I learned much, and gained more, through my involvement with these children. They have a tremendous fund of love and affection, which they unstintingly pass on to others. The enormous dedication of the Brothers of St John of

God was a lesson to me and I very much appreciated their kindness in asking me to preside at the opening, on their Golden Jubilee celebration in 1996.

* * * *

The Community School Programme

Two years before I was appointed Minister for Education, Donogh O'Malley had announced the free post-primary education scheme. The scheme was immensely successful. This was not simply because it was free, as many schools at the time were already free, but because a large section of the population, never previously involved with post-primary education, were now told that education was their children's right. Free school transport was provided and education was no longer confined to the better-off in society.

An enormous amount of work lay ahead, however, if it was to become a reality. I was faced with many formidable practical problems, such as the urgent need for many more teachers and schools and the need to expand the school transport system. One humourous incident stands out in my memory from this time. As CIÉ did not have enough buses they had to contract some work out to private individuals. Some of these drivers insisted on carrying adults if they had vacant seats, even though they weren't insured to do so. CIÉ finally had to let one man in the Midlands go over this rule. The driver thought that the Department of Education was responsible, so he arrived in Dublin and parked his bus outside our offices, displaying a large poster with the words 'HUNGER STRIKE' on it. The driver sat in his bus explaining to all and sundry how he was being victimised by the Department and was determined to continue his hunger strike until he got justice. Some time later as my driver was walking back to the Department he noticed a young lad sitting in the driver's seat. He asked him where the owner was – 'Gone for his dinner' was the reply!

For historical reasons the emphasis in Ireland had always been on academic education. Vocational education was often bedevilled by the assumption that where it began liberal education ended. At the time only a two-year Group Certificate course was available to day pupils in vocational schools which didn't help matters. Under the free scheme parents now largely opted for secondary schools where pupils could pursue Intermediate and Leaving Certificate courses and had the prospect of proceeding to third-level. I agreed with an American educationalist who said that the nation that disposes excellence in plumbing and tolerates shoddiness in philosophy will have neither good plumbing nor good philosophy; neither its pipes nor its theories will hold water. School subjects do not become of little intellectual value just because they can be applied to the essential purpose of earning a living. I wanted to change public perceptions about vocational education. As a step forward I introduced the Leaving Certificate to upgrade vocational schools in the public domain.

I felt that secondary, vocational and comprehensive schools were all just as satisfactory and had no ideological hang-ups on the matter. My only concern was that a school was large enough to provide equal educational opportunities. Sharing facilities was one way of achieving this aim and I was particularly taken by a scheme of common enrolment in Ballinamore, Co Leitrim. The management and staff of three schools – Diocesan, convent and vocational – pooled their resources, to provide a system of post-primary education from which the children would derive maximum benefit. I felt that this model could be repeated in small towns throughout Ireland, but at the time Vocational Education Committees (VECs) could share facilities yet couldn't contribute towards costs unless they were under their own management. In an effort to help foster co-operation, I introduced the Vocational Education (Amendment) Bill in 1970 so that the vocational schools could share costs and management with private schools. Meetings were held in a number of areas in an effort to foster co-operation but the general response was disappointing. Distance between schools, discipline problems and insurance, were just some of the arguments against it. Common enrolment was accepted only in Ballinamore and in Boyle, Co Roscommon.

It was clear that another solution had to be found and the onus was on me to find it. I knew that if a school was large enough provision could be made for a comprehensive curriculum. To cater for these needs, I introduced a new type of school, the community school. Rather than building separate secondary and vocational schools or rebuilding two or three small schools, we would now build one large community school. The community schools would have facilities catering for many specific subjects, such as science laboratories and technical drawing workshops. It seemed like an ideal solution.

Financially, demands on education resources were understandably great at the time and we were very fortunate to have an application for a World Bank Loan accepted. To speed matters up, an integrated team, including architects and engineers, was appointed to assist in the implementation of the programme for community schools.

Cardinal W Conway, Archbishop of Armagh at the time, wrote to me requesting information on the project. I replied, explaining what was involved. The Cardinal, apparently, then passed copies of my letter to superiors of Catholic schools for comment. A national newspaper secured a copy of the letter and published it before I had the opportunity of discussing the concept with everyone involved. In such circumstances this, to many, radical proposal, met with a very emotive response.

The Opposition alleged that I had kept the Catholic Church informed, while keeping the Protestant Church in the dark and accused me of sectarianism. The religious orders claimed that I was planning to take control of their schools, while the VECs accused me of placing their schools under the control of the religious orders. Teachers in both the secondary and vocational schools were worried about their positions. In a welter of emotive outpourings the educational value of the proposal was all but lost. Opposition became so widespread that the education correspondent of one newspaper wrote that 'the grand design of the community schools, the National Blueprint, was as dead as a pork chop'.

I was firmly convinced of the merits of the proposal and I was determined to see it through. Basically both the religious communities and the VECs were opposed to the community schools concept because of their fears in respect of ownership and management. They had all given wonderful service to the Irish people in the field of education and I was anxious to clarify matters as quickly as possible. I held meetings with the Education Committee of the Catholic Hierarchy, with bishops and other religious leaders of different denominations, with VECs, and with the teaching and other interested bodies. I patiently explained to all of them what I had in mind and, more importantly perhaps, what I had not in mind, such as, for example, a State takeover of schools, a suggestion that was going the rounds.

In the meantime I decided to proceed with the project. I selected the two rapidly growing areas of Tallaght and Blanchardstown, now Coolmine, as suitable locations for community schools. From two relatively small villages they had become towns in their own right, with little or no educational facilities. Both areas were in the Archdiocese of Dublin. Dr John C. McQuaid was the long-standing Catholic Archbishop of Dublin and, as he was not a member of the Hierarchy's Education Committee, I discussed the projects with him individually, explaining what I had in mind. He gave me his support, which was crucial at that time.

Archbishop McQuaid was a conservative in doctrinal matters and understandably yielded to none in that respect. He was noted for not replying to media criticism of himself or of his actions. This gave those who disliked him a field day, ensuring that the image of the autocrat grew and grew. This was not the man I came to know. I found him a caring man who had founded charities for the poor of his Diocese when few, including the State, were showing any great concern for them. He was held in high regard by his priests and was particularly noted for his kindness to any of them in difficulty. In the field of education I found the Archbishop to be a man of vision. I had decided that two parents, one of whom would be a mother, should be elected to community school boards. His quick reaction in supporting my decision ensured its general acceptance nationwide and so for the first time parents were officially appointed to Irish school boards.

At a subsequent meeting of the Catholic Bishops' Education Committee I was criticised for having announced parental involvement in the new schools without discussing the matter with them. I reminded them that at a meeting of bishops in Maynooth it had been decided that each bishop would make decisions regarding community schools for his own Diocese, and that Dr McQuaid had accepted my view on parental involvement. The committee was not impressed.

The Archbishop bore a grave mien at public functions and was punctilious in expressing respect for the State but he had, however, a sense of humour that belied the stern exterior he portrayed. I was told one story about the time he caught up with three students on the avenue of Blackrock College, one of whom was mimicking his style of walking, with one shoulder lower than the other. He touched the student on the shoulder saying: 'Wrong shoulder, sonny.'

Winning the approval of the various governing bodies was important but another crucial factor was winning the trust of the parents. I understood that parents in areas designated for community schools would need to be convinced that the new system would help their children succeed in a rapidly changing world. I decided to send a high-level official to attend meetings in these areas, to explain what we hoped to achieve and hopefully to put to rest the various myths circulating.

While some of the objections to the programme could be anticipated we also met with some rather weird ones. In one instance a prominent individual referred to the World Bank Loan, stating that one of the directors of the World Bank was a Swede and that contraception and abortion were rife in Sweden. He maintained that a loan from such a bank would be a telling factor in introducing contraception and abortion into Ireland!

The Opposition in the Dáil continued to attack me on the spurious sectarian issue. In one instance I was accused of discrimination in not appointing a Protestant to the Board of a Dublin community school. I replied that nobody worth his salt would wish to be appointed to a Board except on the basis that he had a contribution to make. Indeed, in a later discussion I had with a representative group of Protestants it was made very clear to me that they didn't wish to receive any such appointment simply and solely because they were Protestants. The

Protestant community was obviously satisfied with my explanation of the community school project. A deputation, made up of various Protestant denominations and led by Dr Simms, Church of Ireland Archbishop of Dublin, with whom I had an excellent rapport, subsequently met with me and requested two community schools. I was glad to agree.

As the Fianna Fáil Árd Fheis of 1971 approached, however, motions opposing the project arrived at headquarters. I must admit that I was somewhat perturbed at this stage. I was aware that some of the VECs and religious communities would have considerable influence on delegates throughout the country. There could be no certainty as to how the Árd Fheis decision would go. Beleaguered as I still was in Dáil Éireann and by pressure groups outside it, I knew that if the Árd Fheis voted against the concept I could be left high and dry and could only proceed under considerable difficulty.

I prepared with care for the occasion. I spoke in some detail and explained exactly what was involved. I pointed out that the document on community schools had not been intended for publication and had been sent to the Catholic Hierarchy in response to their request for information. I stated that there was no question of the religious orders being asked, much less compelled, to move out of education and the same applied to vocational schools. There was also no question of confiscation of school buildings. I was already spending a large amount of capital acquiring new school buildings but if I had four times as much money I could spend that too. I also stated that there was no basis for suggestions that community schools meant a State takeover of education. The Department of Education would not be represented on the proposed boards of management and the schools would be as independent as any existing post-primary school. The only area the State would take over were the bills. I ended by saying that I meant to ensure that this was no empty formula but a practical reality.

I won the Árd Fheis vote by an overwhelming majority and the community school scheme was well on its way. By June 1972, I could name 50 centres in the Dáil that were being listed for community schools, including one in Ardee, Co Louth.

The 1973 Fine Gael/Labour Coalition Government misinterpreted the controversy surrounding the programme and, believing there was wholesale opposition to it, took tentative steps to stop their development. They soon learned the reverse was the case. Needless to say, I was pleased with the success of the project. Overcoming tough and emotional opposition in the Dáil and across Ireland was stressful and difficult, but the public seal of approval stamped on the scheme made it all worthwhile. There are now 81 community schools in Ireland and

I was delighted when Tallaght Community School invited me to their celebration of 30 years of community education in 2002.

* * * *

The Unions

When I joined the Drogheda branch of the INTO in April 1939, teachers' salaries were a regular item on the agenda. In 1920 a salary scheme had been agreed, which the INTO regarded as being fair and equitable. This happy state of affairs didn't last long. The new Free State Cumann na nGael Government cut teachers' salaries and in the early 1930s a Fianna Fáil Government did likewise. Consequently agitation for the restoration of the 1920 salary scales formed an important part of our activities.

In 1945 Irish male teachers were paid £147 pa, and after many years reached a maximum of £318 pa, while female teachers received £134, with a maximum of £258. Hence, when salary scales in Britain granted men a starting salary of £300 and a maximum of £750 pa, and women £270 up to £600 pa, the Irish teachers' patience ran out. The INTO Executive refused the Department of Education's final offer and a special congress was held in Dublin, which I attended as a delegate from Drogheda. A majority of the delegates, including myself, supported the rejection.

A strike was declared and Dublin national teachers went out on strike March 1946. The Government and the then Minister for Education, Tomás Deirg, refused to consider a further increase. Finally, as a result of a letter from Archbishop McQuaid requesting the teachers to return to work – the strike ended in October 1946.

When I entered the Dáil in 1957 the 1946 strike was a distant memory but teachers' salaries were still a contentious issue. I became good friends with Donnchadh Ó Briain, TD Limerick who was Parliamentary Secretary to the Taoiseach and attended all government meetings. The strike came up in conversation one time and I said that I'd found Tomás Deirg's unbending attitude very difficult to understand. Donnchadh told me that he'd never felt so sorry for anybody as he had for Tomás Deirg during that strike. He had watched him being vilified and condemned by teachers. He assured me that at government meetings Tomás had fought like a Trojan for the teachers, but that the then Taoiseach, Éamon de Valera, said that the Government could not give way and that was that. Tomás Deirg, Donnchadh told me, was a man of high principles. He'd been placed in charge of the Department and he would take responsibility for decisions himself. Never, by even a murmur, did he suggest that matters would have been different had he had his way. Things are not always as they seem.

Not much was achieved by the 1946 strike in the short term but the issue continued to gather momentum and had been incorporated into the debate over parity of pay for all teachers. During my membership of the INTO I was a strong advocate of pay parity for secondary, vocational and national schoolteachers. When I was appointed Minister for Education in July 1969 relations between the three teaching organisations over this issue, particularly between the ASTI (Association of Secondary Teachers in Ireland) and the INTO, were at a very low ebb. There were three distinct salary scales for teachers, the secondary teachers being on the highest scale, the vocational teachers next, with national teachers on the lowest scale. For years the INTO had been campaigning for a common scale. Their claim was strenuously resisted on the grounds that the differential had always been there and that secondary teachers had a university degree as opposed to the national teachers two-year training course. The INTO argued back that national teachers had a highly professional training course and that the one-year course for the Higher Diploma in Education did not compare at all favourably to it.

In May 1968, a Government-appointed Teachers' Salaries Tribunal had recommended that there be a common basic scale of salary for all teachers, with allowances for qualifications and for posts of responsibility. The Tribunal's findings were accepted by the Vocational Teachers' Association (VTA, later TUI) and by the INTO but were rejected by the ASTI, who staged a strike in February 1969. Under the strike settlement the Department had committed to granting special allowances to secondary teachers. The other teaching bodies then threatened to strike. Dr Louden Ryan had been appointed chairman of a committee to try to find a way out of the impasse.

Dr Ryan had found that the secondary teachers' settlement departed from the Tribunal's findings. The ASTI then argued that, mistake or not, it was a signed agreement and must be honoured.

This was the dilemma I faced when I became Minister for Education. Offers of concession on any side would be met with strike threats from the other parties.

My relations with the ASTI, who, in the prevailing atmosphere, would have been suspicious of an INTO member in any case, understandably became very strained. Demands were made that I resign my INTO membership. I was not, of course, an active member at the time but the thought had never entered my head to resign. I felt the demand was questioning my integrity but Ministers came to expect outbursts of this nature in times of difficulty, so I simply ignored the matter. When I addressed the Secondary Teachers' Congress for the first time, however, I briefly referred to allegations that I didn't cherish all the teaching bodies equally. I denied that this was so and I let it go at that. I was treated very courteously by the President and the Standing Committee at the Congress but I won't pretend that the general feeling towards me was particularly pleasant. I heard later that a small number of teachers actually left the hall as I started speaking.

I'm afraid this mood prevailed during much of my term as Minister. Indeed on one occasion I prepared two speeches for Congress, one conciliatory and the other much more forceful. When I sat down after speaking, Tom O'Dea, President of the ASTI, noticed my two scripts and asked, 'Why two?' I told him that as I was always last to speak, I had decided to take note of the trend of the debate and to use the speech I deemed appropriate. Fortunately I found that the conciliatory speech was the one for that occasion.

I remember at the height of the community schools' controversy a speaker at the ASTI Congress lauded the excellence of the religious orders' contribution to Irish education, and wondered, at length, why I should be interfering with them. When he resumed his seat he was given a standing ovation. I was well aware that the speech and the applause was a not too subtle attack on me. The ASTI had frequently rejected applications by the religious orders for membership. Indeed, that same year there was a motion on the agenda from the religious seeking admission. As I expected it was very heavily defeated.

With these experiences at the ASTI Congress I wondered what my reception would be like at the VTA Conference. As I travelled to the conference I heard on the radio news that the VTA had decided to take strike action. There wasn't much point in having my blood pressure rise, so I simply adopted a wait and see attitude.

I was received in a very friendly fashion when I arrived and there was no mention of strike action. When the dinner ended the President made a very strong speech in which he tore the Department's policy to shreds. This was followed by an even more caustic and censorious speech by the Vice-President. I then spoke and having noted the comments of the previous speakers, simply expounded on aspects of my policy and talked about what I hoped to achieve in the coming year. I usually weigh up situations as I find them and I most decidedly did not mention a strike, and neither did they. The friendly attitude towards me was very apparent and I had a most pleasant evening. There was no reference whatever to a strike and none took place.

As to the INTO Congress all I need say is that I got a very warm welcome there. Delegates were all pleased and proud to have a member of the organisation as Minister for Education.

Throughout 1970 the education calendar was marked by threats of strike action, and suspension of these, pending negotiations on salary scales. Marathon negotiations took place and strikes continued to be narrowly avoided. A salary proposal I made in July 1970 was turned down and strikes continued to be threatened and narrowly averted into the new school year.

Proposals were put to the ASTI in January 1971. The ASTI threatened another strike in February and I was aware that events hinged on whether the schools of the religious orders would close in the event of a strike. Mother Jordana, Head of the Convent Schools' Association, announced that convent schools would remain open. However, the Clerical Managers had decided to close and their Chairman, Father Hughes SJ, had circulated notices to the newspapers. I was unable to contact Father Hughes, so I immediately approached Archbishop McQuaid. His office tracked Father Hughes down and after they spoke Father Hughes decided to reverse the decision. He also offered to approach the newspapers to cancel the closure notices, but the Archbishop told him he would organise it and the notices were retrieved. I was relieved at the outcome but more needed to be done so I quickly moved to copper-fasten the position by proposing some financial compensation be given to teachers affected by the breach of the 1969 'allowances' agreement. It offered teachers more money, but was limited to teachers already in the service to ensure future teachers were channelled into the new framework.

On February 15, the ASTI rejected these proposals. On February 16, however, their decision to strike was postponed pending negotiations involving the Irish Congress of Trade Unions (ICTU). Finally, on March 1, 1971, despite some disagreement in its ranks, it was reported that the ASTI strike was off.

The common salary scale was now an accomplished fact but the deep-seated antagonism that continued between the teacher organisations concerned me. It would be extremely difficult to develop a co-operative system while such attitudes persisted. The main protagonists were the ASTI and the INTO, and the fact that I was a national teacher and had been embroiled with the ASTI on the pay issue wasn't helping matters.

Whenever I met the three organisations as a group I could be reasonably sure that either the INTO or the ASTI would take umbrage at something the other said and little progress would be made. I resolved to tackle what, to many, appeared to be the impossible task of improving union relationships. Prospects could hardly be termed bright but I was determined to do the best I could.

The three unions were distinct organisations. I had been an INTO activist for years and I knew exactly how it operated. By now I was also well-tuned into the manner in which the ASTI and the VTA conducted their affairs.

The ASTI had an executive of 72 members and a Standing Committee of about 12 members negotiated with me and the Department. Before coming to a decision on important matters, the Standing Committee referred back to the full executive. In an emotional atmosphere a few vocal members could, and sometimes did, secure the defeat of the Standing Committee's recommendations and this further complicated matters. The ASTI President, Tom O'Dea, however, was a formidable figure and a tough negotiator, who was ultimately to play an important role in reaching a peaceful solution.

The VTA was led by Maurice Holly and Charles McCarthy, both good negotiators. Charles regularly used the phrase 'meaningful negotiations' and, in fact, I think he probably coined it. The problem was that his interpretation of 'meaningful' was often at odds with the Department's. While the VTA would naturally like to see more co-operation between the teaching bodies, the battle between the ASTI and INTO didn't perturb them over much, as the VTA would benefit from any financial injection aimed at settling their dispute. It was on fairly good terms with both unions.

The INTO was led by its President and Executive Committee. Its Chief Executives were Seán Brosnahan and Matt Griffin, again very able negotiators. I had known them both for years and this was to prove very important to me in the delicate negotiations that lay ahead.

A meeting was about to take place at which the three organisations would be present. There was one item on the agenda about which the INTO and ASTI were at loggerheads and both had refused to budge an inch. I asked Seán and Matt to meet me a few days before the meeting and, after a long discussion, I prevailed on them to withdraw their opposition. After consulting with their Executive they agreed to do so.

When the meeting started the ASTI repeated their demand. After what appeared to be a few moments hesitation, to the surprise of the ASTI and the VTA, Seán stated that the INTO would agree. Charlie McCarthy of the VTA quickly concluded that something had been planned. He said, 'If you had a halo on you, Seán, I would pray to you.' It was a step forward on the road to reconciliation.

I also met privately on a number of occasions with a prominent member of the ASTI in an attempt to formulate a plan through which friendly relations could be cultivated.

After considerable negotiation, the executives of the ASTI, the INTO and VTA (TUI) agreed to meet me at the Department. The plan was that they would then meet together in a separate room, in an attempt to sort out their differences.

On the fateful morning the INTO and the VTA representatives arrived but the ASTI delegation failed to materialise. After an interval I heard from ASTI headquarters that they were not coming. I got in touch with them and after some discussion they agreed to attend. Meanwhile the delegates from the INTO and the VTA had settled in the 'negotiation' room. When the ASTI delegates arrived their President, Tom O'Dea, stated that they saw little purpose in attending the meeting as whatever the ASTI proposed the INTO would oppose and stalemate would ensue. I pointed out that there was little to be lost by talking and got them to join the others.

A department official met one of the ASTI delegates on his way to lunch, and asked him how the discussions had gone. He replied that when they sat down to start the discussions it was as if the floor were covered with eggs, that they were determined not to break any eggs, and that they had broken none.

From then onwards discussions continued. Members of each union recognised that they had much more in common than they had realised or had been ready to admit. Slowly but surely they began to co-operate with one another. I remember telling my friend George Colley, then Minister for Finance and the Public Services about it. He said he was pleased to hear it, but jokingly warned that he could foresee a future day when Ministers of Finance and Education could have cause to regret it, when faced by the demands of one powerful teachers' union.

The teaching bodies came together, however tentatively, many years ago. I was pleased to have helped commence the peace process between them.

* * * *

It is strange to think now that relatively few colleges and institutions offered third-level courses of a technological nature by the seventies. Almost all such awards were external. I was delighted when there was a demand from industry, as well as from students, for more specialised courses with recognised Irish qualifications. To cope with this need, Regional Technical Colleges (RTCs), some of which I officially opened, were under construction.

To get the RTCs off the ground quickly students who had completed the Intermediate Certificate course could enter RTCs and complete the Leaving Certificate course there. With RTCs available throughout Ireland for the first time, new opportunities existed for students to access third level education, and to improve their career prospects, while studying in their own areas.

The next point to establish was an awards system. The Higher Education Authority (HEA) had been set-up on an ad hoc basis by my predecessor, Brian Lenihan. Government approval for higher education development plans and for general allocation of State funds for third level could now be sought from the HEA instead of from the Minister. I steered the legislation through the Oireachtas establishing the HEA on a statutory basis.

I then recommended to the Government, in January 1971, that legislation should be prepared to establish a National Council for Educational Awards (NCEA) and in February I established an ad hoc council. One of its main functions would be to grant awards to students who had successfully studied at third-level institutions other than universities.

The first students to study for the National Certificate, a third level course under the aegis of the NCEA, were enrolled at Regional Technical Colleges at Athlone, Carlow, Dundalk, Sligo and Waterford in 1970. Ninety-three students were awarded the National Certificate in 1972. I attended the official opening of the National Institute of Higher Education (NIHE), now the University of Limerick, by An Taoiseach, Jack Lynch, in September 1972. With the establishment of the NIHE, technical and technological education had reached full maturity. In a few short years it had developed from the two-year Group Certificate day course to the very apex of third-level education.

The Fine Gael/Labour Coalition 1973/77 subsequently formed a committee to bring the NIHE in Limerick under the aegis of the National University. I strenuously opposed this proposal in the Dáil, pointing out that the NIHE would undoubtedly be absorbed by the long established and largely academic National University system. I believed that the NIHE could only become a university when its roots ran strong and deep. I'm glad to say that the proposal was dropped.

In the modern world the demands made on our schools are constantly changing and the needs of the disadvantaged change with them. I believe that, to this day, Ireland's educational system is one of which we may well be proud. The challenge, for the future, is to ensure its continued growth and development, so that, in keeping with the ideal outlined in the Constitution, 'we may cherish all of our children equally'.

Ten

The Arms Crisis

There had been violence in Northern Ireland throughout 1968 and early 1969 but when the General Election took place in June the situation was relatively calm. The election was fought on internal domestic issues and Northern Ireland scarcely figured in public debates. After Jack Lynch appointed me Minister for Education in July 1969, I thought that my only problems would be educational ones. I was hoping that our election victory would ensure a long and peaceful term in government. I was to be quickly disabused of that notion. Within a few short weeks rioting began and erupted fully with the Battle of the Bogside in Derry. We were soon facing a totally changed set of circumstances. At the time I felt that the Northern question would play some part in our lives but I never thought that it would assume such extraordinary proportions in my party's future or in my own life. I had no inkling that the Troubles would last for decades to come.

As the violence in the North worsened public feeling ran high. The Government had to constantly reiterate its policy of seeking reunification of Ireland by democratic and peaceful means only and not by armed intervention. Dating back to the Government of Ireland Act 1920, which had partitioned Ireland between the Irish Free State and a six-county Statelet, to be known as Northern Ireland, the reunification of the country was a primary policy objective for Fianna Fáil. Successive leaders, de Valera, Lemass and now Lynch, had worked assiduously to try to convince the British Government, as well as world public opinion, of the logic of a United Ireland. Throughout my life I longed to see Ireland truly united, but I believed it could only be achieved by peaceful and democratic means, so I had no problem accepting our party policy. Indeed it had helped to convince me to join Fianna Fáil in the first place.

Northern Ireland, with a population two-thirds Unionist and one-third Nationalist, had been established to assuage the fears of the large Unionist population, who had strenuously opposed the 1920 Act, and to secure a base to safeguard 'Britain's back door' in case there was another war. In the Dáil debate on the Treaty in 1921/22, the partition issue was rarely referred to. This was largely because the British Prime Minister, Lloyd George, had made a promise that he would establish a

Boundary Commission to deal with it. The Irish delegation had been led to believe that the Commission would transfer large Nationalist areas of Northern Ireland to the Irish Free State, thus ensuring the eventual demise of the Statelet. The hopes for the Boundary Commission proved illusory. I was very young at the time but I still have a hazy memory of the disappointment felt at the collapse of the Commission and of the recriminations which followed for quite a long time afterwards.

In the 50 years following the Statelet's establishment the Unionist party maintained control of the new Northern Irish parliament at Stormont. They formed a government exclusively from their own members. Unionists, however, were still fearful that the increasing Nationalist population would eventually overwhelm them at the polls so they set about strengthening their position. They abolished the proportional representation voting system, laid down by the British Government, replacing it with the single vote/single seat constituency system. The composition of constituencies was also gerrymandered, for example in Derry City, where Catholics outnumbered Protestants by two to one, Catholics could only elect eight members to a twenty-member council. The voting system for local elections was loaded in favour of high ratepayers – mainly Unionist. Local Authorities were responsible for allocating public housing and Nationalists often found it very difficult to obtain a home. Finding employment was another problem. The end result was that emigration was higher within the Nationalist community.

I found this discrimination very disturbing. I remember discussing it with a small group of people, including an Unionist and his wife, who was the daughter of an Orange Order Grandmaster. I said that progress could be made towards peace and reconciliation if discrimination ceased. 'Alleged discrimination,' the lady immediately replied. I found her response disconcerting. When I later told a relative of mine, who was born in the North and who lived in Belfast, about it he wasn't a bit surprised. He said that during a bus strike he gave a lift to two old ladies standing at a bus stop in an Unionist area. In the course of conversation one lady had asked him if he could tell them what this discrimination that some people were speaking of, was about. I suppose it had to be taken into account that the two communities in the North lived completely separate lives. They only spoke to their own kind, went to their own churches and schools, read their own newspapers and knew little or nothing about the lives of the opposite group. As the years passed Nationalists became more and more frustrated by their subservient position and the seeds of violence were sown.

There had been sporadic incidents of sectarian violence during the early decades of Unionist rule but it wasn't until the late 1950s that a more serious period of violence broke out. Members of the IRA, operating from the Republic, launched attacks on RUC police stations in border areas. The RUC and the B Specials, a militia-style Unionist police force, were the police arm of the Northern State. The deep prejudice that some of their members harboured against Nationalists manifested itself in small niggling ways on a daily basis. One priest told me that when a local RUC sergeant caught some boys raiding an orchard the Unionist boys were allowed to go home, while the Nationalist lads were detained for a number of hours. It was countless small incidents like this, combined with more serious ones, which made the RUC completely unacceptable to the Nationalist population and a target for attack. The raids on the RUC stations, however, were a totally unacceptable act to our Government and would not be tolerated. I fully supported the measures taken by the then Minister for Justice, Charlie Haughey, to defeat the IRA. The subversive campaign had soon been called off.

The 1960s had brought a gradual improvement in relations between the Unionist and Irish Governments. In January 1965 the Taoiseach, Seán Lemass, went to Belfast to meet the Northern Prime Minister, Terence O'Neill. This was the Irish Government's first official recognition of Northern Ireland and I was pleased they were going to meet as I thought this was a step in the right direction. A 'stand off' attitude was not productive and while progress might be slow, I believed it would come. Many Unionists disagreed with this view. In a foretaste of later developments, one of the leading Unionist protesters against the visit was the young Ian Paisley.

Northern Ireland was profoundly influenced by major social and political changes taking place throughout the world in the late 1960s. 1968 in particular was a year of upheaval worldwide, with anti-Vietnam war protests in the US, student riots in Paris and elsewhere, and the Soviet crushing of Socialist revolt in Czechoslovakia. As I had watched these events on television, listened to discussions on radio and read about them in the newspapers, I remember thinking that if the situation in the North, where Nationalists were suffering from similar discrimination and lack of political power, was not quickly resolved, more violence would be inevitable. Thankfully a number of Nationalists started organising effective and, most importantly, peaceful campaigns for better civil rights in the North. The principal demands of the Civil Rights Movement were to have one man/one vote in local elections, an end to discrimination in housing and jobs, the disbanding of the B Specials and an end to the Special Powers Acts which gave the RUC sweeping powers. The more moderate members of the Unionist community joined the movement.

The first civil rights march had taken place in August 1968 in reaction to discrimination in the allocation of local housing in Coalisland, Co Tyrone. Living in a border county I knew a lot about the problems facing the Nationalist community. I was well aware that the lack of houses for Nationalists was simply a device to force them to emigrate, so my sympathies were fully behind the Civil Rights Movement. They marched three miles from Coalisland to Dungannon and it had passed off peacefully.

A second march had then been organised for Derry on Saturday October 5, 1968. It went ahead despite an official ban and was blocked by Unionist protestors. This led to violent rioting which had lasted throughout the weekend.

Four days after the October '68 riots in Derry the Taoiseach had met leading Nationalist politicians. They urged him to put pressure on the British Government to drop its policy of not interfering in Northern Irish affairs and to quickly introduce reforms. Jack Lynch had been doing this from the outset and of course continued to do so throughout the upheaval in the North. At first the door was firmly closed. The British denied that Lynch had any right to intervene but his persistence forced them to change their attitude and to accept his right to represent the views of Nationalists.

In the weeks following the riot the Unionist Government announced a package of reforms, including a fair system of house allocation and universal adult voting rights. In response to this the Northern Ireland Civil Rights Association (NICRA) agreed to postpone further marches. However, a militant left-wing group, the People's Democracy, had organised a march from Belfast to Derry on New Year's Day 1969.

The march had started off peacefully but on the fourth day the marchers were attacked by militant Unionists and also assaulted by members of the RUC and the B Specials. The violence, which was seen both nationally and internationally on televisions around the world, caused further rioting in Derry. The television pictures had stirred up mixed emotions for me. I was extremely concerned that the Unionist Government was still refusing to accept the Nationalists' right to peaceful protest and I was glad to see the unacceptable activities of the RUC and B Specials shown throughout the world. However, I feared that the involvement of the Peoples' Democracy would further alienate the Nationalists and the Unionists. I was also worried that the riot would effect the progress being made in discussions between the Irish and British Governments and the NICRA. Unfortunately this was the case. The Civil Rights Movement was portrayed as a Nationalist plot to bring down the State and Prime Minster O'Neill's moderate reform policies lost support. By April 1969, following a general election, O'Neill had been replaced by a more hard line régime.

Tensions began to heighten over the summer, with the traditional Orange marches going ahead on the Twelfth of July. Appeals made by Nationalists to prevent the Apprentice Boys' march in Derry were ignored. As the march neared the Catholic area of the Bogside a riot began which went on for two days. Watching on television at home, I was shocked to sees petrol bombs and stones raining down and police using CS gas to quell rioters. It was a disturbing portrayal of the deeply ingrained hostility the Unionist Government felt towards the Nationalist population. It became known as the Battle of the Bogside.

Rioting spread to other parts of Northern Ireland. In Belfast for example, an entire street, Bombay Street, in a Catholic area was burned to the ground. Hundreds fled across the border to the safety of the Republic. As tension mounted in the Republic, and particularly within the Fianna Fáil party, there were more calls for armed intervention and the country was in ferment. The violent events taking place in Northern Ireland were about to lead to extremely serious political consequences, and even potential catastrophe, in the Irish State.

* * * *

As Taoiseach and as a relatively new leader of the Fianna Fáil party Jack Lynch faced an extremely difficult task. He was the first Fianna Fáil leader not to have had any involvement, personal or family, with the struggle for Irish Independence or with the Civil War. In the eyes of some party supporters, whose families had been actively associated with both, the lack of a Republican pedigree was a problem. They felt it led to a want of aggressiveness towards Stormont and the British Government, which they believed essential at the time. They were insistent that his predecessors, Éamon de Valera and Seán Lemass, both names synonymous with Irish Republicanism, would have acted differently. My study of de Valera's and Lemass' speeches and actions *vis-à-vis* Northern Ireland, shows that this viewpoint was without foundation. Fortunately for the future of the country, Lynch had the courage to face up to such criticism – both from within the party and without.

It was understandable that Fianna Fáil party supporters were touched to the quick as they watched the violent assaults on Nationalists which were regularly portrayed on television. Some party members demanded that the Government rush to the aid of the beleaguered Nationalist community. A small minority advocated armed intervention by the Irish Army. Members of the Government differed in their approach to the North. A very small number also favoured a more militant stance but the vast majority supported the party policy of ending partition by peaceful and democratic means. I believed that militancy would create a disastrous situation. Even if we had sufficient military power to force a solution on Unionists, the one thing we most certainly would not end up with would be a United Ireland in its full sense.

The Taoiseach reacted quickly to the escalation of violence in the North and called a Cabinet meeting on August 13, 1969. We discussed the situation in Northern Ireland and a variety of responses were considered. Immediate practical actions such as the setting up of field hospitals and the provision of emergency accommodation for refugees fleeing across the border were agreed.

I remember meeting a group of young people a few days later who had fled across the border and were temporarily housed in the Dominican Friary in Dundalk. While I was chatting with them a priest joined us. Out of the blue one young lad pointed to a car and asked the priest, 'Will we hijack it Father?' This attitude was new to me then but it later became commonplace.

It was also decided to request that a UN peacekeeping force be brought in to help restore order. We all agreed with this decision. If the request was granted I thought that at least a neutral force would be there and this would raise the morale of the Nationalist population. I knew, however, that the prospect of success was minimal given the British Government's power of veto at the UN but in the circumstance every possible solution had to be explored.

There was concern about the state of the Irish army, which was much below peacetime strength. The Minister for Defence, Jim Gibbons, and the Minister for Finance, Charlie Haughey, were instructed to bring the army to an acceptable level of readiness as soon as possible. The possibility of incursions into the North was raised but quickly dismissed. As far as I can remember the matter was raised in a rather haphazard way and was given little or no consideration.

Kevin Boland proposed that we bring home Irish troops on UN peacekeeping duties in Cyprus and call up the second line reserve. This was also rejected and Kevin Boland verbally resigned from Government. I wasn't particularly perturbed as Kevin left the meeting. On another occasion he had walked out of a government meeting because he felt he hadn't been given enough money for Social Welfare. He had returned his official car to the depot, gone home and apparently helped make up hay in a nearby field for the rest of the day. He had returned to the Dáil the following day.

To take our troops home from Cyprus and to call up the reserves would, in my view, have been interpreted by the Unionists and British Government as a sign that we were preparing to use military force in the North. Kevin Boland is on record as being opposed to such action but he obviously didn't see the contradiction involved at the time. If we'd agreed to his proposal it would have involved us in a futile and dangerous gesture. Kevin was later persuaded to reconsider his resignation. He resumed his ministerial responsibilities a few days later.

The Taoiseach then presented the draft of a speech he proposed to make on television later that day. Amendments were proposed and a consensus arrived at. Some commentators may now find part of the final version of the speech to be less than diplomatic but it must be remembered that it was a very emotional time and nobody raised any objections. In retrospect I think it was just as well that the speech was somewhat tough.

The speech was then returned to the Taoiseach's office. Basil Chubb in *Cabinet Government in Ireland* states that a vote was taken to decide on whether the Taoiseach's draft or an amended draft should be used and that the amended draft was carried by a small majority. No source is given for this statement. I have no recollection whatever of such a vote. Those with a knowledge of Cabinet procedures would be aware that to decide on a matter of such vital importance, by vote, would be inconceivable. During my time in the Cabinet, votes at Government were extremely rare happenings and were never used on such serious matters.

The meeting ended with all of us reasonably satisfied. Neil Blaney later claimed that the speech was no longer the Taoiseach's but really expressed his and like-minded minister's views. This is of course nonsense. The Taoiseach made the speech on television and so it was the Taoiseach's speech. I'm sure that Jack Lynch wished to have the views of government members, but it must also be kept in mind that if he disliked the finished product nobody could insist on his making the speech. Indeed if he had wished to deliver his original draft and said so, he would have had no difficulty in so doing.

I watched the television broadcast later that day as the Taoiseach stated that the present situation in Northern Ireland could not be allowed to continue. The Stormont Government was no longer in control of the situation and the RUC were not an impartial police force. He said that the Irish Government could not stand by and see innocent people injured or perhaps worse. He called on the British Government to join with the Irish Government to review the constitutional position of Northern Ireland and to discuss reunification of Ireland, as the only permanent solution. In the meantime he urged the British Government to apply immediately to the United Nations for a peacekeeping force. The

Taoiseach's logical approach to the Northern crisis had a calming effect
and gained the support of the vast majority of the Irish people.

As a result of the Government's decision the Minister for Foreign
Affairs, Patrick Hillery, went to London to meet his counterpart, and to
seek British government support for the UN force, or failing that, to
seek agreement on an Anglo-Irish force to maintain order. The British
side still disputed our right to express any views on happenings in
Northern Ireland. It rejected our request for the use of a UN force,
insisting that Northern Ireland was 'a matter of domestic jurisdiction'
for the UK.

Dr Hillery went on to press the Irish case at the UN Security
Council, and while unable to make much progress because of Britain's
veto power, he nonetheless gained valuable publicity for Ireland's
stance.

At the Government's next meeting on August 16 a decision was
made which at the time seemed to me little more than routine, but later
due to different interpretations, took on a significance which nobody
present then could have predicted. I think it appropriate therefore to
quote from the Cabinet Minutes. They state that:

> 'A sum of money – the amount and channel of the disbursement of
> which would be determined by the Minister for Finance – should be
> made available from the exchequer to provide aid for the victims of
> the current unrest in the Six Counties.'

This minute has been interpreted by a number of later commentators
as giving the Minister for Finance the authority to use the money as he
wished.

The reality is quite different. The Government had decided that
the victims of the unrest in the North needed aid. This instruction to
the Minister for Finance, Charlie Haughey, who had been appointed
about six weeks earlier by Jack Lynch, was to make money available
for that purpose. This was a normal procedure in Government. Again
as per normal, the allocation of the money would be decided by the
Minister on the basis of need and also on the availability of money.
The channel of disbursement was also left to the Minister, but to be
carried out within the confines of an instruction, in a statement issued
by the Government Information Bureau, on the same day, August 16,
1969. Indeed on the following day this statement was summarised on
the front page of the *Sunday Independent*:

> 'In Dublin, Mr Haughey is to have immediate talks with the
> Chairman of the Irish Red Cross, as to the administration of the Aid
> Fund.'

The inclusion of the Irish Red Cross in the administration of the fund money clearly indicates the type of aid envisaged by the Government – humanitarian not armed.

The Taoiseach announced that he had decided to set up a Cabinet Sub-Committee to keep the Northern situation under review. He named Neil Blaney, Joe Brennan and myself, representing border constituencies, and Charlie Haughey as its members. I had no prior knowledge of this decision, which was announced in a relatively informal manner. I was pleased to be a member of the Sub-Committee and I hoped that my considerable knowledge of the northern situation would be of some help. As to the Cabinet they simply accepted the new committee, presumably looking on it as I did, as a positive measure. There was little, if any, discussion of the matter.

We held our first meeting shortly afterwards. So far as I can remember we had an informal discussion about the North and how to counter misleading statements and publicity from Unionist sources so we could clarify the factual position. Seamas Brady, a journalist friend of Neil Blaney, was appointed to help with publicity. We then arranged a time and place for our next meeting and departed.

Joe Brennan and I duly turned up for the second meeting. We sat down and waited for Blaney and Haughey to arrive. Neither came, nor did they send a message explaining their absence. At first I thought the delay was caused by some urgent business in their departments, but as time passed without any word from them I thought the whole thing strange to say the least. Joe Brennan became very annoyed and expressed his resentment in no uncertain terms. He said that he was busy with department work and was returning to his office. I agreed with him, as I too was very busy, and we both left. I was irritated by the failure of my colleagues to turn up, but it never dawned on me at the time that their action was anything other than bad manners. I quickly became immersed in my own work and the whole episode faded from my mind.

The committee never met again and, effectively, ceased to exist. I didn't raise the matter with Haughey or Blaney nor as far as I know did Joe Brennan. If they wanted another meeting they could look for it. Reviewing the whole affair with hindsight I think it would be reasonable to assume that they had come to the conclusion that Joe and I would not be suitable partners for their future plans.

In view of the importance attached to this committee, its alleged activities and decisions, which are to be found in books written about the period and in individual statements, I believe it is essential, in the interest of historical accuracy, that the public should be aware of the actual situation. As I was one of the four members of the Sub-Committee

I feel I am in a good position to deal with it. The Sub-Committee had no authority to make money available to purchase arms for any purpose and, in view of its early demise, it is patently obvious that a non-existent Sub-Committee could not be involved in any activity whatever. If anybody used the name of the Sub-Committee to lend authenticity to illegal activities then it was without my knowledge and without the approval of the Government.

In view of the later emphasis given to the Sub-Committee it is interesting that neither I nor, to the best of my knowledge, Joe Brennan were approached by any commentators to verify or refute the accuracy of accounts of the committee until many years later.

As I have said before the achievement of the reunification of the country by democratic and peaceful means was the policy of the Lynch Government 1969/70. As a member of that Government and also, as a member of the Cabinet Sub-Committee on Northern Ireland, which met only once, I wish to make it crystal clear that at no time did the Government agree to, sanction, or involve itself with the procurement of arms, other than for the legitimate forces of the Irish State. If any individuals were led to believe that they were acting on behalf of or in accordance with orders from the Government, or of the Sub-Committee, in procuring arms for any other purpose then they are mistaken in that belief.

Around this time, Mícheál Ó Móráin, then Minister for Justice, informed the Government that he had a report from his security people that a member of the Cabinet had had a meeting with the Chief of Staff of the IRA, Cathal Goulding. I was very surprised and was wondering who it might be when Charlie Haughey said that he had been asked to meet a person whom he didn't know and that nothing of any consequence had been said at the meeting. He dismissed the matter with a wave of his hand and there was no further discussion about it as we got on with the meeting.

In the weeks and months following the August violence a number of Nationalists, ranging from politicians such as Paddy O'Hanlon and Paddy Devlin, to IRA activists and their associates, came south looking for guns to protect themselves from the RUC, B Specials and Unionist extremists. Around that time I met Paddy Kennedy, Republican Socialist Member of Stormont, in the Russell Hotel in Dublin and we discussed the northern situation. As far as I can remember there was no mention of arms at the meeting. Nor did any other individuals make such a request to me. It may be that because I supported party policy I was categorised as being opposed to the supplying of guns. Jack Lynch and the Government also continued to reject any suggestion that weapons should be made available to northern Nationalists.

In later times it has been suggested that a meeting in Bailieboro, Co Cavan, in October 1969, at which money for the purchase of arms was apparently discussed, had government sanction. This is not so. I had no knowledge of this meeting for quite some time after it took place, and I'm sure this also applies to many of my Cabinet colleagues. If some Ministers met the people involved, before or after that meeting, they did so of their own volition.

The only intimation I later had of something peculiar going on, was when Ó Móráin came into the Ministers' dining room where Jim Gibbons and I were having lunch one day. It was early in 1970, probably February, and Ó Móráin said to Gibbons that some of our colleagues were 'doing something' which they shouldn't be doing. He left what they were doing unspecified and I didn't ask. Jim Gibbons agreed with Ó Móráin, but there was no further comment on the matter. I accepted that whatever was wrong Justice and Defence were dealing with it. This episode, apart from my own personal knowledge, clearly indicates that it was not government policy to approve of, or condone, the illegal importation of arms. It also confirms that neither Ó Móráin nor Gibbons were involved.

I heard nothing further but then an unusual and potentially serious incident, about which I knew nothing at the time, occurred in my own constituency in April 1970. Although Dundalk is just a few miles from the border the army barracks were largely unoccupied. From 1958 it had been used for FCA (the local army reserve force) training. With the crisis in Northern Ireland, regular troops had returned in Autumn 1969, but in small numbers.

On April 2, 1970, 500 rifles and other military equipment arrived at the Dundalk barracks, from, it was claimed, army sources. It has been alleged that the rifles were sent for the use of civilians in the North. The whole matter was shrouded in mystery, but one thing is certain, the Irish Government which had refused individual demands for arms, would not countenance the indiscriminate distribution of 500 rifles. I later learned that when the lorries arrived at the barracks, the authorities were suspicious because they had no escort. When it was discovered that there was no official documentation with the arms, the consignment was not accepted, but the lorries were allowed into the barrack yard for investigation. The Dundalk military authorities had reported the matter to Dublin and when the Taoiseach learned of it, he'd ordered the lorries to remain there all night and to return to Dublin the following day. Later that evening a group of men had assembled at the barrack gate demanding the rifles. Fearing a raid, army personnel were confined to barracks and the gates remained locked. The group of men were dispersed by the Gardaí.

Taking account of what I was told, and the fact that the rifles had serial-numbers, which could easily be identified if they were captured by the authorities in Northern Ireland, the whole episode was a highly irresponsible one. It, clearly, could not have had the sanction of the Taoiseach nor of the Government.

The next event of note occurred at a cabinet meeting on May 1, 1970. The Taoiseach informed us that serious allegations had been made against two of our colleagues, Neil Blaney and Charles Haughey. They were accused of attempting to illegally import weapons for the use of the Nationalist community in Northern Ireland. He said that he had discussed the matter with them and both had vehemently denied the allegations. We were devastated and were under no illusion that if the allegations proved to be true this would not be the end of the matter. It could only result in the Taoiseach asking for their resignations. Neil Blaney was there that day but Charlie Haughey was ill in hospital. Nobody made any comment and we then turned to an item on agriculture. I can still clearly recall Neil Blaney, Minister for Agriculture, vigorously arguing a point on the subject. It was as if the Taoiseach had said nothing of any significance. I was deeply shocked by the revelations, and in view of the allegations made, whether they were true or false, I was amazed that Blaney could apparently ignore them. Perhaps his attitude may have been to show contempt for Jack Lynch. In any case, this, to me, extraordinary display by Neil Blaney underpins my memory of that day.

After the meeting small groups of like-minded Ministers gathered together and discussed whatever views they had on the allegations. To me Neil Blaney was an enigma. Admittedly I was never particularly close to him, but prior to the outbreak of violence in the Six Counties in late 1968 I had not known him to take any particular interest in Northern Ireland, except perhaps, in delivering floods of demagogic oratory at Ard Fheiseanna or on election platforms. In a speech in November 1968 he had attacked the Northern Ireland Government and cited partition as being the root cause of their problems. When the Taoiseach had then delivered his speech in September 1969, outlining Irish government policy on Northern Ireland, Neil Blaney had obviously not agreed with it. In December '69 Blaney had spoken out again in Letterkenny. He stated that Fianna Fáil had never taken a decision to rule out force if circumstances in the Six Counties demanded it. This of course, begs the question as to when the Fianna Fáil party had ever taken a decision to rule force in and what force was he referring to? Éamon de Valera, Seán Lemass and other Fianna Fáil stalwarts never accepted the use of force, even if force were possible, as a credible means of ending partition. On a practical level Blaney would have known that the Irish Army was a depleted, below strength, and poorly equipped force. The Letterkenny speech was a dangerous and intemperate one, capable of inflaming public opinion and leading to catastrophe. However, Blaney appeared to get away with it. In the highly charged atmosphere, such speeches were loudly acclaimed by some of the members at grass roots level. Having tasted the adulation, and perhaps believing that Lynch's downfall was imminent, Blaney had apparently decided that the Republican card was the one to play to further his leadership aspirations.

I was also surprised when I heard of the allegations against Charlie Haughey. When Haughey was Minister for Justice in the early 1960s he had crushed the IRA. So much so that they were still a largely spent force when violence broke out in the North some years later. That an intelligent man should involve himself in activities to reactivate the IRA by supplying them with money and arms didn't seem credible. Many people believed that Haughey's action would only have been as a result of his reaction to Neil Blaney. By this stage, Blaney was actively involved with the Nationalists and his Letterkenny speech, with its strong emotional appeal, could have appeared to Haughey to boost Blaney's prospects in the hoped-for leadership struggle. Haughey may have felt that it was necessary to challenge Blaney – on his own ground. If that were so it was a serious error of judgement. At the time an emotional speech on the Nationalist situation in Northern Ireland could be relied upon to raise the roof at a Fianna Fáil meeting. However, I was well aware, as Haughey should also have been, that while the applause appeared highly supportive it was, in fact, superficial. I knew that in the cold light of day only a tiny proportion of our membership supported violence. Subsequent events were to prove me right.

On May 5, 1970 Liam Cosgrave, leader of the Opposition, informed the Taoiseach that he had received information that Cabinet Ministers were involved in an attempt to import arms illegally, for use in Northern Ireland. I was, of course, unaware of this meeting until it entered the public domain.

As it happened, I left my Dáil office rather late on the night of May 5. When I was walking down the stairs I saw Neil Blaney leave the Taoiseach's office and enter Kevin Boland's office, which was next door. I was thinking of the Taoiseach's statement at the Cabinet meeting a few days earlier and as I left I had an uneasy feeling that something serious was afoot.

The following morning my wife, Kitty, was listening to the radio and heard the news of the Ministers' dismissal. She rushed to my room to tell me. Before she had time to say anything I said to her, 'Blaney, Haughey and probably Boland are gone'. When she asked me how I knew I said that I'd had a premonition because of what I had seen the previous night.

At the time the general consensus was that Kevin Boland's resignation was a sudden emotional reaction to the dismissal of the two Ministers. Even then I failed to see why he would have resigned for that reason. Kevin had little in common with Haughey and I knew he was opposed to him as party leader. He also later claimed that when Charlie Haughey told him of a plan to import arms he had denounced it as reckless. Quite clearly Boland had little in common with the two Ministers concerned and was not admitted into their circle. I was later given a different version of events. Blaney had apparently said to Boland that he had been dismissed because he was a Republican. Boland had immediately replied that Jack Lynch would not dismiss him because he was a Republican and he wrote out his resignation there and then. I never heard Kevin Boland's name mentioned in respect of the illegal importation of arms.

The dismissal of Neil Blaney and Charles Haughey from the Cabinet entailed one of the most drastic and difficult decisions ever faced by a Taoiseach. It called for all his reserves of courage to accomplish it. At the time some elements of the Opposition and the media branded Jack Lynch a weak and indecisive leader because he failed to promptly dismiss the two Ministers allegedly involved in the arms conspiracy. They claimed that he had waited until Liam Cosgrave intervened. Before reaching such a conclusion I think it would be well to examine the situation in which Jack Lynch found himself at that time. Rumours abounded. Vague and imprecise official information was available to him. Some from sources noted for exaggeration. There was not sufficient evidence to put any of the issues beyond all reasonable doubt. Two very senior Ministers, Blaney and Haughey, one appointed to the Cabinet on the same day as the Taoiseach himself, and the other occupying the most important department of Government – Finance – were accused of illegal activity, with both vehemently denying involvement. In the face of their denials it would need considerable evidence to enable a Taoiseach to dismiss them.

With hindsight, commentators have firmed up the vague quality of the information and evidence available, to fit their theories. The reality is that nobody could be certain of anything at the time. The dismissal of two long-standing Ministers causing, as it would, an upheaval in Government, and increasing tension in an already violent Northern Ireland context, would be folly without substantial evidence being available. It was not a time for a knee-jerk reaction. It may be claimed that Cosgrave's intervention forced the Taoiseach's hand, but his information simply supported what Jack Lynch already knew at this point. There is no reason to assume that he would not have taken similar action when he had fully satisfied himself of the need for it. The statement he made at the Cabinet meeting on May 1 bears out this contention. When the Taoiseach felt that the accumulated evidence was sufficient he acted. The Taoiseach's approach of continuing his investigation until the evidence, in his view, was irrefutable and then to act, was the only sane course to follow. Time has proved it so.

In the early hours of May 6, Jack Lynch issued a statement:

> 'I have requested the resignations as members of the Government Mr Neil T Blaney, Minister for Agriculture and Fisheries, and Mr Charles J Haughey, Minister for Finance, because I am satisfied that they do not subscribe fully to Government policy in relation to the present situation in the Six Counties as stated by me at the Fianna Fáil Árd Fheis in January last.'

A government meeting was called that day in the Taoiseach's room at Leinster House. I have a vivid recollection of looking around the table and seeing the four vacant chairs, like black holes, in the circle. Mícheál Ó Móráin, Minister for Justice, had resigned on health grounds on May 4, unwillingly I understand. There is no doubt that Ó Móráin, with whom I had a very good relationship when I was his parliamentary secretary, was very ill at the time. There is no question of his having been involved with, or supportive of, the illegal importation of arms.

Even though I was now aware of the factual position, as I looked at the four empty chairs my mind was in turmoil. I was filled with a mixture of incredulity at the alleged activities of colleagues, surprise at Kevin Boland's resignation, regret at the resignation of my old colleague from Lands and sadness at the break-up of a united party. I also felt an element of fear for the future of the country and the party. Interestingly, the meeting was carried on in a very businesslike fashion. The Taoiseach wisely decided to fill the vacant positions immediately. He proposed to appoint Des O'Malley, Justice, Jeremiah Cronin, Defence, Robert Molloy, Local Government, and Gerard Collins, Posts and Telegraphs. The proposed appointments were no surprise to me. I was particularly pleased to be retained in Education as I had settled in well there. Despite the traumatic political events in this period developments in our educational system had proceeded apace. The names of the new Ministers were to be announced later in the Dáil.

When the parliamentary party subsequently met at 6 pm it was in a very disturbed state. A vote of no confidence in the Government was to be expected from the Opposition. If they won, it would mean a general election. The Government would need the support of almost all the

party members but under the circumstances nobody knew if all the
Fianna Fáil deputies would vote with the Government. The unease at
the meeting was palpable. I was relieved therefore when a vote on a
motion acknowledging the Taoiseach's right to appoint and dismiss
Ministers was passed unanimously. This appeared to show very strong
support for Jack Lynch. While deputies were aware that this was the
Taoiseach's prerogative, it was felt in this unusual situation that the
motion should also be passed by the parliamentary party. The party
then unanimously agreed to support the Taoiseach's nominations.

During the course of the parliamentary party meeting Kevin Boland
briefly intervened, to ask the Taoiseach if he had evidence against the
dismissed Ministers. The Taoiseach replied in the affirmative and
explained his case. When I learned, much later, that Kevin Boland had
claimed that Charlie Haughey had told him of the proposed arms
importation, I wondered why he needed to ask the Taoiseach if he had
evidence against them. At the time I was satisfied with the Taoiseach's
relatively short explanation. To be frank my mind was concentrated on
the practicalities we would be faced with, particularly in the Dáil. I
have little doubt that similar thoughts filled the minds of the other
deputies present.

The essence of Boland's response to Lynch's reply was that if he
had known this earlier he would not have resigned. I got a clear
perception that he regretted his hasty action. As the day went on Boland
was interviewed by journalists and his replies were very conciliatory.
There were soon rumours throughout the House that the Taoiseach
would recall him to Government. At that point I would not have been
averse to this because of my long association with him. All in all the
only interpretation of Kevin's attitude that day, was that he was seeking
reinstatement to office.

When the Dáil assembled at 10 pm that evening, however, the
Taoiseach announced that he had asked the President to accept Kevin
Boland's resignation. Kevin was then aware that his post was being
filled.

Two days later on May 8, when Kevin spoke in the Dáil on the
motion to ratify the appointments of the new Ministers he launched a
bitter attack on the Taoiseach, proclaiming his own righteousness and
dismissing ours. To justify the stand he was taking, he moved further
towards extremes. In the process he forfeited the friendship and respect
of many of the deputies who had admired him for his contribution to
his country and party over the years. I'd had considerable regard for
Kevin Boland, from the time we were both elected in 1957, but I'm
afraid his actions during this period put paid to that. He had resigned,
of his own volition, at a critical time, without informing himself of the

reality of the situation. Sadly his temperament later drove him to resign from the Dáil, to start a new political party, Aontacht Eireann, and finally to fade into political oblivion.

In the meantime I knew that the Opposition was keeping a close watch on events. I expect that they hoped, in such an unprecedented situation, that Fianna Fáil would be unable to count on the support of all their members and that the Government would fall. Even though the new Ministers were confirmed by majority votes, the Opposition still obviously felt that a no confidence vote in the Government itself could result in a defeat for the Fianna Fáil party.

As expected they submitted a vote of no confidence later that day. In an attempt to add to the Government's difficulties the name of Jim Gibbons was incorporated in it. Jim Gibbons, as Minister for Defence, figured prominently in the Arms Crisis controversy. He had been elected to Dáil Eireann, as I was, for the first time in 1957 and over the years Paddy Lalor, Jim Gibbons and I, became friends. I found Jim to be an intelligent, well-read man, with a rather sardonic humour, who, might I add, could be difficult at times. He was a decent, conscientious person and by no stretch of the imagination could I believe he was involved in the illegal importation of arms. Thankfully the Government successfully circumvented the attempt to involve Jim by simply submitting a motion asking the Dáil to vote on confidence in the Government.

Since the subsequent debate had no time limit, it was open to any deputy and I decided to speak in support of the Taoiseach and government policy. I pointed out that Jack Lynch had taken action when there was the slightest imputation against government Ministers. He had shown himself to be a leader with the strength of character, judgement and firmness of purpose to take the right decisions in the interest of the nation. I stated that while the people in the North, both Orange and Green, wanted peace there was a high level of fear, distrust and uncertainty amongst them. Cognizance had to be taken of the plight of the Nationalist people but equally we could not discount the views of one million Unionists who did not wish to become part of a United Ireland and who felt that their future lay with Britain. There was something deeper there than the physical partition of a line on a map, there was a partition of the mind. I also commented that we had a right to be involved in any solution to the problem. The time had come for Britain to call a meeting of the Irish Government, their own Government and representatives from the North to try to resolve the matter of unity.

My speech was designed to bring a much needed realism into the highly charged atmosphere. Nevertheless, it was a difficult speech for a Fianna Fáil Minister to make. I was well aware that elements of the party throughout Ireland, including in my own constituency, were still convinced that if Jack Lynch and his Government would only adopt a militant stance, partition would come to an end. It is gratifying to note that many of these people now accept the Downing Street Declaration of the 1990s, which expresses the same views and underlines the same difficulties as those embodied in the Northern Ireland policy of Jack Lynch's government in 1970.

I was very pleased and relieved when we won the vote of confidence. The immediate crisis passed, and the air of tension in the House eased.

In assessing Jack Lynch's leadership during those critical months of 1969/70, some commentators have since concluded that he lost control in the early stages and regained it only after the dismissal of the Ministers. On the contrary, Lynch's conduct of affairs from the initial stages of the Northern crisis in 1968, demonstrates his strength of character. Faced by powerful antagonists, with their own agendas, rampant intrigue, strife in the North, demands from Nationalists for assistance, calls from Fianna Fáil supporters to send the Irish Army across the Border, and scarcely knowing who his friends were, Jack Lynch refused to waver from his stated policy. I believe this was his greatest achievement. Concessions to the more militant sentiments would have gained him popularity in the short-term, but he knew such an approach would spell disaster for the Irish people in the long-term. Harry Truman, the former President of the United States, said of himself and the office he held: 'The buck stops here.' Ireland was fortunate that in our case the buck stopped with Jack Lynch.

Once the Arms Crisis erupted the Taoiseach dealt with events quickly and decisively. Within the space of a fortnight, two Ministers had resigned and two had been dismissed, four senior Ministers had been replaced, his leadership of the party had been endorsed and he had won a critical vote of confidence in the Dáil, so that the Government would continue in office.

Blaney and Haughey were arrested on May 28, 1970. The three other defendants, Captain James Kelly, John Kellly, a Belfast Republican and Albert Luykx, a Belgian-born businessman, were arrested the previous day.

The charges against Blaney were dropped at District Court level. The trial of the other four took place that Autumn. Evidence from witnesses was in some cases confused and contradictory. The trial ended in late October. All were acquitted, but the judge stated that the Attorney General would have been remiss in his duty had he not brought the matter to court.

After the defendants had been acquitted, Jack Lynch's opponents within the party engaged in a display of what I can only call triumphalism. Lynch, who was in New York attending a UN meeting, was depicted as a weak, but vindictive, leader, who had pursued a mean course of action against his colleagues in Government, and been responsible for their arrest and arraignment. The fact that only the Attorney General could decide on whether a case should be brought before the courts was ignored. Lynch was called on to resign and prominent party members were publicly indicating that, in such an event, they were ready and willing to take over the party leadership.

Shortly before the Taoiseach was due home from America, on October 26, I had a phonecall from Paddy Lalor. He said that he had been approached by an active party supporter, Dan Mullane. Dan had asked him if we proposed to leave Jack Lynch to his opponents and to do nothing to help him in his time of need. Paddy was anxious to help and I agreed with him. We met in Dublin with amongst others George Colley and Dan Mullane. We rang two former senior Ministers, Sean McEntee, who gave us his support, and Paddy Smith, who did likewise and came to the meeting. We decided to try to get the parliamentary party to go to Dublin airport to greet the Taoiseach on his return. We rang all the TDs and Senators, except the tiny number whom we knew were opposed to Lynch, requesting them to attend.

The vast majority of the parliamentary party duly assembled and Jack Lynch, who presumably expected to arrive home to an empty airport, was visibly overcome by the size of the crowd and the enthusiasm of the welcome. I learned quite recently that a campaign was waged at the time, to convince Dublin TDs and a small number of TDs throughout the country, that they should not attend Jack's homecoming. I was not aware of this on the day but was pleased that some of those approached retorted that to do as requested would be an insult to the leader of the party. Paddy Lalor and I just wanted to ensure that the party leader received the support that was his due. But, looking back on that time, when many believed that the Taoiseach's reign was about to end, I am, now, convinced that this episode was the turning point in the struggle. Thereafter the work of Government proceeded normally and Jack Lynch continued as leader of Fianna Fáil for the next nine years.

At the time, the events leading up to and surrounding the Arms Crisis of 1970 were confused. The subsequent comments and behaviour of some of the principals involved means that it is now possible to summarise the situation more clearly. It later emerged that Haughey's co-defendants appeared to believe that they had been acting with government approval. During the trial they appealed to Haughey to acknowledge this in court. He refused to do so.

The reason for Haughey's refusal is clear. When the Taoiseach first raised the issue of the attempt to illegally import arms at Cabinet on May 1, Neil Blaney made no comment. Later that year in a Dáil speech after the trial Blaney said: 'I have no guns, I have procured no guns, I have provided no money for guns.' Similarly, Haughey, both in his evidence at the trial and to the Public Accounts Committee of the Dáil the following year, denied any knowledge of the attempt to import arms and also denied that any public money could have been used to achieve this.

As to any suggestion that in some way the Government authorised or condoned supplying arms to civilians in the North, the evidence is to the contrary. Kevin Boland, for example, later said that Haughey had told him of the plan to import such arms. Why would that be necessary if the Government as a whole knew or approved such behaviour? Or again there is the episode that I recounted of the guns arriving at the barracks in Dundalk in April 1970. It later transpired that it was Blaney who had asked that this be done. When Jack Lynch found out he ordered that the guns be returned to Dublin.

Suggestions have also been made that it was the Cabinet Sub-Committee that in some sense provided the necessary authority for importing arms. While it is clear from Captain Kelly's subsequent accounts that he had numerous meetings with Blaney, and also met Haughey, he never, however, met the Sub-Committee. I certainly never met nor spoke with him.

There have also been references to Kelly acting as a Liaison Officer between the Cabinet Sub-Committee and the Northern Defence Committees. His subsequent behaviour suggests that he believed he had some form of official approval for his actions. Yet, when he was arrested on May 1, Kelly refused to give any information to the police, asked to see the Taoiseach, but then also refused to speak to him. Whatever he might have been led to believe from his meetings with Blaney and Haughey, they had no authority to approve covert arms' imports, as is clear from their later denials.

At no stage did the Irish Government approve or condone the attempt to import arms, and, when sufficient information was available about it, the Taoiseach, with the full support of the Government and the Fianna Fáil party put an end to it.

* * * *

All through this momentous and unnerving period the Fianna Fáil organisation was in ferment in my Louth constituency, as elsewhere. Strangely enough, however, while the Taoiseach was still attacked for inaction there was little or no support for the dismissed Ministers. The more extreme elements focused on the end of partition which they believed was nigh. Among such elements the affectionate name for the Old IRA – 'the Boys' – was used to describe the new IRA and their exploits were greeted with a certain pleasure. When asked if they agreed with violence these individuals replied that they didn't, but.... The 'but' meaning that, in these circumstances they might do so. As the death toll in the North mounted, however, there was a bit of backtracking but at Cumann and Comhairle Ceantair level, whenever calls for practical armed support were made, some acclamation still invariably followed. To these people Jack Lynch would never be aggressive enough.

My long experience of the organisation in Co Louth told me, that no matter how many members applauded extreme speeches, basically the vast majority were a sound, sensible lot, who loyally supported the Taoiseach and government policy of ending partition by peaceful means. However, firm action was needed to reinforce this. Meetings of Cumainn and Comhairli Ceantair were held where I, with my constituency colleagues, Frank Aiken and Senator Joe Farrell, stressed support for the Government's policy on the North. I spelled out the line I believed in myself and the direction I thought the party should take. I pointed out that those who advocated military intervention had given little thought to its consequences. Did they wish to pit poorly equipped Irish soldiers against the armed forces of a major military power, or had they given thought to the dangers to Nationalists in the ghettoes of Belfast and other parts of the North? On one occasion when a Cumann member asked an ardent advocate of army intervention if he would go there himself or send his sons there, the man's ardour cooled rapidly. The majority of members did not condone violence. It was possible to contain the situation and to avoid a split in the organisation. The odd outburst that occurred from time to time could be safely ignored.

* * * *

Throughout the Arms Crisis period in the Republic the situation in the North remained relatively calm. The British Government had finally responded to Nationalist appeals for a more neutral security force. Responsibility for security in Northern Ireland was transferred to the British army. Peace lines were patrolled and relative calm was restored. Tensions remained high in some areas and occasional incidents took place, but, on the whole, the British army had been accepted as a basically neutral peacekeeping force.

In the following months more progress was made. Civil Rights reforms were introduced and a relatively peaceful period was sustained.

This situation quickly changed for the worse after the election of the Heath Government in London on June 18, 1970. Unionists had always supported the Conservative Party, so Nationalists were automatically suspicious of the new Government's potential policy on the North.

Their worst fears were quickly confirmed. At the end of June the army raided a Nationalist area in Belfast, searching for weapons. The first killing occurred that weekend with more killings in the subsequent weeks. Within a short time Nationalists regarded the British army as a hostile force.

By the end of 1970 the number of deaths had reached 20. As the IRA became better organised and equipped, the violence increased and the death toll mounted relentlessly, reaching 172 in 1971, and rising to 467 in 1972.

The climax of an attempt at a military solution came in August 1971, when, on the advice of the Northern Ireland authorities, internment was introduced and several hundred people, believed to be IRA members, were imprisoned. This action was denounced by the Taoiseach and he demanded to meet Mr Heath.

The first meeting took place in early September. At that stage the British Government continued to hold the view that Northern Ireland affairs were a solely internal matter for the British authorities. Nothing concrete was achieved at the meeting.

Throughout this period both the British and Irish Governments were involved in negotiating their entry to the EEC (now EU). If they were successful membership would automatically bring changes in the North-South relationship. Customs' borders and other barriers between Ireland and the UK would have to disappear in a Common European structure. It is also relevant that the primary driving force for the creation of the EEC was to make future wars in Europe impossible. The Treaty admitting the UK, Ireland and Denmark to the EEC was signed in Brussels on January 22, 1972.

Membership of the EEC should have brought some hope that tensions in the North could be resolved but unfortunately, just eight days later, on January 30, a terrible event took place. It became known as 'Bloody Sunday'. The British army, acting against the advice of the police, attempted to confine a banned Civil Rights Movement march within the Bogside area. When the marchers began breaking through the blocked route a unit of British army paratroopers, who had been drafted in, opened fire. They killed 13 people.

The Bloody Sunday deaths triggered off a wave of protests throughout Ireland. There were angry demands for action to protect the Nationalist community in the North, and bitter denunciations of the British Government. On the day of the funerals, a massive demonstration was held in Dublin. It culminated with the burning down of the British Embassy.

The Irish Cabinet had decided to attend Mass for the 13 victims in St Eugene's Cathedral in Derry on February 2, to show solidarity with the relatives. We also wanted to express our abhorrence of the murders and to impress on the British Government the need to carry out reforms – rapidly.

The sight of the 13 coffins, with hundreds of grieving relatives and friends was a heartbreaking sight that I will never forget. The people's detestation for the British troops was palpable. It was a far cry from the Nationalists' initial attitude to the British soldiers. When they had first arrived in 1969 they were regarded as defenders of the Catholic population. By this stage the 'no go' areas were fully operational in Derry City.

The Nationalist population greeted us with enthusiasm. As I moved among the people, after the funerals, speaking to many of them, one incident stands out clearly in my mind. Nationalist civilians were carrying out police work and I spoke to a man who had the job of directing traffic at a crossroad, his hand signals obeyed by all. He was a pleasant individual, rather poorly clad, unemployed for most of his life, proud of the 'no go' areas and of his position as traffic controller. I remember thinking to myself that here was a man with previously little to do but chat all day long at street corners with his unemployed colleagues, ignored and scorned by officialdom, treated with contempt by the better off. Now, suddenly, for the first time in his life, he was somebody, receiving at least some of the respect due to him as a human being. There would be no going back for him.

I returned to Dublin determined to redouble my efforts to achieve peace in Northern Ireland, so Unionist and Nationalist alike could live in harmony together. I felt that now was the time for the British Government to call a meeting of all interested parties to try to find an agreed solution. Two years had passed since I had first made this call in my Dáil speech, and the urgency was now self-evident.

A major change in British policy was announced that March. The Northern Ireland Parliament was abolished and direct rule from London was introduced. Over the following months discussions began to take shape which were to lead to the setting up of a new type of Northern administration, in which power would be shared between the Unionist and Nationalist communities.

The escalation of violence in Northern Ireland from 1970 onwards had also had repercussions for security in the Republic. It was apparent that IRA members and supporters were active throughout the country. Special Criminal Courts, sitting with three judges and no jury were established to deal with IRA members, since it was an illegal and subversive organisation.

The Government also introduced an Offences Against the State (Amendment) Bill in December 1972 to give extra powers to these Special Courts. The Opposition parties were opposed to the Bill because of the proposed restrictions on the civil rights of individuals. As the debate continued the expectation grew that a small number of Fianna Fáil members, such as Neil Blaney, Des Foley and Paudge Brennan, opposed to Jack Lynch, would vote with the Opposition. In this case the Government could be defeated and a general election would be necessary.

I remember standing in the corridor in Leinster House, looking out over Dublin City and wondering if the Bill would plunge us into an election, so shortly after we had weathered the storm and controversy of the Arms Crisis. It was December 1, 1972. As I stood there I heard a muffled explosion across the city. For the first time, bombs had gone off in Dublin.

Fine Gael changed its position on the Bill and decided to abstain from voting against it. The Offences Against the State (Amendment) Bill was carried with a comfortable majority, and the immediate threat of a general election had been averted. But one consequence of our EEC membership from January 1, 1973 was that Paddy Hillery resigned from the Government and the Dáil, in order to take up his position as an EEC Commissioner. This left the Government short of a majority. Rather than risk defeat on some issue in the Dáil, Jack Lynch decided to call a general election.

Eleven

General Election

The 1973 General Election, scheduled for February 28, was to create serious problems for the Fianna Fáil party in County Louth. The convention to select candidates to contest it was duly held, chaired by Paddy Lalor, and nothing untoward happened there. The sitting deputies had rarely been opposed since I was elected in 1957 and, at this convention, Frank Aiken and I were selected unanimously. While I was naturally pleased, the selection of a sitting TD was a fairly routine matter. Frank thanked the delegates, wished me well and hoped we would succeed. Everything appeared as usual. With hindsight, some recalled that Frank had said something along the lines of possibly not being in the contest but nobody paid any attention to that at the time. There was nothing in the atmosphere that night to prepare me for the problems ahead.

Frank usually prepared the Election Address, while Senator Joe Farrell, Director of Elections and I, with the help of our organisation generally, dealt with all other aspects of the election. Matters proceeded as per normal. I was deputed by the National Executive to preside at the Kildare convention in Naas. On my way there Joe and I called at Leinster House where we met Frank. As the election date was approaching, I asked him if he had prepared the Address. He told us he hadn't done it yet. This was very unlike him and we were both perturbed. I remember thinking that he didn't look well and wondering if he had the flu.

Nominations closed on a Thursday and on the Monday night of the same week I had a telephone call from George Colley asking me if I knew anything about Frank's position regarding the election. I told him that I wasn't aware of any change of plan. George then told me that Frank did not propose to stand for the election. I was flabbergasted and told him that I found that very difficult to believe. George then said that the Taoiseach wished to see Joe Farrell and myself the following morning.

It was now late on Monday night and the weather was atrocious. Snow had fallen heavily and the roads were covered with ice. My car had returned to Dublin earlier in the day so I had no transport and Joe Farrell, who lived 12 miles away, had no telephone. I hoped to have the car back the following morning, weather permitting, but how I was going to reach Joe was the immediate problem. Fortunately a constituent called to see me and he drove me into Dundalk depositing me on Joe's doorstep.

Joe Farrell was one of Frank Aiken's closest and loyal friends. When I gave him the news he was dumbfounded. Frank hadn't taken either of us into his confidence. We had no idea why he'd made such a drastic decision. We discussed the matter for half the night and decided to speak with Frank the next day after we'd spoken to the Taoiseach. We decided to try to get him to change his mind, but knowing him as we did, we both knew that the reason for his decision must have been very serious indeed.

Joe and I travelled to Dublin together the next day and met Jack Lynch and George Colley in the Cabinet anteroom to discuss the news. We were told that Frank had decided not to stand because the Taoiseach and the National Executive had sanctioned Charlie Haughey's candidature in the General Election. Frank had also stated that he proposed to make the reasons for his decision public.

Frank Aiken was a man of high principle and a thorough gentleman and during the time we represented Louth together, from 1957 to 1973, we had an excellent relationship. He'd been the Commander of the Fourth Northern Division in the War of Independence and having done more than one man's part to avert the Civil War and failed, he threw in his lot with the Republican anti-Treaty forces. Before the Civil War ended he was Chief of Staff of the Republican forces. I had learned, over the years, that when he made up his mind on what he regarded as a matter of principle Frank was unshakeable. Once Frank believed in the merits of what he was doing he was impervious to criticism. It was this attribute which enabled him to successfully fight for causes on unpopular issues in which he believed, including an attempt to have Red China discussed at the United Nations. I can well remember the statements castigating him for this stance, the jeers in the pubs and at the crossroads, the forecasts that he would be swept from his seat in Louth because of it. It was only when the Pope expressed a view similar to Frank's that the clouds dispelled. Today the media eulogise Frank's successes. He is the angel of détente; the man who almost single-handedly was responsible for the Anti-Proliferation of Nuclear Arms Treaty, who was far-seeing about Red China. All now bask in the reflected glory. I often wonder what he would think of it.

Joe and I were very deeply disturbed as we left the anteroom and went to another room in the House where Frank was waiting for us. Here we were being told a few days before nominations closed that one of our candidates had decided not to stand for election. It was a potentially disastrous situation. Should we fail to find a new candidate it would mean handing a second seat to the opposition parties and our whole organisation would be in turmoil. As we sat down with Frank we immediately launched into every possible argument we had to try to get him to change his mind but without effect. I pointed out that with nominations closing on Thursday he was proposing to let down the Fianna Fáil organisation and the people of Louth generally, who had supported him for 50 years, but to no avail. Finally, in my frustration and in an attempt to shock him, I said that if that were his attitude I would also withdraw and let the whole lot go to blazes. His reply was that that would be my own decision. I knew then that his mind was made up.

Given his personality, our attempt to have him change his mind had always been unlikely to succeed. Joe and I had no choice but to accept his decision. However, at the time, I couldn't agree with the stance he had taken. During his long career as a Minister, no matter how difficult the problems that beset him, at local, national or international levels, the Fianna Fáil organisation in County Louth had supported him absolutely. The organisation had defended him, on every occasion, without exception. They had selected Frank as their preferred candidate to contest the election and I simply couldn't understand his attitude in all these circumstances. It saddened me because I felt that it was not the way that a 50-year period of exceptional public service should end. I suppose I can only repeat what he said to me — that it was his decision and I must respect that.

Joe and I reported our failure back to the Taoiseach and George Colley and we discussed how we should proceed from there. Time was of the essence. It was now Tuesday and nominations closed on Thursday. The immediate practical problem was whether we could manage to hold a selection convention to choose another candidate. The weather was exceptionally bad, with packed snow on many roads in the constituency. To call a new convention, in the short time available and in such conditions, would be well nigh impossible. The decision reached was that the Comhairle Dáil Ceantair would be empowered to appoint a replacement for Frank Aiken. Many members of the Comhairle Dáil Ceantair didn't have telephones but we did finally succeed in gathering a full muster. Joe Farrell was selected as the replacement candidate. I was relieved that we had a new candidate, but we were all traumatised and I hoped that I would never face that situation again.

I learned later that it was at a Fianna Fáil function held after the dissolution of the 1973 Dáil that Frank had intimated to Jack Lynch that he would be unhappy if Charlie Haughey were a Fianna Fáil candidate in the forthcoming election. I don't know if Frank told Jack at this point that he wouldn't contest the election in such an eventuality but I think it was strange that Jack did not tell me about this conversation. If he had, we could have tried to find a way out of the impasse at an early stage. It is possible, of course, that Jack thought Frank had informed me of his position or maybe when Jack heard that Frank had been selected at the convention he thought that the difficulty had been overcome. In any case Jack Lynch and the National Executive would have been faced with an almost insurmountable problem if they had tried to refuse Charlie Haughey the right to stand in the 1973 election. Haughey had successfully contested a vacancy at the Ard Fheis in 1972 and had been elected Vice-President of the Fianna Fáil party. I understand that Frank Aiken was offered the vice-presidency of the party by Jack Lynch but had turned it down.

Joe managed to persuade Frank not to go public about the reason behind his decision before the election. His reason for standing down could have split Fianna Fáil and perhaps affected the election result. In such circumstances the great work Frank had done for the country, and for the constituency, would be forgotten and he would be remembered, only, as the person who spilt the party. The public was left under the impression that Frank withdrew for health reasons.

We found out later that when Frank had decided not to stand, he had then involved himself in a strange venture. He had travelled to Dungannon with his daughter, Emer, to ask John Hume to stand for election in Louth, in his place. Apparently Frank intended to request the Fianna Fáil convention in Louth to endorse Hume's candidature as an independent. The purpose was to show Northern' Unionists that, by electing Hume, the people of Louth approved of Hume's policies. Emer was completely unaware of her father's intentions until they were on their way home. She asked him if he had consulted with his friends or with the Fianna Fáil organisation in Louth before visiting the North, and when he told her he had not consulted with anybody she was very much taken aback. She later told Joe Farrell of the episode and Joe immediately told me. To put it mildly we were both amazed. It was most uncharacteristic of Frank. It was fortunate that John Hume didn't accept the proposal. It would have been highly unlikely that the Fianna Fáil party in Louth would have selected John Hume as a candidate in preference to one of its own members. Had such been the scenario Unionists would have interpreted it as a rejection of Hume and his policies, the exact opposite of Frank's intention. The plan was badly thought out and was most unlike what we would have expected from the solid, sound Frank Aiken we had known so well for many years.

We knew nothing of this venture at the Comhairle Dáil Ceantair meeting at which Joe Farrell was selected, but immediately afterwards

Joe received a phone call from Austin Currie simply saying that 'that' was off. Joe didn't know 'what' was off, but we soon knew that Currie was referring to the Aiken/Hume proposal.

It is worth noting that despite the upheavals of the early 1970s and our traumatic experiences immediately prior to the 1973 General Election, Joe Farrell and I were the first two elected in our three-seat constituency, polling 51.17% of first preference votes between us. My election was the only result to be announced on the lunchtime radio news and it looked as if Fianna Fáil would sweep the country and confirm the oft-repeated election saying that, 'as Louth goes so goes the country'. However, it was not to be. Fianna Fáil won 69 seats, while Fine Gael and Labour had 73, with two seats going to others. The general impression before the election was that Fianna Fáil would fare badly because of the Arms Crisis, but in fact the party received a higher vote than in 1969, when it had won. The result, in my view, was much more affected by the Fine Gael pact on transfers.

From out of this intense period of problems and difficulties I can remember one funny incident. Unknown to me, a rumour had circulated throughout Drogheda, just before the election, that I would lose my seat. I didn't hear anything about it until the election was over but one man who was obviously happy with the rumour was a Councillor in Drogheda. At lunchtime on the day of the count, he asked a friend if there was any news. When he was told that my election was the only one announced for the whole country, before the lunchtime adjournment of the count, the Councillor opined that the people of Louth must have holes in their heads.

A few days later, as I was walking down West Street, the same Councillor rushed across the road, grasped me by the hand, congratulated me on my excellent vote, and assured me that nobody deserved it more. One should be gracious in victory, so I thanked him for his good wishes, without further comment.

The election result in Co Louth was phenomenal. A couple of days before nominations closed we were to all intents and purposes in crisis, with the sudden withdrawal of our longest-serving member. Yet within two weeks the voters had given us the highest share of the vote that the party has ever received, before or since. I believe this happened because, in spite of the turmoil and strife, we had convinced the people of Louth, a border constituency, that our policy for reunification of the country by peaceful and democratic means provided the only solution to partition. There were no 'ifs and buts', no foot in one camp and one in the other, just a simple straightforward message –unity by peaceful, democratic means. Through their support, the voters in Louth endorsed, without any doubt, the policy of Jack Lynch and his Government. I had always been proud of the men and women of our organisation, but never more so than in 1973.

I was pleased to be returning to the Dáil, but, I must admit, disappointed with the overall result. It was clear that we would be replaced by a Fine Gael/Labour government, and I wondered how I would fare in Opposition – for the first time in my political career.

Twelve

Life in Opposition

Immediately after the election I returned to my office in the Department of Education. Under our political system a number of days elapse between the results of a general election and the recall of Dáil Eireann. This gave me time to clear my desk and bid farewell to my officials. Years later, when I took over from an outgoing Minister, I learned how important it is to be careful with personal documents. I opened a drawer in my new desk and found some letters addressed to a coalition constituency colleagure of mine. They could have been politically useful but I was not tempted. I tore them up and threw them out.

During this period deputies drop into Leinster House to sign the roll. An usher once told me that at each election his colleagues run a competition on who will be re-elected and who won't, and they are never far off the mark. As the new Dáil gathered for its first meeting I chatted with many of my colleagues. Deputies come from different age groups and many walks of life, some are very industrious, others less so. I remember one deputy asking a colleague why in heaven's name did he write so many letters. The deputy asking the question continued to be elected until he retired. There were quite a number of new faces replacing old colleagues of mine, which I regretted, but such is the way of political life. Fine Gael and Labour deputies were jubilant at the prospect of power after 16 years in Opposition. Fianna Fáil members who had been re-elected were happy enough to be returning at all. There is initially some sympathy for those who have lost their seats, but in the hurly burly of Leinster House I'm afraid they are soon forgotten.

A coalition of Fine Gael and Labour took office under Liam Cosgrave as Taoiseach. Fianna Fáil had been in office since I was first elected in 1957 so this was my first time to sit on the Opposition benches in Dáil Éireann. I found it a very traumatic experience to change sides in the House after 16 years in the Government and to see a totally new set of Ministers taking our places on the Government benches. The work I had been immersed in for years suddenly came to an end. I was very sorry to leave the Department of Education as I had a deep interest in education and understood its importance. To have to break off from direct involvement when I believed I had more to contribute was very difficult. Problems and pressures can weigh down on Ministers and may, at times, become oppressive, but I was soon to discover that after only a few weeks in Opposition these memories quickly dissipate.

Sitting on the opposition benches reminded me of my first years in the Dáil and having to listen to opposition deputies in a full flow of oratory, while we, as government backbenchers, had to exercise restraint in order not to delay business. At the time, I remember saying to a colleague, Paudge Brennan, that I would like to be on the other side of the house for a while. 'Oh', he replied, 'never say that. I spent some years in Opposition, and it was the most frustrating time of my life.' I could now bow to his greater experience.

It took time to adjust to my new role but the human being is nothing if not resilient and I quickly got used to it. I was fortunate that, whatever my role, deep down I was the same person, who, man and boy, had lived among his neighbours in the parish of Dunleer and who had always been treated, whatever my official standing, as one of themselves. The trappings of office never overly affected me. I remember one incident that drove this home to me. My son, who is a national schoolteacher, takes a particular interest in football and helps to transport the boys to the various football grounds to play matches. When I was a government minister I returned home from Dublin one time to find that one of the cars had cancelled and there was a transport crisis. We had a family car and I offered to help carry some of the children to a field at Tullyallen. When the game ended, one of the boys, who had travelled over with my son, said, 'Pádraig, I'm in a hurry home. Could I have a lift with you? Mr Faulkner won't be returning home for some time yet!'

Having adjusted to my new life in the Dáil it wasn't long before the thought uppermost in my mind was that those now seated on the Government benches might not last long in Government anyway. This helped to spur me on to greater efforts to ensure that Fianna Fáil returned to office.

To achieve this one of the first problems to be dealt with was party morale. Except for two relatively short periods of coalition government, 1948/51 and 1954/57, Fianna Fáil had been in office since 1932. For many years Fianna Fáil Ministers had been in the full glare of media attention and had become household names. Suddenly, with defeat at the polls, these well-known figures all but disappeared from public view and were replaced. The Fianna Fáil organisation found it almost impossible to cope with the new situation and party morale plummeted. Complaints flowed into headquarters about the alleged inactivity of our new front bench, of our failure to get publicity, and of our propensity for letting the Government away with everything. It took quite some time to make our people accept the reality of political life. Opposition parties can speak as long and as often as they wish, but governments can act, and, so far as the media is concerned, actions speak louder than words.

Slowly but surely, however, the natural optimism that was part of the Fianna Fáil psyche began to emerge and the challenge was taken up by all of us – front bench, parliamentary party and party members alike. We quickly set about updating old policies and formulating new ones, all contributing towards the compilation of an election manifesto, while dealing with policy and other matters as they arose in the Dáil. This all kept me very busy.

The new Coalition Government created controversy almost immediately when James Tully, the new Minister for Local Government, revised the constituencies. The revision, known as Tullymander, among other things, changed substantially the number of three and five seat constituencies. The objective was to give Fine Gael and Labour an advantage where possible, thereby underpinning the new Coalition Government for many years to come.

Personally, I was not particularly perturbed by the revision though a number of my colleagues who could be badly affected were unhappy. As far as I saw it the Coalition had sufficient seats to ensure a full-term in office and by the end of that period much could change. On one occasion, on my way out from RTÉ after a political broadcast, I met Ted Nealon, whose political allegiance was unknown to me then, but who later became a Fine Gael deputy and a Junior Minister in a Coalition Government.

He suggested that in the new circumstances it would be difficult for Fianna Fáil to ever regain office as a single-party government. I accepted his point should an election take place immediately, but pointed out that if the Government lasted its full-term and if its popularity waned, as it undoubtedly would, the new revision would spell disaster for it. I would have to wait four years to find out.

For a short period after the election of 1973 I shadowed my old Department of Education. I had the opportunity of speaking on the Education Estimate, which I had prepared myself. I was pleased to have an opportunity to put my work in the Department on record but I'm afraid I spoke for a rather long time, much to the annoyance of a Fine Gael deputy who was waiting to speak after me. Jack Lynch, Leader of the Opposition, then appointed me to his front bench as Spokesperson on Social Welfare. Des O'Malley became Spokesperson on Health and we decided to set up a committee to deal with both departments. The committee consisted of a number of deputies as well as experts in social welfare and health from outside the Dáil. We held regular meetings for the purpose of developing health and social welfare policies. Much research was needed and discussions with my colleagues on the committee kept me very active.

I had a strong interest in social welfare having learned a lot, over my 16 years in the Dáil, about the problems and difficulties confronting old people, people who were ill, unemployed people and those on low incomes generally. I remembered, years before, when the means test in social welfare cases was very rigid, the case of a man who failed to get an old age pension because he owned a small piece of land. He wrote to me saying he would give the land to the Minister, for the rest of his life, in exchange for the pension, but the property would have to be returned to his family when he died. I'm afraid the Minister was not impressed!

I spent long hours researching my subject and obtaining advice and help from experts. At the time, spokesmen for the Opposition were on their own. They depended on their own research and on the aid of interested voluntary people, with little assistance from public funds. I learned, belatedly perhaps, that, in order for democracy to function properly, much more needed to be done to provide assistance to those in Opposition.

As Spokesperson for Social Welfare I decided to visit Liverpool again. I'd first visited my uncle's home there when I was 16. The return fare by boat from Dublin had been 16 shillings, about a quarter of the average weekly wage. In later years I'd gone there on holiday and got to know the city even better. I wanted to find out how social welfare problems were dealt with in Liverpool and if any of their solutions could be applied to similar situations in Ireland. I spent some time carrying out research in a multi-racial and impoverished area known as Liverpool 8. I discovered that many people there were unaware of their rights under the Social Welfare Acts and giving information in newspaper ads was no use, as they didn't read newspapers and others couldn't read at all. The financial loss was very great indeed and it made me conscious of finding out if a similar situation existed at home. I also studied the American system but it was too far removed from my concern for the rights of the weaker sections of our community to be of much help to me.

As opposition spokesperson I was critical of the Irish Government's performance in the field of social welfare and my research enabled me to make constructive speeches in the Dáil on the subject.

* * * *

As the period in Opposition and my research into Social Welfare issues continued I was delighted in 1975 to be appointed as a member of the

Childhood home at the Trean, Dunleer, Co Louth.

Pat and Thomas Faulkner, my grandfather and father, 1927.

Aged 3, 1921.

My mother and father, Elizabeth and Thomas, 1955.

As Group Leader, LDF Dunleer, being presented with a cup on behalf of the Dunleer Group LDF Athletic Team, 1942.

Éamon de Valera arriving in Drogheda for a Fianna Fáil function. I am in the centre with Aly Farrell to my left.

Dev speaking at a bye-election meeting in 1954.

First time as a candidate, addressing the bye-election meeting at Dundalk, Co Louth, 1954.

Rannafast 1951. **Front Line:** *Pádraig Faulkner, Éamon de Valera, Paddy MacNamee (President of the College who had the unique achievement of being seven times President of the GAA), Jack Dennedy, Secretary of the College, Father Devlin.*

Pádraig Ó Fachtna ag bronnadh an **Fhocloír Gaeilge Beárla,** *le Niall Ó Dónaill, ar Éamon de Valera, Uactarán na h-Éireann. L Mac Ugo, Pádraig Ó Fachtna, Niall Ó Dónaill, Éamon de Valera, Matt Crowe.*

Minister for Education 1969-73.

Paddy Lalor (Minister for Industry & Commerce) visiting the Electrical Factory in Dunleer with myself and Jimmy Sharkey.
(Photo courtesy of Tony O'Malley Pictures Ltd)

Speaking at UNESCO Conference in1972.

On my 21st Anniversary as a Deputy in Dáil Éireann. **Back Row:** *Joe Farrell, Joe and Mary Sharkey, Kathleen and Jimmy McShane.* **Front Row:** *Pádraig and Kitty Faulkner, Mary and George Colley.*

Being appointed Minister for Lands and the Gaeltacht, by Éamon de Valera, Uactarán na hÉireann, in the presence of An Taoiseach, Jack Lynch.

Greeting the Pope on his visit to Ireland in 1979.

Ceann Comhairle 1980/81.

*Conferring Ceremony 1992 – Doctor of Law –
with former President of Ireland, Patrick Hillery.*

Conferring ceremony with former Taoiseach Jack Lynch.

Celebrating my Golden Jubilee, 1948-1998, with Kitty.

At the official opening of the new student services building, Dundalk Institute of Technology, 2002. The building was dedicated to me in recognition of my contribution to Irish education.

Council of Europe in charge of the Fianna Fáil parliamentary delegation. The situation in Northern Ireland had deteriorated rapidly and by January 1976, 1,400 people had died and numerous others had been injured. The Council of Europe had set up a committee to investigate the matter with Mr Dankert, of the Netherlands, as Rapporteur. The committee, and particularly Mr Dankert himself, did an excellent job in identifying the major difficulties and in bringing them before the Assembly. The Dankert Report recognised that a solution could be based only on partnership and participation and that the only form of democracy in Northern Ireland would be one that enabled both communities to share the power and burden of government together. I agreed with Mr Dankert on this point because, in essence, it was quite similar to Fianna Fáil policy. When I discussed it with him we didn't of course agree on everything, but I felt the issue was getting a worthwhile airing.

As Fianna Fáil differed with the Coalition Government on certain aspects of Northern Ireland policy, there was much media speculation on a possible clash between the Government and the Opposition during a debate on the Dankert Report in Strasbourg. I believed that our differences should be debated in the Dáil and not at an international forum. I met with Eddie Collins TD, Fine Gael, who was the leader of the Government delegation, and suggested that we should present a united front in Europe, with each party making its respective speeches but avoiding point scoring. This was agreed and adhered to, much to the dismay of one Irish journalist, Raymond Smith, who had already reported, in a national newspaper, that Fianna Fáil proposed to introduce divisive amendments. No doubt much to his disappointment, I basically stated that my party was totally opposed to violence and that unity in some form, by agreement, was the only road to lasting peace. We accepted that the vast majority of Loyalists were opposed to unity with the Republic and that unity could not be achieved without their consent. At the same time it had to be taken into account that a large majority of the Irish people wanted unity. Smith later wrote an article highly critical of all the Irish delegates to the Council of Europe.

It was very noticeable that the British Conservative and Labour parties, who disagreed publicly and vociferously at the Council of Europe on a large number of policy issues, agreed on Northern Irish policy, the Labour party being in Government at the time. The British Conservatives, whose full name was the Conservative and Unionist Party, strongly supported the Unionist population in Northern Ireland. Interestingly when the Labour party were in Opposition they had expressed support for Irish reunification.

For the next few years our northern policy continued to be based on peace and reconciliation and if, on rare occasions, someone strayed a little, they were soon brought back into line by our front bench. I was interested to read the views of a Dutch political scientist published in the *Sunday Times* in 1977:

> As for the solution to the Northern Ireland problem it seems less important what solution to adopt than how the solution should be arrived at. It seems to be most important that the Northern Ireland people have the feeling it is their own solution and not one imposed by British or Irish governments.

I agreed with this. Efforts to impose a solution were doomed to failure. They had failed and would fail in the future. I believed that a solution could only be made by Unionists and Republicans acting together with the help of the Irish and British Governments.

With this in mind I was surprised and curious when, on my arrival in Strasbourg to attend the Council of Europe in April 1977, I was informed that Bill Craig would be interested in meeting me. Craig had held the powerful Home Affairs position at Stormont during the time of the Civil Rights marches, from which position he had antagonised the whole Nationalist population, who detested him. When we subsequently met he put proposals for a new devolved Government at Stormont, where among other things, Catholics would be included, as of right. By this stage in his career Craig was a rather lone figure, his vanguard organisation collapsing. When I got back to Dublin I sent Jack Lynch a note giving him details of the meeting and little notice was taken of his proposals.

Years later, in March 1980, I received a document from Craig, prepared by himself, David Narry and David Trimble, entitled 'Towards the Better Government of Northern Ireland'. Stripped of the verbiage it appeared to support government by Unionists, with safeguards for Nationalists. It was now obvious to me that nothing concrete, or that would form the basis for agreement, would come from this episode and we never met again.

As I had realised when the Troubles first started in 1969, efforts to resolve the crisis in the North would always have a high priority on our political agenda. Every avenue was worth exploring – no matter how nebulous.

* * * *

After we returned from the Council and midway through the Coalition Government's term of office Jack Lynch reshuffled his front bench.

My brief was changed to Spokesperson on Local Government, opposite Jim Tully, TD, Minister for Local Government. I had an excellent back-up team to assist me and I got to work forming a committee of Oireachtas members and experts in Local Government affairs, which I organised into an effective unit. As time passed and a new election drew nearer, I concentrated more and more on policy matters so as to be prepared for any eventuality.

The general mood of the party was good during this period. We had overcome the negative reaction to the loss of the 1973 election and our organisation had been reinvigorated throughout the country. Many potential new candidates were emerging and we were now looking forward with quiet confidence to the future. In the reshuffle Des O'Malley took over as Spokesperson on Industry and Commerce and Charles Haughey was introduced to the front bench as Spokesperson for both Health and Social Welfare. I had a hazy feeling that something was afoot behind the scenes between Lynch and Haughey but I was somewhat surprised at his appointment. I knew of Haughey's ability and capacity for hard work and innovation, but nevertheless, his well-known antipathy to the party leader made it difficult to understand what motivated Jack Lynch in making his decision. I believe it may be that he thought the move would make for greater unity in the party or he was simply signalling that bygones were bygones. Whatever the motivation the party leader had made his decision and as such it wasn't questioned, though not everybody was happy with it. It was rumoured afterwards that Haughey had been offered Foreign Affairs, but had rejected it. This rejection was interpreted by some deputies and by some elements of the media, as a desire on Haughey's part to come into the mainstream of political affairs, rather than to be on the periphery.

Generally speaking affairs ran relatively smoothly except on one occasion when a clash of views between Jack Lynch and Charlie Haughey at a meeting resulted in Haughey leaving the room. I met him later in the corridor and, as I was returning to the meeting room, I suggested that he should return with me. On the way back we called in at another meeting, where Haughey launched into a vitriolic attack on Jack Lynch. This embarrassed many of those present, including myself. The bad feeling on Haughey's part was suspected, but the verbal attack was so unexpected that nobody commented. It was a clear sign that despite Haughey's return to the front bench little had changed in their relationship, at least so far as Charlie Haughey was concerned. During the period in Opposition Haughey made himself readily available to the party organisation and, while attending functions throughout the country, made contact with prominent members which was to stand him in good stead in later years.

The front bench continued its discussion on the content of the election manifesto, putting the finishing touches to various aspects of it. We wanted to make sure that we would be ready the instant the General Election was called.

Thirteen

Fianna Fáil
Election Manifesto

Fianna Fáil scored an outstanding victory in the 1977 General Election, returning with a huge 20-seat majority. I feel this phenomenal result was largely attributable to the immense personal popularity of Jack Lynch. Our clear policies on inflation and other issues also proved much more acceptable to the public than the mishmash of policies offered by the Coalition partners. I was delighted with the election result especially with the outstanding result in my own constituency, where we won three seats out of four, with Eddie Filgate taking the extra seat. I, like Jack Lynch himself, did have some qualms about the ultimate effect of such a big majority, but they were tiny in the light of the magnificent victory in Louth.

Jack Lynch was elected Taoiseach by the Dáil in July 1977 and he in turn nominated 14 Cabinet ministers, while the Government appointed seven Junior Ministers. George Colley was appointed Tánaiste and Minister for Finance and the Public Services and Charles Haughey was appointed Minister for Health and Social Welfare, two big-spending Departments. Haughey, I understand at his own request, did not get a Junior Minister, which, to say the least, was highly unusual in the circumstances. It appeared to me that he wanted to have a completely free hand in his Department, with no other politician directly involved.

I was appointed Minister for Tourism and Transport and Posts and Telegraphs. I was very pleased with my appointment which was a particularly challenging one. Communications, especially, were in a sorry state. My Junior Minister, Tom Fitzpatrick, had been our Spokesman on Posts and Telegraphs, which was a valuable bonus.

While in Opposition from 1973 to 1977, front bench members like myself had surrounded themselves with advisory committees to research and develop policy. I had put forward proposals for the Manifesto based on my research on Social Welfare and Local Government. Policy issues were regularly discussed at front bench meetings and, before the 1977 General Election, the final draft of the Election Manifesto had emerged. The Fianna Fáil Manifesto of 1977 was a comprehensive document proposing a wide range of reforms in all areas. Its immediate emphasis was on dealing with the high levels of unemployment, inflation and government borrowings.

When we took office the initial package of reforms and changes outlined in the Manifesto were immediately introduced. For example, additional funds for construction and the initial phases of youth employment schemes were introduced to boost employment. I was delighted when our target of creating 20,000 jobs in 12 months was reached. Inflation fell and the state borrowing requirement was also lower than in the Coalition years.

As part of the Manifesto, Fianna Fáil had also promised to abolish rates on domestic dwellings, which we duly did. Rates were a matter which cropped up regularly in my work as a deputy. That they were unfair was obvious. Outdated valuations ensured that there were substantial differences in rates' charged on the same houses in the same areas. When a family went to the trouble of improving their residence their house's valuation rose, and so did their rates. An old lady living alone on a modest income in a large house would pay higher rates than a family in a smaller dwelling with several members working, and so it went on. Carrying out a total revaluation of the country would take too long and in the meantime domestic rates, which bore no relationship to peoples' ability to pay, would remain, so Fianna Fáil abolished them.

I was delighted to see the policies in the Manifesto we had been working on for some years being put into practice. It was an invigorating time and I still find it hard to believe now that this same Manifesto was, sometime afterwards, to become the whipping boy for all our economic ills.

The main focus of the Opposition parties' subsequent attack on the Manifesto was the rates' issue. They called the plan an election gimmick, claiming that it was adopted without due consideration or in-depth analysis and would seriously damage Local Authority' finances. These charges were untrue and we denied them. The Opposition knew that we had been dealing with the issue of abolishing rates, in public, for years.

As time progressed, claims were made that we had impoverished Local Authorities and frustrated them in their attempts to retain reasonable levels of services. When in fact, Local Authority spending continued to account for a growing share of available resources right up to the mid-80s. While opposition parties regularly and persistently condemned the Manifesto, Fianna Fáil councillors were deluged with hostile propaganda from all quarters. They lacked a briefing from headquarters on the positive results which flowed from our Manifesto policies, so many had little alternative but to allow what were, in effect, unsustainable charges to go unanswered.

To this day, I have no doubt these accusations do not stand up. The fact is that the trend in developed countries like Ireland was that, despite the economic growth taking place, local government spending was rising faster than national income. Rates were providing a smaller and smaller part of the necessary revenue. Our approach was to provide Local Authorities with a block grant in lieu of domestic rates, the councillors to decide how it was to be spent. It they wanted to spend over the grant they could raise the excess through their own local initiatives. This would require them to face up to the cost of their own extra spending decisions, rather than looking to the Government to meet it with higher grants.

I am convinced that through the abolition of rates, Fianna Fáil got rid of an anomaly-ridden, inequitable system and opened an avenue to a fairer and more controlled method of Local Authority financing and spending.

It is also very interesting to note that all the major political parties had committed to abolishing rates on domestic dwellings before the election. In the lead-up to it the Fine Gael party had first promised to remove rates over a four-year period. Then a subsequent joint Manifesto issued by Fine Gael and Labour had promised to abolish rates over a two-year period. The swift and very opportunistic reaction by the Coalition partners to the Fianna Fáil stance could hardly have been as a result of their profound re-examination of the domestic rates' problem. Nor could they assert with any credibility the dire consequences they predicted if our policy was implemented.

It is also noteworthy that a perusal of the newspapers after the 1977 election shows that none of the Coalition members interviewed gave the rates' policy as a reason for their defeat. Their reasons included the Coalition's policy on farm tax, the high level of inflation, unemployment and the timing of the election. Their policy on domestic rates wasn't mentioned for the obvious reason that it was very similar to ours. However, as time passed and their policy had faded into the realm of forgotten things, as often happens to the policies of defeated parties, the Opposition went on the attack.

Similarly, the major newspapers in their commentaries on the election result also emphasised other factors, with only one paper mentioning rates. The *Sunday Press* observed that a government could not expect to win on soaring prices and high unemployment, a theme echoed by the *Sunday Independent*. Only *The Irish Times*, the following day, made a reference to voters being able to calculate the benefit to themselves of the abolition of domestic rates, as part of a more general resumé of the reasons for the Coalition Government's defeat.

These statements and the comments in the media show that what subsequently became part of accepted history, about the negative effect of abolishing rates, has little or no foundation in fact.

The abolition of rates was not the only policy in the Manifesto to be attacked. A veritable tirade of ill-informed criticism and misinformation targeting the Manifesto emanated from opposition parties, at local council and national level. This was bolstered by the uncharacteristic failure of the Fianna Fáil leadership to defend party policies. I feel that this was obviously designed to make the Manifesto, and especially its chief architect, Martin O'Donoghue, the scapegoat for the Government's failure to deal positively with critical problems which subsequently arose, such as the OPEC crisis in 1979 and the consequent deterioration of the Irish economy.

I think it is relevant to take the following into account when dealing with the tirade of criticism directed at the Manifesto. Charlie Haughey was elected Taoiseach in December 1979. He advocated the need for belt tightening by the people but failed to follow this policy in the conduct of the public finances. The Coalition Government that replaced Haughey in 1982 also promised and failed to stabilise the Nation's finances. They doubled the national debt while in office up to 1987. The urge to make the Manifesto a scapegoat for the Government's, and then the Opposition's, failure to deal positively with the economic problems and to allow the chorus of criticism to continue unabated must have been particularly strong. Both sides needed an excuse, and what better one than the Manifesto? With the propaganda machines of the three major parties ranged against it, it is hardly surprising that the public impression of the 1977 Manifesto was unfavourable.

The propaganda became so all-pervading that a member of the 1982/87 Coalition Government went on to use the Manifesto to excuse the immense increase in public debt. He claimed, in Dáil Éireann, that our 'Manifesto policy' had resulted in rapidly inflated State borrowing requirements. A complacent media accepted his statement and passed it onto the public without any reference to the Coalition's total failure to deal with public finances, or, indeed, to the Manifesto itself.

The misleading emphasis on just some elements of the 1977 Manifesto ignores the fact that the really important impact of the programme was on the longer-term major reforms. These reforms included modernisation of the telephone system, railway development, such as the DART, ending tax discrimination against married couples, the programme for promoting equality between men and women in the workplace, as well as many other reforms.

The negative attitude towards the Manifesto persists to the present day. It is reinforced by the writings of some social observers, most of whom uncritically recorded the myth as fact. In reality the Manifesto introduced many of the major reforms necessary for Ireland's progress today. I am still convinced that it was an excellent programme that brought many lasting benefits for the Nation.

* * * *

In 1975, the Fine Gael/Labour Coalition Government had decided to place an embargo on pay claims in the public service. I was to discover that this would create serious political problems for me on my new appointment.

All the public service unions had been perturbed by the embargo and as time passed they felt that their pay had fallen behind salaries in similar jobs. When Fianna Fáil returned to office in 1977 the new Government negotiated 'A National Understanding', which provided for negotiations on increases, on the grounds of serious inequity or of productivity. Offers were made and settlements reached. I had felt that the issue of public servants' pay could be dealt with in a more sympathetic and creative manner than an embargo, so I was pleased that the vast majority of public servants regarded our approach as fair.

The post office workers, however, resented the decision to restrict wage increases to increased productivity. They claimed that the Government had introduced something new and they now demanded compensation for past changes and for future productivity or they would go on strike. The postal workers were looking for substantial increases, ranging from 31% to 51%. The union had essentially placed itself outside any realistic negotiating position. In my INTO days when a pay increase was sought, the union would identify what would be a satisfactory increase and would then demand something a bit higher. Both sides were often satisfied by the final outcome. A demand for increases ranging from 31% to 51%, however, could have virtually wrecked the economy and would never be possible.

Civil servants and public servants had already accepted increases varying between 7% and 9%. Obviously if the postal workers were granted the huge increases demanded, all the other service unions would demand more money. The quick fix, easy solution is often to pay up and smile. As a Minister, however, I was convinced that to concede to these demands would be disastrous. I simply could not accept them. I explained to the union several times that if their demands were conceded the other unions would demand the same additional rises and the resulting inflation would seriously reduce the real value of their own incomes.

The pay increases demanded were discussed with the Union at

Departmental Council level on 12 occasions. While they were unable
to justify the very large claims, four separate offers were made in respect
of the various grades involved but to no avail. To say I was feeling
frustrated at this stage would be to put it mildly. All the normal rules of
negotiation seemed to have been abandoned. When strike action was
first threatened I had immediately brought the matter to the Employer
and Labour Conference, in accordance with the National Understanding. I had already intimated to the Post Office Workers' Union
(POWU) that they could take their case to Arbitration and I guaranteed
that I would accept the Arbitrator's findings. I repeated this offer in a
radio broadcast but it was rejected. It is important, however, when
involved in such situations to present a veneer of calm in public, which
I tried to do.

On the Conference's advice, negotiations had continued and I made
improved offers. Yet while negotiations were still in progress a strike
started, on February 19, 1979. This was breaching the Conciliation
and Arbitration systems in place, as well as the National Understanding
to which the POWU was a party. The decision to strike was wrong and
not in the interests of the POWU itself. It meant no further direct
negotiations between the union and the Department, future dealings
would have to be through an intermediary.

I discovered later that strike action was precipitated by the actions
of a radical group in the Central Sorting Office in Sheriff Street, Dublin.
They had threatened to breakaway if the union accepted less than the
increases demanded. When a breakaway union began to take on the
semblance of reality, the Union Executive apparently succumbed and
a strike was declared. As a life-long member of a union, I was only too
well aware of how easily a few strong willed members can, for a time
at least, frustrate progress.

The Central Sorting Office group announced its intention of
remaining on strike, whatever the Executive decided. As the Sorting
Office was a key area and could paralyse the whole Irish postal system,
the strike could continue indefinitely. I was disturbed by this, but as I
had already explained to the union, several times, there was no way I
could concede to their claims.

As deadlock was reached the matter became a government issue
and my attitude during the strike was dictated by government policy
with which I fully agreed. Both the Taoiseach and I were under
considerable pressure from all quarters. The leader of the Opposition,
Garret Fitzgerald, called on the Taoiseach to remove me from office.
Jack Lynch replied, at a public meeting in Carlow, that when a Minister
was facing unwarranted criticism, it was not his interpretation of
leadership to renege on him, '... it would indeed be a weak-kneed

leader who threw Ministers to the wolves to save his own skin'. I very much appreciated his statement. It was typical of the man.

I was worried about the effect the strike was having on the economy and also on the families of the postal workers, who were bearing the brunt of it. Business people were constantly demanding that the strike be brought to an end as the employment of more and more people was being jeopardised. I met with business leaders and I explained why I could not simply accept the union's demands. I finally asked if they wished me to end the strike at all costs – thankfully no hand was raised in favour.

The Irish Congress of Trade Unions (ICTU) was understandably loath to get involved in a strike by one of its members. However, as time passed, Congress became very concerned. I could understand the ICTU stance but I was very glad when they finally got involved. I must admit I admired the fortitude of their representatives, sitting in my office, night after night, sometimes into the early hours of morning. I well remember on one occasion when I left my office to discuss certain aspects with the Minister for Finance, and was gone for about an hour, they simply pulled the chairs back to the table when I returned and resumed our discussions, without a murmur. They were tough negotiators but when a set of recommendations, which I had accepted, was finally reached I know they also put tremendous pressure on the striking union. The POWU, however, rejected the recommendations, which especially annoyed the ICTU negotiators. Congress then expelled the POWU on the grounds that it had breached the National Understanding.

Later the ICTU re-entered the negotiations in the capacity of honest brokers. How the ICTU could negotiate on behalf of a union that had been expelled from Congress created a difficulty. The problem was overcome when the Secretary of the POWU claimed that his union was unaware of its expulsion as due to the Post Office Strike the union had not received official confirmation of such action by Congress! I was only too well aware that this was codology but I had to work with what I had got, not what I wanted, and in the circumstances, codology was acceptable.

Discussions resumed and after much effort by all concerned, the Congress was able to draw up a set of recommendations acceptable to both parties. Pay offers involved average increases from 9%-15% and the POWU returned to work in June 1979.

I was naturally pleased when the long strike ended. I had a deep and genuine feeling for the members of the union and particularly for their families. This had helped me to maintain a balanced judgement when under pressure, and considerable provocation, from the

Opposition and the media. The Opposition raised the strike issue on a regular basis. They knew that the union demands were ridiculously high, but they simply blamed me, as the Minister, giving the impression that if one of their number was in my place the issue would be successfully dealt with. I doubt if anybody believed them.

The publicity surrounding the strike had obscured public awareness of another task that had been demanding a great deal of my time and energies – the modernisation and reform of our telecommunications.

Fourteen

Posts and Telegraphs

As I took up my appointment as Minister for Posts and Telegraphs it quickly became obvious to me that the Department had had a low priority rating under previous governments. Why such a situation should prevail in an enormous Department, employing over 28,000 people, about half the total Civil Service at that time, is difficult to appreciate. Not to mention that it should have been patently obvious by then that the postal and telecommunications services were vital to the Irish economy. The need for radical change was self-evident years before 1977. Ireland had been caught napping and I needed to take immediate action to make up for lost time.

When I took over as Minister, Ireland had the lowest telephone density in the EEC, only 15% of the population. New connections were at a premium and cabling was inadequate. Subscribers had difficulty even making and, indeed, sustaining local calls. A heavy downpour of rain in Sligo could cut Donegal off from the rest of the world. Exchanges were antiquated. Engineers and highly qualified technicians were employed but there were too few of them. They could barely keep the services operating properly, not to speak of developing them. To cap it all I inherited a very difficult and protracted dispute involving the engineering staff in the Department. Thankfully, following a return to negotiations, that dispute was settled.

It was obvious that a major effort was required to raise the standard of the Irish telephone service and the first step was to get some funds. In my Dáil speech I outlined the programme proposed for the following five years at an estimated cost of £350 million. Legislation was enacted and the money was authorised. While I was pleased with this, knowing the tight control on extra spending by the Minister for Finance, I knew that much larger funds would be needed in the not too distant future.

It didn't take me long to realise that the management structures in Posts and Telegraph were inadequate. A number of new appointments were made to not only increase efficiency but to underline our desire to speed up the development project.

I was also aware that good staff relations were crucial if we were to get anywhere so I tried to deal with existing staff rules, regulations and other grievances. These rules and regulations were too specific and created ill-feeling and distrust. I appointed a mediator to examine them and a mediation committee that could recommend on grievances.

If real progress were to be made, however, I was convinced that immediate steps had to be taken to give telecommunications and the postal services the freedom to operate as commercial businesses. I recommended to the Government that a review group be set up to examine the feasibility of achieving autonomy. Personnel at the Department, which had been starved of capital for years, now believed that a new era was dawning and worked with great enthusiasm on the project.

The Review Group was set up on July 8, 1978 and delivered its excellent report on May 28, 1979. They recommended that both the telecommunication and postal services should be taken out of the Civil Service and that two semi-state bodies should be set up to operate them. The estimated cost of modernising the telecom service was £600 million, to be spent over a five year period. This would cost more than the total amount spent on telecoms in over 50 years, since the foundation of the State.

On July 3, 1979, in record time, the Government not only accepted the basic recommendations but increased the funding to £650 million. I was delighted that the Government had recognised the growing importance of telecommunications and was making it a top priority.

The Review Group had concluded that the service was undercapitalised structurally and they commissioned the Bell Telephone Corporation to examine it. Bell recognised that the inadequacies could not be remedied quickly but urged all speed in the implementation of policy. I agreed with these findings but the task of implementing the accelerated programme was a formidable one. The rate of telephone connections would have to increase from just over 40,000 a year to well over 100,000. Many factors could effect success. For example during the postal strike, as stores were controlled by the Post Office Workers Union, work on connections had virtually come to a halt while the strike lasted.

Pending the setting up of the statutory bodies, the Department of Posts and Telegraphs would have to be split into three separate units, one dealing with telecommunications, one with posts, each headed by an interim board, and the third dealing with residual ministry functions. This division of the Department could not be done quickly. It involved consultation with staff unions and associations. The removal of over 26,000 people from the Civil Service to the control of two semi-state boards was a major operation.

As regards appointment of a chief executive and senior management, I believed that the boards should have the same freedom as they would have if the statutory state-sponsored bodies were already in being. It was obvious that if the Board couldn't compete with the private sector for the high-grade staff required it would not be able to recruit staff of the right standard.

It was vital to start organising each board as soon as humanly possible. The basic function of the interim telecommunications board would be the management of the telecommunications service and its development, to ensure it met the targets set in the accelerated five year programme. I realised it was desirable to have worker directors on the board, elected by their co-workers. As we didn't have the necessary arrangements in place for an election I appointed the Irish Post Office and Engineering Union (IPOEU) secretary to the Board in the interim. At a later date I assured the staff that the nominated directors would be replaced by elected directors. I also gave an undertaking to the staff organisations that there would be full consultation with them on any proposals or changes affecting them.

The calibre of the personnel appointed to the two boards was fundamental to their success. I discussed the matter with Jack Lynch and asked for a free hand in selecting personnel and that no considerations would be countenanced, other than proven ability and suitability. I told him that I wished to appoint people, who had already proved successful in their own businesses and I would submit the names to the Government before approaching them. The Taoiseach gave me his full support.

To me, the telecommunications system was somewhat akin to an industrial project, while the postal service resembled a marketing concern. I chose candidates for board membership accordingly.

The choice of a chairperson for the telecoms board was crucial. I knew that finding someone of the required calibre and reputation, willing to take over the enterprise, could be a major difficulty. Successful business people could well feel that failure in this unknown, and very rocky, field could tarnish their business reputations. A full-time chairperson would be desirable but on the other hand, the most suitable person might not wish to take on a full-time post. I decided to leave the question open as I felt that a very successful businessman could scarcely be expected to abandon his business to the care of somebody else while he took on the onerous task of developing Ireland's telecommunications system.

Michael Smurfit, Chairperson and Chief Executive of the Smurfit Group, was an outstanding success in his own business, with a high public profile. To my mind he would be the ideal man. I met him in August 1979 and offered him the chairpersonship of the telecommunications board. Being a very busy man and recognising the immensity of the task involved, he was not overly enthusiastic. I pointed out that the development of the Irish economy was largely dependent on a first-class telecommunications system and that I was convinced that he would be a key figure in achieving this. I thought by his reaction, that, with some encouragement, he would be willing to accept the position. I went on to make the point that the Government had underpinned its belief in the enterprise by making £650 million available to finance it. He promised to consider the matter and to get in touch with me again.

We discussed the matter on a number of other occasions. Michael Smurfit was inclined to take up my offer but before coming to a decision he wanted to have a number of matters clarified and confirmed. These matters included the period he deemed necessary to achieve success, the salary of the Chief Executive, the type of company (limited liability) and so on.

When we met again, in early September 1979, I agreed to quite a number of his suggestions and proposals, including the length of his contract, for seven years, and the level of the Chairperson's fee, which, incidentally he did not propose to take himself.

As time was of the essence, I wished to establish the Board as quickly as possible. However, before Michael Smurfit could give me his final decision, he ended up in hospital, with an injured back. Liam Ó Réagáin, Secretary of the Department, and I decided, in the circumstances, to visit him in hospital. It was strange to be carrying on negotiations in a hospital bedroom. Normally I would never have considered pressurising somebody recovering in hospital but we were determined to get the new system in place quickly. I greatly appreciated his willingness to continue talking, despite his obvious discomfort. He was finally persuaded to accept the appointment, commenting that he needed it like a hole in the head. I could sympathise with him.

I went on to invite others, such as Denis Brosnan, Chief Executive, Kerry Co-operative Ltd and S. de Paor, General Secretary, IPOEU and Dr John Scanlon, Professor of Electronic Engineering UCD to accept board membership.

For the postal services board I felt that Fergal Quinn of Superquinn, a salesman par excellence, was the ideal person to chair the new An Post. With his acceptance I appointed the remaining members of the Board including Terry Quinlan, Secretary of the POWU, J H Ryan and Tony Halpin, Managing Directors respectively of Carroll Industries and Beamish & Crawford.

While I wanted to announce the names of the new board members, of each board, as quickly as possible, the difficulty I experienced in finding women who would qualify held up the announcement for the best part of a month. It became obvious that few women at that time got opportunities to develop their initiative at top level in industry or in business, with a resultant loss to our economic development generally. I did, however, succeed in finding women who had many skills to offer and the interim boards were established. The appointments were announced on October 30, 1979.

As I remember it, the Irish Post Office Engineering Union (IPOEU) was enthusiastic about the change. They were convinced that the elimination of civil service restrictions would enable the telecommunications system to develop rapidly, particularly as funds were now available. The Post Office Workers Union (POWU) had doubts. While they were concerned about civil service restraints, particularly in pay negotiations, they were not anxious to lose the security of civil service membership. However, all eventually accepted the situation and a change of historic proportions took place.

On March 14, 1979 I launched a Post Office/Office of Public Works joint initiative. A high percentage of the sites needed were quickly acquired and a number of buildings were erected. The accelerated building programme provided for the erection and extension of some 560 buildings. It was a large number but I was determined to get the work done. By the end of that year almost 420 of the sites had been acquired while 90 buildings were in the course of construction and our target was to place contracts for 130 to 140 before March 1980.

Telecommunications has always been one of the fastest changing industries. In the late 1970s the latest advance was the development of digital electronic telephone systems. Having considered my department's assessment I decided that Ireland should adopt this technology. It was a key decision. No other country had a fully developed digital system at the time and many of the major producers were keen to win the contract. Tenders came in and towards the end of the year it was apparent that the choice would be the French Alcatel System and Ericsson. I was quite happy with this. We had a highly talented group in the Department who knew exactly what was needed. The Secretary of the Department, Liam O'Réagáin, ensured a smooth and efficient transfer in record time.

While all this was going on, Ita Meehan, an assistant secretary was preparing the extremely complex legislation that would take more than 26,000 employees of Posts and Telegraphs out of the Civil Service and establish An Bord Telecom and An Post on a statutory basis. Considerable work had already been done on a Green Paper that had been circulated to other relevant departments, but some of them had not yet replied by the end of 1979. I was anxious to have all comments back as quickly as possible, but I had to accept that some departments are slower dealing with such documentation than others.

When I left the Department in December 1979 the task I set myself on taking office – giving Ireland one of the most modern communication systems in Europe at the time – had reached a very advanced stage. The works in progress included the installation of a major new computer controlled trunk exchange, the extension of international subscriber dialling and the building programme, which was proceeding rapidly. The key technological decision to change over to a digital network had also been taken. Productivity agreements had been negotiated with the telecommunication workers and the interim Bord Telecom and An Post had been set up.

In spite of the difficulties I had encountered during my term as Minister, the groundwork had been well and truly laid. I could hand over to my successor, Albert Reynolds, confident in the knowledge that all the necessary decisions had been taken to get the most up-to-date and efficient Telecom service up and running.

I was pleased with everything that had been accomplished in a short span of time and very appreciative of the enthusiastic way in which officials, workers, and the public-spirited people who accepted positions on the new Boards, had pressed ahead to develop the new systems.

Fifteen

Minister for Tourism and Transport

While the programme of major reforms and development was under way in Posts and Telegraphs, I also had another department, Tourism and Transport, to cope with. This meant different personnel, another building, new problems, and also of course, new development opportunities. It had previously been known as the Department of Transport and Power, but post-election the energy section had been transferred to another ministry. New name panels were erected in the building's entranceways, with the discovery that the word 'Tourism' had been placed before 'Transport'. I can't say if this was intended to put a new emphasis on Tourism, or was merely accidental, but it certainly aroused the ire of the transport personnel, who felt that the importance of their responsibilities was being downgraded. This was, to say the least, ironic as our new Government also envisaged major developments to meet the nation's transport needs.

In the seventies tourism had begun to be recognised as an important source of income. However, the Troubles in the North were creating problems for the fledgling industry. Many people, particularly in Britain, assumed that the Republic suffered from the same level of violence as Northern Ireland. I remember relatives of mine from Liverpool who came on holiday to County Louth each year telling me that people were horrified when they told them they were coming to Ireland. They asked them if they really intended risking their lives by coming here. When my relatives said that they came to the 'border county' of Louth each year they were stared at in disbelief. They couldn't, for a time, convince their friends that a very enjoyable and perfectly safe holiday could be had here.

This kind of attitude was very serious. Britain would have been, by far, the most important source of tourists. Visitors came in large numbers and they spent large sums of money. They were also some of the most popular tourists. When Irish people rail against things British I believe it is invariably the British Establishment that they have in mind, never the individual Briton or the British family. Indeed, tourists from Britain coming here for the first time in the late 1970s with preconceived ideas as to what to expect were often moved by the warmth of their welcome. Regular visitors from Britain, of course, took the welcome as the norm.

With all this in mind I decided to target the British market, with the able assistance of Bord Fáilte. I spent time in London, being interviewed on many radio shows, outlining the different types of holiday available here and underlining the warm reception visitors would get. The interviewers co-operated to an exceptional level and did everything they could to help me convey my vision of Ireland as a tourist venue. I was delighted when visitor numbers from Britain substantially increased.

I was well aware that the US was another rich source to be tapped for potential tourists. I personally felt that visitors from America didn't mingle with locals to the same extent as the British. You could get the impression that they spent their time constantly flitting from place to place, their cameras flashing and with numerous destination tabs covering their luggage. The reality, of course, was quite different. They stayed at the larger hotels, bought highly priced Irish goods and left behind them an Irish economy enhanced by large amounts of much-needed dollars.

I travelled to the US as part of our campaign. Given the size of the country my focus was naturally on the major cities. The presence of a government minister usually helps to ensure good coverage and this was evidently the case as large numbers attended the functions arranged for my New York visit.

Kitty and I went to Sunday Mass in St Patrick's Cathedral, an impressive building, that owed much to the pennies and cents contributed by Irish immigrants. A girl read the lesson, and when she finished, she welcomed my wife and I by name. We were pleasantly surprised that even in such a large city our presence didn't go unnoticed!

I was similarly surprised when I phoned to contact a former pupil who had emigrated to the US, years earlier. Before I identified myself she greeted me by name. I asked how she knew me, and she said, ' I knew your voice'. I'd often heard former pupils remember events from their school days, but never to that extent!

We visited other US cities before returning home, and I met a number of Americans who had visited Ireland. One man that I got to know well was fourth or fifth generation Irish and had developed a keen interest in the Irish language. He'd bought an Irish language grammar from a New York shop and later attended language classes. He finally came to Ireland to hear the language spoken, and spent quite a while in Donegal. It was striking to hear his Irish spoken with a

Donegal accent, while his English came with a very pronounced New York flavour.

When I was in New York I particularly noticed the desire some of its citizens had for panoply and display of all sorts. I had thought that it would be taboo in the great American Republic but it was quite the opposite. Old family names are titled, and I use the word advisedly, the first, the second, the third and so on. At a function at which I was Guest of Honour, I became the 'Honourable' for the first and only time in my life.

I felt it would be worth making a special effort to encourage Americans with Irish ancestors to visit Ireland, to trace their family roots, and we emphasised that aspect in our promotions. In later years I had the pleasure of assisting many Americans with this search in my own district, as I had always had a deep interest in local history.

Continental Europe was another area largely untapped for tourism purposes at the time. I visited several European cities, and opened a Bord Fáilte office in Paris which was a great help in attracting French tourists. Strange as it may seem, my most vivid memory of that occasion was the alarm on the faces of the Irish officials, when they saw me chatting with the owner of an Irish satirical journal. They needn't have worried.

One Bord Fáilte representative looking after Irish tourism in Germany had produced beautiful scenic views of Ireland on posters, all of which had clouds floating in the sky. Germans coming on holiday to Ireland knew what to expect, few complained about the weather and left well satisfied.

Encouraging tourists from abroad did not mean that I ignored Irish people who went on holiday at home. Traditionally large numbers of people from Northern Ireland visited the various holiday resorts in Donegal, the Midlands and the South. However, relatively few people from this side of the border went to the North, which I felt was a pity. Few people living in the Republic had any in-depth knowledge of the people in the North, Protestant or Catholic. There was a perception among Catholics south of the border that all northern Protestants were a narrow-minded lot who wouldn't bid a Catholic the time of day. I had quite a different experience.

County Louth is part of the Diocese of Armagh. As a member of Dáil Éireann for Louth I was invited to the consecration of Dr William Conway as Bishop of Neve at the Cathedral of Armagh. To cross the border by car, it was necessary to have a document stamped by the British customs, and stamped again on departure. The British customs hut closed at 8 pm. If you left later, with no exit stamp, you would have great difficulty with any subsequent visit. My companions were Senator

Larry Walsh and some councillors.

On the way there I remember we passed by a scheme of houses in a rural area in County Armagh. It was the month of July, and all the houses were bedecked with Union Jacks, telling us that the occupants were Protestants.

We arrived safely in Armagh City and enjoyed the day but, on our way home the car engine stalled. None of us had the slightest idea what was wrong. I'll always remember how relieved I was when Larry Walsh lifted the car bonnet and gave the engine a few hard slaps and it started up again. We set out once more but the car engine stalled again – just as we reached the scheme of houses, with all the Union Jacks flying. We looked at one another in silence. Finally I said there was nothing for it but to seek help in one of the houses.

We found a mechanic in no time at all and he came over to look at the car with his two sons. He asked us if we'd had a good day so he obviously knew where we'd been. The mechanic said the pump was faulty and he could take it off and repair it, but we wouldn't reach the border by 8 pm. In the circumstances he started up the engine, told us what to do if it stalled again and assured us that if we followed his instructions we would arrive home safely. He refused to take any payment for his work or for his advice so we thanked him and set off once more. As we moved off our reaction was one of relief, as if we had successfully crossed some hurdle. I said 'that was a decent fellow' – all enthusiastically agreed!

As we were climbing the hill south of Newry the car stopped once more. As I got out of the car whom should I see but the mechanic and his sons in their own car, who had stopped behind us. He helped us again and we made it home with no more trouble.

If any of us had got preconceived ideas as to how we would be treated we were taught a salutary lesson that day. I have no doubt that the memory of this episode made me keener than ever before to encourage people here to holiday in Northern Ireland. Among other things, they could then have a better understanding of the people there. I met the British Minister dealing with tourism in Northern Ireland and we agreed to co-operate in a joint tourism venture which would encompass Counties Down, Armagh and Louth. We jointly published a booklet, 'From the Mournes to the Boyne', setting out the delights to be experienced in this area.

I have always felt that the more all the people of this island intermingled and got to know each other, the nearer we would be to a solution without violence. Too many people were pontificating on the North who hadn't the faintest idea about the reality of the situation there.

We had all – Bord Fáilte, my officials, myself – put a major effort into promoting Irish tourism and our efforts were having some success. In 1978 we had a record number of foreign visitors, higher than the peak reached in 1969, before the start of the Northern troubles.

While I was happy that we were making headway with tourism I was also conscious of the need to press ahead with developments in the field of transport. Noel McMahon was Secretary of the Department of Tourism and Transport at the time and his advice was excellent. Radical changes were taking place in the transport area and one of the main areas of concern, as ever, was the traffic problem in Dublin. Traffic was slowed to an unacceptable level and the congestion was intolerable. Trains ran slowly and irregularly, with the result that very few people used them. I was convinced that a highly efficient service on the suburban lines would result in a rapid increase in passengers and traffic congestion would be relieved. CIÉ had been pressing for years to have the Howth/Bray railway line updated by replacing diesel with electric trains. I thoroughly examined their proposals and having studied a new electrical system in Newcastle, England, I recommended the new system.

The Government favoured upgrading the system but there was considerable opposition to electrification because of the cost. I continued to argue my case and whenever I felt I was facing defeat I asked that the discussion be adjourned. I returned to each meeting with more and more files in attempts to prove the efficacy of my proposal. I finally succeeded in convincing the Government. The decision to proceed with the new system, now known as the Dublin Area Rapid Transit (DART), was announced in May 1979. I was delighted and immediately asked the chairman of CIÉ, Dr St John Devlin, to call to my office. It was with great pleasure that I told him he had an immediate go ahead for the project.

The original estimated cost of the DART was £46.4 million and the estimated completion capital cost, at 1979 prices, was £46.1 million, so the scheme remained within the estimated budget. In later years there was criticism of the final cost of the project, £87 million, but, in fact, it was right on target. The critics failed to take into account the increase in costs due to factors such as inflation and the devaluation of the Irish pound.

It was intended that a fast and frequent train services would operate on the Howth/Bray electric line from 7 am until midnight, with the capacity to carry 25,000 passengers per hour. The cars would have the most advanced technology available. There was an enormous amount of work involved, including the rebuilding or lifting of 40 bridges. Nearly 1,500 people were employed when peak construction was underway with many of the materials made in Ireland.

I must admit it gives me great pleasure, even now, to travel on the DART and to remember the struggle for its acceptance and the final outcome. In later years I was happy to be told that the number of passengers had reached over 15 million a year.

A less happy memory that has always remained in my mind from my time in Transport, was the disastrous explosion on the oil tanker 'Betelguese' in Bantry Bay. I can still recall the unfortunate victims and the continuing fear that the ship would break up and cause a major oil spill. Fortunately there was an official in the Department with a phenomenal knowledge of the tides around the coast. So valuable was he that he was still working there, despite being over the retirement age. After the explosion a large part of the ship remained intact. A high risk strategy of towing the ship out to sea had to be adopted. Our expert official was able to chart the route which the hulk should take and the exact spot where it could be sunk without danger to the coastline. I can well remember listening to the early morning news for days, until to the great relief of all, we heard the hulk had been safely sunk.

A less dramatic but much happier maritime memory was my decision to give a grant, for the first time, to the Royal Naval Lifeboat Institution. During the six years that I taught at Clogherhead, I had seen at first hand the risks run by the lifeboat men and the courage they showed in going out in raging seas.

When I look at the canals now I am also glad to recall that I requested the Government to approve the transfer of the Grand Canal system and the Royal Canal from CIÉ to the Office of Public Works. The Government agreed and, over the years, our canal system has been transformed.

* * * *

I had the honour of representing the Irish Government at the inauguration of Pope John Paul I. The new pope had decided against a coronation, which had been the norm. The inauguration was an awesome spectacle. I was especially proud and honoured to be present on such an auspicious occasion. Numerous countries had delegates present, some dressed in their national costumes, all adding further colour to the event. I have a vivid memory of the newly elected Pope as he slowly passed by our delegation. I cannot say that I thought he was ill, but his appearance, in the heat of the day, coupled with the very heavy vestments that he wore, brought clearly to my mind the tremendous physical and mental burden he had undertaken. Sadly he died within a short time.

A new Pope was elected, taking the name of John Paul II. He decided to come to Ireland on a pilgrimage to Knock Shrine and visit a number of other venues in the country, all closely associated with Christianity. On the day of his arrival I was at Dublin airport with the Taoiseach, Jack Lynch, and the rest of his Government to greet him. He shook hands and spoke to each of us in turn. As I spoke with him I had an immediate feeling that someone very special had come amongst us, not just because he was Pope, but also I felt I was in the presence of a wonderful personality.

From the beginning it was clear to me that we had here a charismatic leader, with a common touch as the following incident portrays: Bobby Molloy's two little daughters stood behind the line of Ministers and shortly after the Pope had passed me by, they managed to squeeze through the line to present him with a bouquet of flowers; at the last moment their courage failed and one of them began to cry; I could hear the Pope saying, 'Oh! That bold Pope!' to comfort them – the crying stopped and smiles reappeared.

I was extremely pleased when I was told that the Pope had decided to come to Drogheda. As soon as the welcoming ceremony at the airport was over, I left for my constituency. As I neared the town I could see the fields thronged with people, thousands upon thousands of them. I was due to read a prayer during the Mass but the roads were so full of traffic I reached the altar with the greatest difficulty.

The Pope got a tremendous welcome on his arrival and was presented with the Freedom of Drogheda by the Mayor of the town. It was a very special occasion for me, with thousands of people praying along with me and an incalculable number watching on television. Never in my whole life, especially in my younger days, could I have anticipated or even dreamt of such an occasion.

During his sermon, Pope John Paul II called for an end to violence in Northern Ireland, a call that came to all of us from his heart, a call that is still remembered as one of the major items of his visit. Unfortunately, the call was not responded to immediately, but I have no doubt that, echoing through the years, it has played its part in helping to produce the peace process of today.

Sixteen

The Battle for Leadership

After Fianna Fáil's election victory in 1977, there were 62 deputies on the government backbenches. I think Jack Lynch was aware of the potential problem from the moment we won the election. At the time he said that the Government majority was too large. Governments with small majorities concentrate deputies' minds on survival. When, as in 1977, a large majority ensures the government's security, in-fighting, with its attendant problems, usually follows. This is particularly the case when many government deputies are elected to the last seat in a constituency. The slightest adverse change in public opinion can mean defeat. All in all it's a volatile situation.

In Éamon de Valera's and Seán Lemass's periods in government such a number would have presented no problem. They were both heirs to the Republican tradition, products of the Irish fight for freedom and the Civil War, with total control of the parliamentary party and the organisation countrywide. Jack Lynch, on the other hand, did not have a Republican background. While he fully subscribed to Fianna Fáil policy on Irish unity and, like both de Valera and Lemass, spurned violence as a means to its achievement, the right wing of the party only grudgingly accepted him. A ludicrous situation pertained. If Jack spoke on the Northern question in the same terms as de Valera such people were critical of him, suggesting that, while the words might be identical, de Valera meant something different. Logic had no place in the emotive atmosphere.

This situation had its origins in the 1966 leadership battle. When Neil Blaney and Charles Haughey had withdrawn as candidates at the eleventh hour, leaving George Colley as the only other candidate, it was not a philanthropic gesture. It was because they had realised that they did not have much hope of winning. Nevertheless neither Blaney nor Haughey had any respect for Jack Lynch and were biding their time, believing that he wouldn't continue for long as party leader. They availed of any opportunity to show their independence. Blaney's speeches on the Northern situation in 1968 were an early indication of these attempts to undermine Lynch's authority.

By 1977, 11 years later, Blaney was out of the party, Haughey was back as a member of the Government, and the decisive nature of the election victory meant that, on the surface at least, Lynch's authority was unassailable. But the continuing trouble in Northern Ireland, meant that the Lynch and Fianna Fáil policy of non-violence was only grudgingly accepted by some.

The ambitions of backbenchers, with little hope of promotion under Jack Lynch, were another factor to be reckoned with. I was aware of undercurrents within the party and of the names of some of those involved, but having a responsibility for two large Departments and all the activities that entailed I had little time for, or interest in, the manoeuvrings of a small group of malcontents. I was to discover, much later, that the dissidents were a disparate group, their individual motivations varying to quite a degree.

The activities of the conspirators were carried out in secrecy, but, as numbers grew, total secrecy was difficult to maintain. In July 1979 a caucus meeting was held, the purpose being to test the level of discontent among deputies. The leadership question was not to be raised directly but by chance an unwelcome deputy entered the room. The result was that the whole matter was raised at the next parliamentary party meeting. When the Taoiseach asked who had attended the caucus meeting Padraig Flynn was the only one with the courage to admit he had been present. I later learned that others involved included Jackie Fahey, who chaired the meeting, Mark Killilea, Tom McEllistrim and Sean Doherty.

Some deputies, such as Tom McEllistrim, Síle de Valera and Bill Loughnane, among others, seemed to believe that because of their Republican family backgrounds, they were the guardians of the Republican flame. They showed their disapproval of government policy on Northern Ireland in a variety of ways. Síle in a speech in September, which ran counter to Fianna Fáil policy, McEllistrim through a party motion on the alleged breech of Irish airspace by British aircraft and Loughnane by claiming that the Taoiseach had in effect lied at a parliamentary party meeting. Other deputies objected to aspects of economic policy. In addition deputies were dissatisfied because they had not been re-appointed to office, others because of a lack of promotional prospects, and a few because of a personal dislike of Jack himself. All seemed to hold the belief that the removal of Jack Lynch would achieve their different objectives.

I believe that the plots and subterfuges in which the conspirators were engaged became, in themselves, enjoyable to the participants. Walking on tightropes generated its own excitement. Holding caucus parliamentary party meetings in such a way as to protect the identity of the convenors and other such stratagems produced their own thrill. One incident I particularly remember involved an attempt to trap deputies and senators into signing a document urging Lynch to resign. The pretence was that there was a further document underneath that carried many signatures, which could not, the conspirators held, in fairness, be divulged except to those who signed. As I was a well-known Lynch supporter nobody approached me nor my close friends requesting us to sign. In fact it was some time before I became aware of it.

As time passed, more information on the conspirators' activities came to light. The threads which caused all the marionettes to dance to a single tune, however, all seemed to lead back to C J Haughey, who rarely identified publicly with the dissidents. I subsequently learned from an informant that Haughey invited selected deputies and their friends to Health and Social Welfare receptions. After most of the guests had departed the deputies were entertained by the Minister and the future of the party was discussed. Each deputy was expected to prevail on another deputy to attend the next function and so the conspiracy progressed.

Strangely enough I was convinced that Jack Lynch's appointment of Michael Woods as Chief Whip had a bearing on the growing sense of discontent. At a time of considerable disaffection in the party I saw this appointment as a tactical error. Michael Woods had been elected for the first time in 1977. There were many competent long-serving deputies who felt that they had a prior claim on the position. A strong feeling of annoyance and indignation permeated the party. This was not against Michael Woods personally, a highly intelligent and excellent deputy, but rather with the decision to appoint a newly elected deputy as Chief Whip. I expressed my unease to the Tánaiste, George Colley, who told me that he had not been consulted. If a long-serving deputy had been appointed there would have been little room for complaint and greater party unity would have been the end result.

Dissatisfaction with Jack Lynch increased. I saw Haughey's mask slip on one occasion at a parliamentary party meeting. The Taoiseach was on official business in the USA so George Colley was standing in for him. Bill Loughnane had continued to maintain that Jack Lynch had lied at a parliamentary party meeting and refused to withdraw the accusation. A motion to expel Loughnane was put to the meeting and I saw Charlie Haughey getting visibly agitated. He evidently feared the loss of a supporter and conferred quickly with a number of dissidents sitting around him. The result was that Jackie Fahey jumped to his feet and proposed that the meeting be adjourned, as lunchtime was approaching. This was agreed.

During the lunch break Loughnane's supporters evidently prevailed on him to withdraw his charge against Jack Lynch. The meeting resumed and the charge was withdrawn, causing the meeting to come to an abrupt end.

The agreement to an adjournment was a mistake for which I must take some of the blame. It weakened the leadership, which would have easily won the vote.

C J Haughey, of course, also signalled his position by, for example, failing to turn up to meet Jack Lynch at Dublin airport in November 1979. His absence was taken to be a message to his supporters that the heave against Lynch was on.

The unease and dissatisfaction in the parliamentary party was exacerbated by the severe effect on the Irish economy of the 1979 OPEC oil price rise. Inflation, which had fallen in 1977/78, rose. This increase, combined with the effects of the postal strike and differences on farmer taxation, had damaged the Government's public rating. Support for Fianna Fáil plummeted. The party vote dropped to 35% in the European election and local election results were also poor.

Two bye-elections took place, one in Cork City and the other in north-east Cork, on November 17, 1979. By Fianna Fáil standards, the election campaigns were very poorly run. Some dissidents, present in Cork, took no active part. I have a distinct recollection of asking Seán Moore TD to call at a hotel in Cork City to check on the campaign in the area. When he asked a number of anti-Lynch deputies why they weren't canvassing they said there was no need to do so.

Fianna Fáil lost both bye-elections. This was a particularly severe defeat in an area that had previously been dominated by Jack Lynch. The mood of uncertainty was grist to the mill of Lynch's opponents. Many deputies were now very uneasy about their prospects of re-election under his leadership.

Jack Lynch returned from America clearly tired of all the hassle. I understand that he had earlier privately decided to resign as leader of Fianna Fáil and Taoiseach in January 1980. He subsequently resigned a few weeks earlier in the belief that George Colley would be elected to replace him.

I appreciated his position but was saddened by his decision. Jack Lynch had led the Fianna Fáil party for 13 years in an honourable, upright and highly commendable fashion. He had steered it safely through some of the most momentous and critical years of its existence, when a false move could have had calamitous results for the whole Irish nation. He had an exceptional hold on the affections of the Irish people, as evidenced by the three General Elections he fought as leader. It is true that Jack Lynch would have had no difficulty in continuing as leader but this does not exonerate those who, in their small-minded, calculating manner, plotted to remove him before he had publicly indicated his desire to go. I found the whole episode shameful and deeply disturbing. Moves to oust a Fianna Fáil leader could, thenceforth, be legitimately taken at any time, and the tradition of continuing with the elected leader until he chose to retire was no more. This resulted in the turmoil and strife which harassed and haunted the party for years.

When Jack Lynch announced his decision to resign, George Colley and Charles J Haughey were the obvious candidates for leader. I had been closely associated with George since his election in 1961. I knew him to be a man of integrity, pleasant and courteous, an able minister and a hard worker. I was convinced he would make an excellent leader and Taoiseach and I had no hesitation in giving him my full backing.

I had never been very close to Charles Haughey on a personal basis. I knew him to be an able administrator, courteous to me personally, and, while capable of being aloof, could mix easily with deputies, should he so desire. He had built up a strong relationship with the party organisation countrywide, which was an asset during the leadership contest and afterwards.

Charles Haughey's ambition to become party leader and Taoiseach was perfectly legitimate. The methods used by his supporters, however, to undermine Jack Lynch and to force him out of office were repugnant to me and strengthened my resolve to do my utmost to have George Colley elected. There was no need for the dissidents' activities. Charles Haughey had proved himself as a Minister. His creative ability helped to devise means of helping people, such as pensioners, in ways that did not put a significant burden on the exchequer. Had Haughey held his hand until Jack Lynch decided on his own initiative to retire and contested the vacancy when it arose, he could still have won the contest. Haughey's real strength lay in the fact that Colley was seen as the establishment man. The large Fianna Fáil backbench contingent felt that he had little to offer by way of ministerial positions while Haughey appeared to be a free agent.

As the campaign got under way I felt that the modus operandi adopted by Haughey's supporters was damaging the unity of the Fianna Fáil party. I had little doubt that if Haughey was elected, the resulting deep divisions would severely restrict his capacity for positive and effective leadership. I put an intense effort into having George elected. I got in touch with quite a number of deputies and I met them in my Dáil office and around the House to request their support. I cannot say how many others made a similar effort. My Dáil office was next door to Charlie Haughey's and I was later told that the names of deputies who called on me were noted. For instance I called on Denis Gallagher seeking his support. Thankfully he had already decided to vote for George. Later I chanced to meet him in Leinster House and we stopped to chat. Our meetings were obviously noted by Haughey supporters as Denis was subsequently overtly informed that his activities were being watched. The implication was that his future prospects would be far from bright if Haughey won the contest, and so it turned out to be. He was not re-appointed to Government. He was an exceptionally fine person and his constituents left the new party leader in no doubt about their anger. In due course he was assigned a Junior Minister's position.

As the voting day approached I continued to do my best to ensure that George Colley was successful. Brendan Crinion, a popular deputy for Meath, was very ill and there was a doubt about his attendance. I asked Bobby Molloy to telephone him and ask him to vote for Colley. I then called on Brendan at his home, and told him that I was voting for Colley, gave my reasons why and left it at that. He attended the meeting and voted for Haughey, which, of course, was his right. I didn't ask Vivion de Valera to vote for Colley, as I knew their fathers to have been close friends and colleagues. I was disappointed when Vivion voted for Haughey.

I called to see Jim Gibbons, who I knew strongly supported Colley, to see how his campaign was going, only to find him reading a book. He told me he hadn't approached anybody, as he wasn't much use at that kind of thing. I reminded him that should Colley lose he would have plenty of time for reading. He later approached his constituency colleague, Liam Aylward, a committed Haughey supporter, with, as might be expected, no success.

Shortly before the election Michael O'Kennedy approached me looking for advice. He wanted to know whether I thought he should contest the election himself. I told him that in view of my support for Colley, I couldn't advise anybody to contest the election if I thought it would harm George's prospect of success. He accepted my point and after a brief chat he returned to his office. I was firmly convinced, at the time, as I feel were most of the party, that Michael would support Colley. I called at O'Kennedy's Dáil office, with Martin O'Donoghue, the night before the election and we discussed the situation. I did not ask Michael to support Colley thinking it unnecessary.

Meanwhile Haughey's key men passed by my door regularly to attend meetings in his office, working as a group to secure his election. Colley supporters, visiting my office, told me that a civil servant was engaged in full-time canvassing for Haughey in the Fianna Fáil rooms on the top floor of Leinster House. This high level of activity apparently prompted Haughey to express the view, at a meeting of his committee, that he would win by a landslide. I understand Sean Doherty told him not to be foolish and that the contest was far from being decided.

On election day when I entered the party room in Leinster House, feeling reasonably confident of the outcome, Jimmy Leonard informed me that it had been publicly announced that Michael O'Kennedy had decided to support C J Haughey. I was shocked and dismayed. Along with many of my colleagues I had been convinced that he would support George. During my conversations with Michael O'Kennedy I had never got an inkling from him that he proposed to support Haughey. The public announcement, from whatever quarter it came, was clearly designed to influence others, especially Michael O'Kennedy's own group. A wave of disbelief, followed by anger, swept through the Colley supporters, especially when it was apparent, in view of the closeness of the vote, that it appeared to have ensured Haughey's victory.

At the time I felt saddened by the event, but, in retrospect, I must accept that Michael O'Kennedy was entitled to vote for whomsoever he wished. He had no obligation to inform me of his decision.

The candidates, Colley and Haughey, were proposed and seconded and without further ado the votes were cast. Jimmy Leonard, TD Cavan/ Monaghan, whispered to me during the counting of the votes that he feared Colley would lose.

It wasn't long before we knew that this was the case. I was, naturally, very disappointed with the result but I knew that George Colley, the establishment man, had had major difficulties confronting him. As Minister for Finance he was, unfairly, being blamed for the deterioration in the country's economic position and for the resulting flagging support for the Government and the party. If Jack Lynch had retired a year earlier most deputies agreed that Colley would have won the leadership without difficulty. However that is politics. Around the corner 'it' is waiting for you, and that 'it' may be anything.

In view of the small majority, six votes, in the actual contest, looking back I believe that if George's campaign had been pursued more vigorously and with better co-ordination we might have carried the day. George, as far as I know, rarely left his office and his supporters, generally, took too much for granted. They relied on the accepted wisdom that he had the full support of the Cabinet and that Ministers would persuade many deputies to vote for him. Apart from a hazy recollection of one gathering, I know of no meeting to plan strategy or to assess the situation. I have often pondered on what might have been if the deputy who had promised to vote for Colley at my request had done so. Or if the deputy who had volunteered that he would be voting for George and the deputy who had denounced Haughey, more than once, had both actually voted for Colley. This, however, is now simply conjecture.

I shook hands with Charlie Haughey, congratulated him and wished him well in his future work as Taoiseach. I added that he hadn't been my choice and that I had worked might and main to have George Colley elected. He told me he was aware of this and that I had been damned effective and then continued that it didn't matter. I didn't take much note of the last phrase at the time.

Brian Lenihan was noted for his loquaciousness, so I have always been intrigued that after the meeting nobody knew which way he voted. Although he was seated close to Haughey, in the party room when the voting took place it was assumed that he had voted, along with most of his Cabinet colleagues for Colley. It wasn't until many years later that he stated in his book *For the Record* that he had supported Haughey.

There was, understandably, jubilation in the Haughey camp of which I had no part. His parliamentary supporters crowded around him for television appearances and media photographs. In the meantime I travelled to George Colley's house to help comfort him in defeat. I had been a close friend of George's for years but, interestingly enough it was my one and only time in his home. In the main, Ministers keep their private and public lives apart. Des O'Malley, Bobby Molloy and Martin O'Donoghue were already there and Ben Briscoe arrived later. We did what we could to console George and each other, but it was a sad gathering.

The new leader went on television to give a brief resumé of the policies he proposed to pursue. In the course of the broadcast he stated that his old friend and colleague George Colley had pledged loyalty to him as the new party leader. This latter statement was to create serious difficulties in the not too distant future.

Charles J Haughey set about forming a new government. I didn't expect to be considered for office, nor to be quite candid, in view of the lead-up to Jack Lynch's resignation, had I any particular desire to be. As I presided at a lunch in the Gresham Hotel for the postage stamp design committee, I was told that Mr Haughey wished me to telephone him at Leinster House. I immediately guessed that an offer of a place in the Cabinet was now likely. Normally a deputy wastes no time complying with such a request, but my mind was filled with conflicting emotions. I had difficulty reaching a decision.

I didn't telephone him. I naturally wished to continue to serve in Government but so many unedifying events had, in my view, occurred that I felt I could not grasp an offer with any enthusiasm. I continued to mull it over throughout the afternoon and evening, balancing the pros and cons. I felt I had to make the decision alone, consulting with nobody. Finally, rather late in the evening, I decided to call on the party leader. I was concerned that if everyone on the Colley side refused to serve, the new Cabinet would be devoid of the balance I believed it needed. I called on George Colley on my way to Leinster House and told him of my decision and my reason for taking it. Des O'Malley was with Colley when I arrived and I had a brief conversation with them. They didn't say what they proposed to do, but I got a feeling that they might follow my example. I left and went to call on the new leader.

Charlie Haughey asked me if I were willing to serve in his Government. When I replied yes we shook hands on it. He asked me my preference as to a department and I replied that having accepted his invitation that was a matter for him. However, I was determined not to take on another heavy department. For the past two and a half years I had shouldered a considerable burden, with responsibility for two departments and an enormous amount of work. Had George Colley become leader I had already decided to ask him for Defence. I had never discussed this with George nor, of course, as I have already said, did I mention it to C J Haughey.

I returned to discuss matters further with George Colley and Des O'Malley and found that they, too, had decided to accept the invitation to serve in Government. When I returned to Charlie Haughey he again asked me if I had a preference for any particular department and when I replied in the negative he said, 'All right, Defence'. Since then I have read, in the media, that I was appointed to Defence on George Colley's insistence. George Colley and I never discussed this matter and it is clear from my discussions with C J Haughey that had I expressed a preference for a particular department he would have been amenable to any reasonable choice. It might be inferred from the Taoiseach's wording that George Colley had discussed the matter with him but, if so, it was without my knowledge.

When I was clearing out my office in Tourism and Transport, George called to see me. He was angry at the Taoiseach's personal reference to him in his television broadcast. He told me that he had prepared a script to be delivered that night, differentiating between loyalty to the Taoiseach, which he accepted, and loyalty to the party leader, which, in view of the conspiracy against Jack Lynch, he had no intention of giving. So far as I was concerned, that was a matter for himself and, as I also felt aggrieved because of the treatment Jack Lynch had received, I did nothing to dissuade him.

On the following morning, as the new Minister of Defence, I travelled to Gormanston Camp to speak to the troops and to familiarise myself with some of the workings of my new Department. During my discussions with army personnel I was told that the Taoiseach was on the phone and wished to speak with me. Haughey asked me if I had seen Colley's speech and when I said I had, he expressed his annoyance with George and asked what I would do if he took action against him. I avoided a direct answer and replied that I thought it ridiculous that two adults couldn't settle their differences sensibly, without going to extremes. He continued to press me on the matter, to no effect. Finally

I offered to speak to George, to which he agreed with the proviso that I wouldn't tell George I had been speaking to him. I couldn't accept such a condition and I told the Taoiseach that unless I could tell George that we had spoken together I wouldn't approach him at all. Haughey finally agreed to this.

I telephoned George and told him that the Taoiseach had expressed considerable annoyance at his speech. I didn't say much about the rest of our conversation. I was anxious that George should remain in the Cabinet and I argued that he could be jeopardising his place there. I pointed out that if he left the Cabinet he would be upsetting the balance there, and reducing our group's strength to influence policy. I advised him to reach some kind of compromise when the two met during the day. George was a very determined character and was noncommittal when our conversation ended.

When I left Gormanston for Dundalk army barracks I had decided that if George was dismissed or forced to resign I would also resign from the Government, but, of course, I hadn't told him my intention. On my way through Dunleer I called in home and told Kitty what had happened and my intention to resign should the occasion warrant it. I was anxious that she would be aware of the position beforehand rather than hear it announced over the airwaves. She agreed with my decision.

I had lunch at the army barracks and I have a very clear recollection of the commanding officer saying how pleased they all were to have a County Louth man as Minister for Defence and wishing me a long stay among them. At the same time, I was wondering if my tenure of office would be the shortest ever. When I returned to my car, my driver, who, of course, knew nothing of what I had in mind, mentioned that he had heard on the car radio that the Taoiseach and the Tánaiste had settled their differences.

One of my most enduring memories during my tenure as Minister for Defence, was when I had the privilege of leading a group of Irish soldiers and their relations on a pilgrimage to Lourdes. Each year soldiers from a wide variety of countries travelled to Lourdes on a particular week. Each individual paid his or her own expenses and I learned from a priest, who was on the pilgrimage, that were it not for the generosity of the soldiers he could not have afforded to travel to Lourdes.

The pilgrimage was accompanied by a FCA band from Kerry. As we all marched together from our hotel to the square at the Grotto, down the narrow streets, with their many storied houses, the music of our pipe band was greatly amplified and attracted enormous attention. People lined the footpaths and many hung out of, even, the highest windows to get a view of the band. The spectacle of the armies of many countries, the soldiers all in uniform, was something to behold. Men trained for war, coming to Lourdes to pray for peace, was an example to us all.

* * * *

Before Charlie Haughey was elected leader of the party and Taoiseach, in December 1979, his supporters claimed that only he had the capacity to ensure the safety of the Fianna Fáil deputies' seats. With this in mind, in January 1980 Haughey made a Ministerial Broadcast. He impressed on the Irish people the strong need to tighten our belts and the urgent requirement for other tough measures to achieve economic recovery and growth in the wake of the horrific OPEC oil price increases, which had rocked the world economy. The tough measures proposed were well received and his advocacy of them proved he had a good grasp of the economic essentials. However, the manner of his elevation to the party leadership and Jack Lynch's election record meant that it was essential for Haughey to win an overall majority at the next General Election. Otherwise he would not retain his credibility within the party and secure his position as leader. Achieving an overall majority dominated Haughey's thinking. Difficult and unpopular but essential decisions were avoided, for fear of losing electoral support. While he displayed toughness and resourcefulness in the battle for leadership, his lack of political courage, was highlighted in the aftermath of the Ministerial Broadcast. As the economy deteriorated and the election loomed Haughey's need to secure an overall majority became the priority. The Taoiseach abandoned the guidelines for recovery outlined in his broadcast and sectional interests had a field day.

Haughey, as I saw it, was now forced into adopting stances which could only prove inimical to Ireland's success. Listening only to what he wished to hear, demanding loyalty but not always returning it, viewing as enemies parliamentary party members who expressed views different to his own and pressurising deputies to conform to his wishes, all added to the discord within the party. Attempting to obliterate the Lynch name from Fianna Fáil history and agreeing to proposals when in difficulty and then ignoring them when he felt strong enough to do so caused more problems. Haughey could be a charming and persuasive person and if he had reached the leadership in the normal way, without the preliminary activities that so divided the party, he would have found that failure to achieve a majority would have been accepted as one of the hazards of political life. The party would have developed in a united, positive and outgoing manner, avoiding the trauma, the turmoil, the emotional shocks of the years to follow.

Sadly it was not to be.

Seventeen

Ceann Comhairle

Following a long illness Joe Brennan, TD Donegal, Ceann Comhairle, died during the summer of 1980. The Dáil was in recess and as we were walking together from Leinster House to a government meeting, Charlie Haughey asked me if I would consider taking the position of Ceann Comhairle. He added that he was quite happy with me as Minister for Defence and simply wanted me to consider the new position. I asked for time to think about it.

I had been Minister for Defence from mid-December 1979 and I was, by now, very much involved in the workings of the Department. On the other hand, I was 62 years old, and the prospect of becoming Ceann Comhairle presented a new challenge for me. Having given considerable thought to the Taoiseach's suggestion, I decided to accept and told him my decision. An interesting aspect of my appointment as Ceann Comhairle is that the father of John Foster, the last Speaker of the Irish House of Commons, was a native of Dunleer, as I am, myself. Kitty had never sought to influence my decisions on political matters, but I think she was happy that I would be able to spend more time at home. She was aware of course that my work as a TD would continue, so the phone and the doorbell would continue to ring and the letters continue to come through the hall door. I submitted my resignation as Minister for Defence and as a member of the Government to the Taoiseach.

On October 16, 1980 the Taoiseach proposed me for the position of Ceann Comhairle. He was evidently pleased with my decision, perhaps more particularly, with the reception my nomination received from the Opposition parties. I must say I very much appreciated the tributes paid to me on that day, not only by the Taoiseach but by the leaders of the Opposition as well – Garret Fitzgerald for Fine Gael and Frank Cluskey for the Labour Party. I was unanimously elected, for which I was grateful. Having worked at ministerial level for a number of years, it was difficult in the cut and thrust of Dáil debate to avoid treading on people's toes. At the end of my acceptance speech I expressed my appreciation for the many kind things which were said about me, since it was very unusual to be praised to such a degree by the Opposition – I light-heartedly questioned whether they were sure it was me they were talking about!

The Ceann Comhairle, as Chairman, presides over sittings of the Dáil. He calls on members to speak and all speeches are addressed to him. He is responsible for keeping order in the House and is Chairman of the Committee of Procedures and Privileges of the Dáil. He is also ex officio a member of the Council of State, which advises the President and is a member of the Commission which exercises the powers and performs the functions of the President in his or her absence or incapacity. Having been a member of the Dáil for more than 20 years, I felt confident about taking on the role, and by the time the first month had passed I felt as though I had been Ceann Comhairle for years.

I decided to tighten up on Dáil procedures, and, while being fair to every deputy, to ensure that Standing Orders were adhered to. I believed that so long as a deputy received fair play he or she would usually react in a reasonable manner. As the meatiest media morsels were, usually, to be had when Standing Orders were contravened I, understandably, was criticised by a section of the media for my stance.

A major problem I faced, as Ceann Comhairle, was how best to handle the Order of Business procedures. Deputies received an Order Paper each day on which Dáil business items were numbered at the start of the day's proceedings. The Taoiseach, or his representative, then told the House of the numbers to be dealt with that day and the order in which they would be taken. The Ceann Comhairle repeated the Order of Business and, in earlier days, then announced the first number on the list and the debate began. A tradition had, however, grown up whereby deputies asked questions, supposedly on the Order of Business, but in reality, on any subject under the sun. In the ordinary course of events deputies submitted questions to Ministers, which were answered the following week when the Minister had had time to compile the information. Asking these questions on the Order of Business was simply an attempt to circumvent normal procedures and occasionally to ask questions which would not normally be allowed by the Ceann Comhairle. This was not in accordance with Standing Orders, and in any case made little sense, so I decided to take steps to control the practice.

Rules and regulations governing procedures in the Dáil are laid down by the House. I knew that it was my duty to interpret them, but it was a matter for the House to make whatever changes it wished and I would carry out its instructions. I was well aware that governments rarely wish to change rules and regulations, and while opposition parties complain about them and express a desire for change they do little about it. After all, they may soon be in Government themselves. I did believe, however, that the possibility of change should be discussed.

For example, there were many occasions when matters of urgency could not be raised immediately because of Standing Orders and procedures. I was determined that any change could only be effected in a systematic way, otherwise there would be chaos.

After consideration I decided to accept interventions from deputies on the Order of Business under three specified headings only, on the Order of Business itself, on any matter on the Order Paper and on legislation promised, in the Dáil, by a Minister. I was only too well aware that should I announce these new conditions formally, they would immediately be opposed by the Opposition parties, fearing a curtailment of their liberties, so I simply wrote them down and kept them on my desk until an appropriate occasion arose. One morning when there was an uproar on the Order of Business and I, apparently, had difficulty in restoring order, I stated that should such a commotion arise again I would state categorically what I would allow. Assuming, as I expected them to, that I had nothing prepared, the Opposition called on me to state my intentions there and then. I announced my decision and not only did I hold that line for the remainder of my term of office, but I later found the conditions laid down by me regularly quoted, as a precedent, by my successors.

In spite of all, I continued to have good personal relations with deputies, including Frank Cluskey, the Labour Party leader, a specialist in the art of circumventing Standing Orders and Rules and Regulations, with whom I had a few verbal battles.

One memorable battle I had was with Joe Birmingham, a Labour deputy from the Kildare constituency, who was the only member suspended during my time in office. Houses had been burned at the Curragh army camp and this episode had resulted in numerous questions, especially from Joe Birmingham. He persisted in asking supplementary questions after being instructed by me to resume his seat until I was finally forced to have him named by a Minister and suspended from the House. I was loath to do this as he was usually an orderly deputy, but, also, because I knew he was unlikely to obey, especially when thinking of the publicity to be garnered from expulsion. He admitted the latter to me later on.

Another incident I particularly remember was when John Bruton submitted a bill on behalf of Fine Gael. When it appeared on the Order Paper I was forced to deal with it in an unorthodox manner. I had previously read of the Bill in the newspapers. As I hadn't seen it beforehand, I assumed it had, unusually, been allowed, on the Order Paper by the Clerk of the Dáil, without my being aware of it. When I reached the Dáil that morning the Clerk approached me in deep distress, explaining that he hadn't seen the Bill and it was on the Order Paper without his knowledge. Bills from opposition deputies, which had financial implications, were not allowed on the Order Paper so we had a problem. If an ordinary Opposition Bill appeared on the Order Paper and the Government did not wish it to have a first reading, they simply voted it down and it disappeared. If I allowed this Bill to remain I would create a precedent. Bills with financial considerations from the Opposition would continue to appear on the Order Paper, with serious implications in some cases. I decided to remove the Bill from the Order Paper, on my own initiative – an unprecedented action. Fortunately John Bruton had given a press conference the day before explaining the low cost of the Bill's implementation. When the matter arose in the Dáil I simply stated that I was only fully aware of the financial implications of the Bill when I read Bruton's speech and the matter was thankfully dropped. I did make some enquiries into this matter to ensure, as much as possible, that it wouldn't happen again.

I can vividly remember one incident as Ceann Comhairle about which I was justifiably annoyed. Numerous questions and supplementary questions had been asked about the horrific Stardust tragedy and as further questions were simply repetitions of the earlier ones, I ruled them out of order. The final questions were submitted by John Boland, TD, Fine Gael Deputy for North County Dublin and when they were ruled out he raised the matter in the Dáil. I informed him that my ruling could not be questioned in the Dáil but that if he wished to discuss the matter further with me he could call to my office. When he arrived I told him that the Taoiseach had replied to numerous questions, that his queries were repeats and that that was the end of the matter. He suggested that the Taoiseach might have changed his mind about taking the questions and I told him that he hadn't done so.

John Boland then approached his leader, Garret Fitzgerald, to tell him what I had said and the Opposition leader raised the matter in the Dáil. The underlying theme of his questioning was that the Taoiseach had consulted me about it. I told the Fine Gael leader that I was surprised by his approach. As a former minister, he would be aware that the Ceann Comhairle's office would be in touch with a minister's office on such matters and a recommendation would then be made by the Clerk to the Ceann Comhairle. C J Haughey at no time spoke to me about the matter. I felt somewhat annoyed when John Boland did not accept my explanation, but Garret Fitzgerald's intervention did not trouble me. When the matter was brought to his attention he had little option but to act as he did. I simply put it down to the cut and thrust of politics.

I was involved in an interesting procedural problem, about which I had no previous knowledge, when I became Ceann Comhairle. When

I was appointed, I actually legally represented Joe Brennan's constituency in Donegal, until the Dáil made the necessary change to substitute my own constituency of Louth. The Government would have found it an easy matter to make the change had they done it immediately after my appointment. As time went on, the Fine Gael party realised that the Government's failure to rectify the position would inhibit the Taoiseach from calling a general election. They then proceeded to resort to all kinds of stratagems to block the change in the Dáil. However, by the time the 1981 General Election was called the change had been made and I was returned unopposed for Louth. The unopposed return is to ensure that while the Ceann Comhairle remains in office, there is no need for him to involve himself in party politics. He or she can consequently act independently and be seen to do so.

Patrick Hogan, a Labour TD from Clare, had been Ceann Comhairle when I entered the Dáil for the first time in 1957. Fianna Fáil obtained an overall majority in that election and could have appointed a Ceann Comhairle from their own ranks, but Éamon de Valera regarded continuity in that office as important and he informed the outgoing Taoiseach, John A Costello, of his view. Costello agreed with him and Hogan remained on as Ceann Comhairle until he retired. Cormac Breslin, a Fianna Fáil TD from Donegal, and Leas Ceann Comhairle, had then succeeded him as Ceann Comhairle. It had also then been the custom to appoint the Leas Ceann Comhairle from a party not providing the Ceann Comhairle.

When the Fianna Fáil Government was defeated in the 1973 general election and the Coalition Government took office, the Fianna Fáil parliamentary party decided that Cormac Breslin should not be a candidate for the position of Ceann Comhairle. This was to keep pressure on the new Government by forcing it to appoint a Ceann Comhairle from its own rather meagre ranks. Cormac Breslin felt very aggrieved and disappointed. Looking back now I believe that this was a short-sighted decision. We should have continued the de Valera policy of continuity so long as we were satisfied that the person concerned was a competent Ceann Comhairle as, indeed, Cormac was. From then onwards, governments have appointed both the Ceann Comhairle and the Leas Ceann Comhairle from their own ranks, when they have found it possible or practical to do so.

Despite the fact that the appointment of a Ceann Comhairle had become a more partisan political matter, I found that in general, deputies acted fairly towards me. For my part I endeavoured to treat all of them equally, as I pledged to do. Every deputy would not agree that I achieved this at all times, but on the other hand if they did it would probably have meant that I was not doing my job properly! Deputies came from a wide variety of backgrounds, they differed in attitudes, ideology, and behaviour, but all in their own way contributed to the working of the Dáil. For my part I was happy and honoured to have had the opportunity to occupy such a privileged position as Ceann Comhairle.

Eighteen

Haughey Leadership Challenge

The 1981 General Election result was a far cry from the result anticipated by the deputies who had supported Charlie Haughey's candidacy for leadership at the end of 1979. The Fianna Fáil percentage of first preference votes nationally fell from over 50% in 1977 to 45% in 1981. Fianna Fáil now had 78 seats while the combined Fine Gael and Labour parties had 80 seats and Independents held eight seats. As Ceann Comhairle, with my unopposed return, I could take no part in election activities in Louth. For election purposes Louth became a three-seat constituency. Four Fianna Fáil candidates were nominated to contest the three seats available with the end result that the Fianna Fáil first preference vote was badly split. This, together with a surge of support for a Sinn Féin candidate on hunger strike in the Maze resulted in Fianna Fáil winning only one of the three seats. This had not happened since I was first elected in 1957. I was somewhat disappointed but in view of the downward trend in the Fianna Fáil vote all over Ireland and organisational problems in Louth, I was not particularly surprised.

Shortly after the results came in, Charlie Haughey told me that he believed he would get enough support to be elected Taoiseach but that he needed my vote. He asked me to stand down as Ceann Comhairle when the Dáil reconvened. I agreed, but realising that his election to Taoiseach was by no means certain, asked him what my position would be if a Fine Gael/Labour Coalition government was likely. If that happened, he told me, I would remain on as Ceann Comhairle. Shortly afterwards I was approached by a representative from Fine Gael who asked me if I would be willing to continue in office as Ceann Comhairle if they formed a coalition government. I replied that it was a matter for my party to decide. I told Charlie Haughey about this meeting and when Garret Fitzgerald approached Haughey asking him to agree, he refused.

On the morning the new Dáil assembled I again met the Taoiseach. By this stage it was clear that he was most unlikely to be re-elected. Even if he had the support of John O'Connell, a former Labour deputy but now an Independent, whom he claimed would vote for him, he had no real chance of winning. But Haughey persisted with the view that he would continue in office. As I would never stand in the way of the possible election of a Fianna Fáil government I accepted the situation. As it turned out John O'Connell was voted in as Ceann Comhairle, and then Garret Fitzgerald was elected Taoiseach.

After the new Ceann Comhairle had been elected I was approached by Haughey to contest the Leas Ceann Comhairle position. To be frank, I found this totally inappropriate, and I immediately declined. He asked me why not, and if I thought it infra dig to accept the position of Leas Ceann Comhairle. I replied that this was obviously the case. Some of my colleagues expressed their sympathy, but I regarded the whole episode as simply part of the ups and downs of public life. Looking back on that period I am still happy with the decisions I made. If I had accepted the Fine Gael offer I would have continued on as Ceann Comhairle, but the post would have sat very uneasily on my shoulders.

So for the time being I returned to the backbenches in the Dáil. It appeared that the 1981 Coalition would last for some years and I began to think of retirement. I had now been over 24 years in the Dáil and if the new Government continued for the usual average of three to four years I would have spent a considerable portion of my life there. I told Charlie Haughey that I was no longer interested in a Cabinet or a front bench position.

When the Coalition Government collapsed suddenly and unexpectedly on its first budget in January 1982, however, I had little option but to allow my name to go forward for the ensuing General Election. It would have been unfair to plunge the local party into the turmoil of selecting a new candidate at such short notice.

As I started campaigning I knew that the fact that my name had not appeared on the ballot paper in the 1981 General Election could have a detrimental effect on my efforts to be re-elected. We also discovered, during the canvass, that opposition to Charlie Haughey's leadership was palpable. Many supporters told me that they wouldn't vote for the party so long as Charlie Haughey was its leader. I replied that I had represented the constituency for 25 years and to adopt that stance would mean voting against me. I am glad to say I successfully persuaded large numbers of these people to vote for the party.

The efficiency of our organisation and the calibre of the candidates stood us in good stead in Louth and helped us to overcome the anti-Haughey bias, which I might add was used to the full by our opponents. I remember an elderly man tellling me that neither he nor his wife would vote for me, this time, because of Charlie Haughey. The inference was that they had always done so previously. I tried to make him change his mind, but without success. I must admit I was perturbed as their change of heart could represent the tip of the iceberg. At another house, in the same street, I met a supporter of mine, and not wishing to pinpoint the other man's house, I asked my friend how people voted in some of the houses in the row. When he reached the house in which I was interested, my friend told me they were very strong Labour supporters. After that I went home content.

Our superb organisation succeeded once again, electing three deputies to the Dáil, with Tom Bellew taking the extra seat. I was pleased that I headed the poll for Louth. In view of our result I hoped that Fianna Fáil would gain an overall majority but it wasn't to be. Fianna Fáil returned with 81 seats, with 85 seats going to the remainder.

As I said before, in the leadership contest between Haughey and Colley many of the deputies voted for Haughey, believing that he would be more successful at the polls than Colley and would ensure their re-election. The result of the 1981 General Election had come as a severe shock to them, so failure to win an overall majority in February 1982, when the tide should have been running with Fianna Fáil, was a disaster. Their faith in Haughey's capacity to deliver was diminishing rapidly. They were also thoroughly shaken by the hostile reception they had received on the doorsteps during the election campaign.

When I look back at the 1981 election results I believe that C J Haughey made a serious political error in refusing to agree to my re-election as Ceann Comhairle. The Coalition Government had been defeated by a single vote. The Ceann Comhairle does not vote in ordinary circumstance, but he has a casting vote in the event of a tied vote. Traditionally, in such circumstances, the Ceann Comhairle votes for the status quo – the Government in office. If I had been in the chair, the Dáil vote would have resulted in a tie and, following precedent, my vote as Ceann Comhairle would have been for the Coalition Government, avoiding their defeat. The electorate had rejected Fianna Fáil in June 1981 and the General Election in February 1982 arrived much too soon for a sufficient change of attitude to ensure an overall Fianna Fáil majority. I believe that the party would have achieved a better result if the election had been at a later date.

Fianna Fáil won the February election but it was to be a short-lived victory. A culture totally alien to the culture permeating the Fianna Fáil party I had known, and of which I was justly proud, now pervaded the party. When the final results of the February election came in rumours began circulating of a possible attempt to replace Haughey as leader. I did not attend caucus meetings where the leadership was discussed. Shortly after the election George Colley phoned me to tell me that a group had decided to contest the leadership with Charlie

Haughey with, as I later learned, Des O'Malley as their candidate. I told George that I was not particularly keen on the proposal. Like George, I was still very angry about the tactics used by the dissident deputies, with whom I was convinced Charlie Haughey was closely associated, in their attempts to depose Jack Lynch. However, I was even more disturbed about the divisions in the party, which had once been such a tight-knit unit. I feared that another battle for leadership would only exacerbate the situation. The methods used in the leadership election had poisoned relationships in the party, but I feared that an attempt to replace Haughey after such a short period in office, whether successful or not, would destroy the prospects for stability. I still hoped that it might not be too late to heal these divisions. I was anxious to help to put a stop to the constant bickering that went on. I wanted to give the party time to settle down.

At the next parliamentary party meeting I thus decided to propose that we should not have a divisive election for leader. I intended to suggest that Haughey should continue in office if he agreed to consult some of the deputies in the opposite camp on the formation of a Cabinet. I hoped that, in such circumstances, the most capable deputies would be chosen both at Cabinet and junior ministerial level. This would give the new Government the drive and the balance that would benefit the country and, incidentally, the party as well.

So far as the Haughey faction was concerned I was irredeemable. They knew that any attempt to force me into supporting him would fail. No effort had ever been made to pressurise me, by for example, threatening to have the local organisation replace me with another candidate at election time, as was threatened in the case of some other deputies. I had an intensely loyal organisation and I was too long a member of the Dáil to be intimidated by any such threats. However, late on the night before the parliamentary party meeting was scheduled I had a phone call from a prominent party member in County Louth. He told me that Ray MacSharry had asked him to have as many letters and telegrams as possible sent to Fianna Fáil Headquarters, supporting Haughey. MacSharry had then remarked that my colleague, Eddie Filgate, was all right, the inference being, since my name was not mentioned, that I was not. When I asked him if he were certain it was MacSharry who had phoned, my informant replied that he was positive. The speaker had identified himself as MacSharry and he recognised MacSharry's voice. The leadership believed that it had done its homework well, and I have no doubt that they would have been dismayed and disturbed that information on their activities in Louth had been relayed to me.

I had represented my Louth constituency continuously for 25 years, and I was furious at any interference in it by outsiders, without any reference to me. However I didn't intend to allow this intervention to alter the difficult decision I had made.

The following morning I told Jim Tunney, Leas Ceann Comhairle, who occupied the same room with me, about the phone call. I said how distasteful I found such interference in my constituency. Shortly afterwards Jim Tunney left the room to get a cup of coffee. He obviously told Ray MacSharry about our conversation, as MacSharry rushed into the office to deny he had spoken to anybody in County Louth. I simply told him what I had been told. He again denied any involvement and we left it at that.

C J Haughey then asked me to call in to see him, which I did. He said he didn't think it was fair that he should be opposed as leader, having borne the heat of the day in the election campaign. I told him I had made up my mind on a course of action but I didn't inform him what it was.

At the party meeting I said that I was very concerned that the party was split down the middle. I pointed out that many Fianna Fáil deputies looked on one another as enemies, conversations among groups of party deputies often ceased immediately on the approach of other Fianna Fáil deputies – that this was not the Fianna Fáil party I had joined. I proposed that an all-out effort had to be made to restore genuine unity and confidence if the party was to have a future. I appealed to Des O'Malley to withdraw from the contest and I asked Charlie Haughey to consult with O'Malley, Colley, Brennan and others in the formation of his Cabinet, to reach a meeting of minds. Haughey agreed to consult with the others and Des O'Malley withdrew his name. Some deputies appeared to be relieved, while I'm sure others were disappointed, but very few blamed me for what I had done.

Haughey now had an excellent opportunity to promote peace but he failed to grasp it. I was very disappointed when I discovered that the promised consultations did not take place. Far from promoting reconciliation, his subsequent decision not to appoint George Colley as Tánaiste ensured Colley's refusal to join the Government. Now that Haughey felt safe, rather than promoting peace his objective apparently was to show all and sundry that he would do whatever he wished. This attitude boded ill for the future of Fianna Fáil. The purpose behind my intervention came to naught yet I didn't regret what I had done. I had learned a valuable lesson from the outcome and I began to consider my own future.

Nevertheless my decision had been an extremely difficult one for me to reach. All my personal friends, particularly George Colley and Tom Fitzpatrick, were on the opposite side of the fence. I knew they could find it difficult to understand why I had made my proposal. In fact Bobby Molloy had rung me at home prior to the meeting to let me know what was afoot, assuming my support. When I told him I didn't think the leadership challenge was wise or in the interests of the party he had accused me of a lack of courage. I ignored this remark and we remained friends. The rest of my friends also knew me too well to be suspicious of my motives and our relations continued to be cordial after the meeting. I have no doubt that Charlie Haughey was pleased with the outcome.

Charles Haughey became Taoiseach once more in early March 1982, as head of a Fianna Fáil government. To be elected, Haughey had needed the support of some non-Fianna Fáil deputies. In addition to gaining the support of three Workers Party' deputies, he also won the support of an Independent, Tony Gregory, after negotiating an agreement with him known as the 'Gregory Deal', which promised various benefits for Gregory's constituency. After Haughey was elected Taoiseach, Gregory immediately read all the details of their deal into the records of Dáil Eireann.

Fianna Fáil were back in power but the Government was short-lived and plagued with problems. The tenuous support of Gregory and the Workers party' deputies could be withdrawn at a moment's notice. Unsurprisingly this was to lead to further convulsions within the party.

Nineteen

The 'No Confidence' Motion

During 1982 morale in the Fianna Fáil party was at an all-time low. By Autumn '82, with a new election on the horizon, fears were widespread about a government collapse. Fianna Fáil deputies no longer believed that the party would gain an overall majority under Charlie Haughey's leadership. Conditions were much worse than had prevailed in February and deputies in marginal seats were deeply disturbed. Discussions took place between individual Fianna Fáil deputies and other political parties with the objective of forming a coalition government. I was completely unaware of these discussions until I read about them in an evening paper. It referred to a possible coalition between Fianna Fáil and Labour. At first I thought this was simply the usual type of speculation indulged in by the papers, but I decided to investigate the matter. By coincidence I met Martin O'Donoghue at Leinster House and asked him if he had any idea who might be proposing this crazy idea. I was surprised to find out that he was very much involved. His argument was that the Labour Party would accept Des O'Malley as Taoiseach.

To me coalition was heresy. I told him I would oppose such a proposal – tooth and nail. Since the party was founded we had provided single party government. If we were defeated in the Dáil we should go into opposition, rebuild the party as we had previously done and continue to give the Irish people a clear choice at each election – a Fianna Fáil Government or a coalition. I had the greatest respect for Martin O'Donoghue as an economist, but I thought that as he was new to political life he couldn't have the same feel for the Fianna Fáil party and its traditions as I, who had been a member for 40 years, had. I believed that the majority of the parliamentary party would never accept it. Thankfully the proposition never came to anything and the Government continued to function, but on very shaky foundations.

In October 1982, as I was about to leave for a Fianna Fáil Comhairle Ceantair dinner in Cooley, George Colley phoned me. He told me that Charlie McCreevy had put down a motion of no confidence in Charlie Haughey, for decision at a parliamentary party meeting. I immediately said that I thought it strange that Charlie McCreevy, one of the leaders in, what I regarded as, the despicable activities against Jack Lynch, and a relative newcomer to boot, should be chosen to sponsor the motion. George replied that, so far as he was aware, McCreevy was acting on his own initiative but that a number of deputies, including himself, were supporting the motion. He explained that he was ringing me to let me know about it before the news became public. I felt that the matter was being approached in the same amateurish fashion as was the previous case. I doubted very much that he could succeed. Charlie McCreevy was acting on his own, and had only told Charlie Haughey what he proposed to do. He had made no preparations to help achieve his objective.

Albert Reynolds was guest of honour at the function in Cooley. During the night he was called to the telephone and later told us about the McCreevy motion. Reynolds thought that McCreevy would get little support. I of course, at that point knew of McCreevy's effort but I kept my own counsel.

On an RTÉ programme soon afterwards, C J Haughey announced that there would be an open roll call vote on the motion. Haughey felt that the Fianna Fáil organisation in each constituency should know how its deputies voted. This was a very disturbing statement and I decided to oppose the open vote. I had no worries about my own constituency, as the vast majority of the members would trust and support me in any action I might take. However, I strongly believed that I belonged to an organisation where it was mandatory, should an officer's position be contested, even in the most insignificant Fianna Fáil Cumann, to decide on the matter by secret ballot. Now we were being informed that in a matter of great significance an open vote would be taken. There had been an open vote once before on Jack Lynch's leadership after the Arms Trial, but the circumstances and objective were very different. When the results of the trial were announced four former ministers called for Lynch's resignation. After Lynch arrived home to the tumultuous welcome at the airport, he needed to know just where he stood with the whole party. The country had passed through a very serious crisis, and he called on those who were opposed to him to publicly challenge him on the leadership. On that occasion nobody objected to the open vote which Jack Lynch won by a very large majority. This time I felt the objective was to frighten deputies into submission by suggesting that their own local organisations would disown them if they voted against the leader. It also heralded the start of a propaganda assault on constituency organisations by Charlie Haughey's leadership group and Fianna Fáil headquarters.

C J Haughey told his Cabinet colleagues that he demanded their full support and as a consequence, two Ministers, Des O'Malley and Martin O'Donoghue, had resigned from the Government. Some time before the meeting I was approached by Tom Meaney TD, a highly respected deputy who now no longer supported Haughey. He asked me to do something to help keep the party united, along the line of what I had done in February. I told him that I didn't propose to take such a course this time. I added, however, that I was very disturbed by the threat to have an open vote and that I was determined to oppose it.

On October 6, 1982 the parliamentary party meeting to discuss the 'no confidence' motion was held. Before the discussion on the leadership motion could begin a decision had to be made about how we would vote, secret or open – by a show of hands. This was a major problem for many of those who favoured a secret ballot. If a deputy raised their hands against the open ballot it would be interpreted as being anti-establishment. Additionally those who strongly supported Charlie Haughey would vote for the open vote, those who opposed him would vote for the secret ballot, which meant that the decision would be made by the so-called middle ground deputies. As Haughey had already stated that he wanted an open vote there was tremendous pressures from headquarters on constituency organisations, which usually meant that the middle ground would support the establishment. Nevertheless before the vote began I spoke on the reasons why an open ballot should not be acceptable to the party. One deputy interrupted me and commented that he was not afraid to raise his hand in public. I replied that now that he knew he was on the side of the big battalions I had no doubt he would be happy to be seen raising his hand. I added that in public life he might not necessarily always be on what appeared to be the side of the angels and he would then be most anxious for a secret ballot. If the party successfully voted down the proposal for a secret ballot they would be giving up their right to a secret ballot on such issues for all time. There would be no going back. As a matter of interest this same deputy had been highly critical of Charlie Haughey, complaining to me on a number of occasions that Haughey had blocked him from standing in a constituency where most of his support lay.

Despite my attempt the motion to support a secret ballot was lost and an open vote was taken. The atmosphere was tense before and after the vote. I had decided to vote against the establishment so I was quite pleased with the support the motion obtained. I supported the McCreevy motion along with 21 other members. In light of the open vote, this was an exceptionally high number. The group became known in the media as the 'Club of 22'. I never regarded myself as a member of any club.

In the short term, the open vote was a successful leadership tactic. It pressurised some deputies into voting for Charlie Haughey who might not otherwise have done so. The tactic, however, backfired. In the long term it proved detrimental to the leader's position, solidifying, as it did, the opposition within the party, which continued unabated until his resignation. The fact that 22 deputies, or over 27% of Fianna Fáil deputies, had defied all pressures and voted against him underlined a deep division in the party. It also identified for the public and, indeed, for the rest of the party members, a group of deputies who had every reason to close ranks and no reason whatever to change their stance. If there had been a secret ballot and even, if the result, had meant an increase in the number of deputies opposing the leader, the deputies' names could not have been positively identified. The result would have soon passed into the realm of forgotten things as the media could have done nothing but speculate on events.

There were vacancies in the Cabinet because of the resignations of O'Malley and O'Donoghue. Around the same time I paid a visit to Leinster House on constituency business, and as I was leaving an usher stopped me and told me the Taoiseach wished to see me. I returned rather unwillingly because I had guessed why he wanted to see me. When I arrived he offered me a Cabinet position, which I declined. When he asked me why, I reminded him that I had previously told him I didn't want any further government office. I simply didn't wish to serve in his Cabinet. He then asked me not to mention his offer. I refused to agree to this largely because I knew he was aware that if I gave him my word I would keep it. However I did not mention it to anybody at the time.

It was becoming more and more obvious that the Government was hanging by a thread. So when the Government collapsed on November 4, after the Workers' Party deputies voted with the Opposition, and Gregory abstained, I doubt if many deputies were surprised. Nonetheless the deputies were not happy to have to contest a third election in less than two years. It is true to say that only the leaders of opposition parties welcome elections, since it offers them the prospect of returning to Government. But for the ordinary deputy the risks are high. Their seat may be lost not only to a candidate of an opposition party but even to someone from their own party. I have a distinct recollection of the Coalition's Government's defeat in January 1982. The Fianna Fáil deputies were clustered together in the House, awaiting the result of the crucial vote. When they learned they had won there were cheers and whoops of joy. But the thought struck me at the time, that if the truth were told, for many of them, their hearts would have been sinking to their boots.

For me the election meant that I was, again, in a quandary. I discussed the situation with my closest colleagues in the organisation in County Louth and for the same cogent reasons that applied in February, I was pressed to stand once again. I finally agreed to do so.

Fianna Fáil put forward three candidates in the Louth constituency. Eddie Filgate had decided to stand down and his place was taken by Seamus Kirk. It was a tough election, with the tide flowing strongly against Fianna Fáil. To further complicate matters during the course of the campaign a decision to impose a health charge of £5 on hospital patients began to take effect. Hospitals, such as Our Lady of Lourdes Hospital in Drogheda, had not been properly informed about who should be levied so they applied the levy to all patients, even medical card holders. The hospital manager then went on local radio to state that this was a ministerial order and was not their fault. This action had a drastic impact on the Fianna Fáil vote in Drogheda and South Louth generally. I was not aware of this until I was told about it in the middle of an election canvass in the town. A Fianna Fáil supporter, a medical cardholder, who had been ill, had been charged the £5. I protested to the Minister concerned and instructions were immediately sent to hospitals pointing out exemptions. However, the election was over before the public knew the real facts.

Under these difficult circumstances I was delighted when the results came in and I once again headed the poll in County Louth. The organisation had worked in its usual efficient manner, successfully keeping our candidates' first preference votes as close to one another as possible in an attempt to retain the three seats won by the party in February 1982. Our total vote, however, had fallen. We succeeded in securing two seats only, with Seamus Kirk gaining the second seat. Fianna Fáil returned to the Dáil with 75 seats, Fine Gael with 70 seats and Labour with 16 seats. A coalition government was formed by Fine Gael and Labour, with Garret Fitzgerald as Taoiseach and Dick Spring as Tánaiste.

As for me, I took my seat on the opposition backbenches once again, spoke in debates on matters of interest to me and resumed the normal work of a deputy.

Twenty

Phone-Tapping

After the February 1982 election, some of the deputies opposed to Haughey's leadership began to suspect that their telephones were being tapped. Later disclosures would confirm that these suspicions were well founded. At the time I had no proof that this might be happening, but in case there was any substance in the rumours I became careful when speaking on the telephone, especially with George Colley. As the only other candidate to contest the leadership when Jack Lynch resigned, and as a deputy who had subsequently been critical of Haughey's behaviour on a number of occasions, I felt George might be a prime target for any such type of surveillance. While the feeling was that any phone tapping was being done on behalf of the pro-Haughey position, it was uncertain whether it was being carried out privately or in some other way. In the wake of the February election for example, when the first challenge to Haughey's leadership was emerging, there were rumours of opponents' homes being watched, and of surveillance equipment being brought in from outside sources.

The first public allegation that such activity was taking place came after the November 1982 election, just after the formation of the new Fine Gael/Labour coalition. *The Irish Times* published a report claiming that the phones of two journalists, Geraldine Kennedy and Bruce Arnold, were being tapped. When the new Minister for Justice, Michael Noonan, was asked to comment he replied that he had nothing to say for the time being. Later, on January 20, 1983 having obviously carried out an investigation, he confirmed that *The Irish Times'* story was correct, and that the tapping had been authorised by his predecessor Sean Doherty. At this point Haughey denied all knowledge of the tapping and of having seen any transcripts.

Personally I could not conceive of a situation where a Minister would involve himself with such a delicate matter as bugging journalists' phones without first consulting his head of government. The question also arose as to who would wish to have these telephones tapped, and why? To some deputies, and to me, the tapping was much more concerned with the internal affairs of the Fianna Fáil party, than with any aspect of public security. Knowing that one of the journalists, Bruce Arnold, was on friendly terms with George Colley, I had no doubt that this was the motive. An attempt was made to justify the tapping on the grounds that there were suspicions of confidential Cabinet discussion being leaked to the journalists. If that was the purpose it failed, since Colley was an honourable man.

In addition to confirming the phone tapping the new Minister also disclosed that Ray MacSharry had recorded a conversation he had with Martin O'Donoghue. A meeting of the parliamentary party was called for Sunday, January 23, to discuss Minister Noonan's statement. MacSharry defended his action, on the grounds that rumours had been floating around about his financial position and that he wished to ensure that his character and integrity were protected. O'Donoghue, who had lost his seat in the November election, was granted permission to attend the meeting. I was surprised when he appeared to me to have a poor recollection of what had been discussed at the meeting. It later transpired that the conversation had taken place three months earlier, shortly after the failed McCreevy challenge to Haughey's leadership. While MacSharry had a record of the conversation, O'Donoghue did not, and at the time of the January meeting he was out canvassing for votes in the Seanad election, due at the end of the month.

Following MacSharry's trenchant defence of his actions, a number of deputies spoke strongly in his support. I sat beside George Colley at the meeting and after listening to some of the speeches I whispered to him that I couldn't remain silent any longer. I stood up and said that as my silence could be interpreted as meaning consent, I wished to put on record that whatever the circumstance I could not condone the recording of a colleague's conversation without his being aware of it. So far as I can recall the discussion ended there.

A committee under the chairmanship of the party chairman, Jim Tunney, was set up, with Michael O'Kennedy, Bertie Ahern and David Andrews as members, to investigate the two matters. The committee in my view should have included more of the Colley grouping.

Only gradually, with the passage of time did a clearer picture emerge about these and other events during that 1982 period, which confirmed my view that they were all connected to Haughey's leadership of the party. It was not until 1992, nine years later that Doherty confirmed that Haughey did know about the phone tapping. And it was some years later again before it became publicly known, through the tribunals, that Haughey owed a large amount of money to the banks at the time. This apparently was the basis for O'Donoghue saying to MacSharry, during the meeting that was taped, that it was Haughey who was in financial difficulties.

All that was for the future. At the time, the immediate fall-out of the phone tapping was that the Commissioner and Deputy Commissioner of the Garda Síochána had to resign their positions. Interestingly enough as the Seanad election progressed Martin O'Donoghue headed the poll on his panel, largely with the votes of Fianna Fáil deputies and councillors. This demonstrated that he had considerable party support throughout the country.

As for myself all these events, coming on top of other happenings during that short-lived government of 1982, brought home to me the way the character of the party had changed. It was no longer the party I had joined so enthusiastically over 40 years earlier. At that point I had confidently believed that all the members were united in their desire to contribute to the welfare of the people and the country. Now there was a reluctance, almost a fear, to talk to more than a few trusted colleagues. A climate existed in which any open and frank debate on issues was viewed as being disloyal to the leader. I was not looking forward to the rest of the year with any great enthusiasm.

Twenty-One

The Ben Briscoe Motion

At the start of 1983 the Fianna Fáil Party was in turmoil. The party's poor showing in the November election, the bugging and other scandals meant that the leadership was once again under scrutiny. The general consensus among Fianna Fáil deputies was that change was necessary and that Haughey should resign. I also believed that Charlie Haughey should relinquish his position as party leader. The media had come to the same conclusion, one newspaper going so far as to write C J Haughey's political obituary.

A meeting of the parliamentary party was held on January 27, 1983. Standing Orders were suspended and the leadership was discussed with a number of deputies speaking their minds. Haughey stated that he would think the matter through and would then do what he thought right. Knowing him as I had for many years, and especially given my experience in the aftermath of the February 1982 election, my view was that he was simply endeavouring to gain time. He had no intention of resigning. He added that he would not be driven from his position by the media. As the meeting broke up he invited party members to call to see him throughout the day, to offer their advice. Quite a number of deputies called on him and as far as I know a majority of them advised him to resign the leadership.

I did not call to see him. I admired C J Haughey's contribution to many of the ministries over which he had presided but he was now, in my view, more than ever a divisive force. Many deputies felt that he was psychologically incapable of healing the rifts within the party and, if the party were to retain any credibility, a new leader was urgently required. I had no desire to meet Haughey to advise him to resign. I was only too well aware that it would be a waste of time and effort.

While the leadership debate was still underway, the party was thrown into more confusion when on Tuesday February 1, 1983 we received the tragic news that Clem Coughlan, a Donegal deputy, had been killed in a car accident. At the parliamentary party meeting the following day Haughey paid tribute to Clem Coughlan and a minute's silence was observed. The Party Chairman, Jim Tunney, then adjourned the meeting and left the room. The majority of deputies were shocked by the Chairman's sudden departure. It was most unusual for the

Chairman to leave a meeting so abruptly after a vote of sympathy had been passed on the death of a deputy. In view of the intense atmosphere prevailing at the time many deputies believed it was a ploy to forestall further discussion on the leadership and to avoid a decision on when the party would reconvene. In my mind's eye I still have a clear picture of Jim Tunney disappearing through the doorway and the thought immediately entering my mind that this was a delaying tactic. Forty-one deputies, including myself, subsequently signed a petition demanding another meeting on Friday, February 4. The petition was presented to the Party Chairman and to the Whip's office, but without result.

Haughey's opponents thought that the Party Chairman's decisions always appeared to suit Charlie Haughey's needs. Jim Tunney's refusal to meet the wishes of the majority of the party deputies to hold a special meeting was looked upon askance by many deputies. They were annoyed, angry, and above all, frustrated by his action. However, I had known Jim Tunney better than most, for quite a long time and had always had a high regard for him. When pressed not to meet Jack Lynch at the airport after the Arms Trial he ignored the pressure and was present to greet the then Taoiseach. During the Colley/Haughey leadership contest he supported Colley. I knew his view was that, as the elected leader of the party, Charlie Haughey was entitled to the allegiance of all of its members. As far as he was concerned adjourning the meeting after the expressions of sympathy on Clem Coughlan's death, was simply following precedent. Jim and I remained on friendly terms. Years later during a conversation with me, he expressed the same view.

At the time I was personally very annoyed by the frustrating delaying tactics being used by the leadership. Our rights as elected representatives were not being respected. We were confronted with the argument that Charlie Haughey had been democratically elected by the party, which was true. The sad fact remained, however, that the democratic process was overshadowed by the activities of the conspirators who had tried to overthrow his predecessor, Jack Lynch. I had accepted the status quo for quite some time, even when it went against the grain to do so. I had endeavoured to help weld the party back into the unit it had been for most of my time in Dáil Éireann. When the leadership question first arose, in early 1982, I had persuaded the party to eschew voting and I had attempted to have the open vote taken by secret ballot in October '82, knowing that serious consequences would follow. I failed and as a result the 'Club of 22' became known as a permanent opposition within the party. After all my attempts to re-unify the party had failed, I felt that for the sake of Fianna Fáil Haughey's only option at this stage was to resign.

The party leader can only be elected or deposed by the Fianna Fáil deputies. When Haughey implied in a radio interview that, should the necessity arise, he would appeal to the party grass roots, the ire of his opponents was aroused. Haughey was attempting to involve the whole Fianna Fáil organisation in a matter that was the prerogative of the deputies.

As a result of Haughey's statement, Ben Briscoe, a Dublin deputy with commendable courage, handed in a motion for discussion at the next parliamentary party meeting, requesting the immediate resignation of the party leader. I decided to support the motion because I was convinced that to save the party from disintegration, in a welter of personal animosities, a new leader was needed.

The Fianna Fáil party was now deeply divided. The old camaraderie, which had been its hallmark, had gone. In the Dáil restaurant tables were occupied by deputies belonging to different factions. Discussions no longer related to how Fine Gael or Labour might be defeated in the next election but rather to the activities of opposing groups within our own party.

At several parliamentary party meetings I had expressed my concern about what was happening to the party. Having been, for a long time, a member of a united party I was deeply saddened by it all. Trust was at a discount. One deputy approached me twice in the foreground of Leinster House and urged me to take a lead in the opposition to C J Haughey. When I asked him, 'Why me?' he replied that I was a highly regarded figure in the party and could wield considerable influence. I asked why shouldn't he give a lead and so far as I can remember was given an excuse of some kind. I must admit I wasn't particularly surprised to hear him laud Haughey at a later parliamentary party meeting.

As the party leader appeared to be about to resign, contenders began to raise their heads above the parapets. Michael O'Kennedy's and Des O'Malley's names were mentioned. Then C J Haughey approached Gerry Collins, who was in hospital. The leader reputedly told him he was resigning and urged Collins to throw his hat into the ring. Adding Gerry Collins's name to the list, was a move obviously designed to split the vote of the most likely winner, Des O'Malley. It was a real stroke of genius. The more candidates there were for the succession, the better the prospects of Haughey's survival. There is little doubt that the failure to identify a single likely successor caused confusion in the minds of many deputies.

I viewed each candidate with certain reservations. Michael O'Kennedy, who the Colley supporters had believed to be on their side in the Haughey/Colley contest had subsequently voted for Haughey and consequently was unlikely to get the votes of the Colley group. In essence, he would have little prospect of victory. Des O'Malley's intelligence and ability were recognised, but his involvement in leadership battles, coupled with his rather abrasive manner, raised doubts about his ability to unite the party. Gerry Collins, despite his ability as an organiser, did not appear to be attracting sufficient support. I thought that other names might surface but did not know for definite who they might be.

In any leadership battle the incumbent leader, of course, has a head start on his opponents. It is the leader who appoints Ministers when in Government and front bench spokesmen when in Opposition. He controls party headquarters and from there, pressures can be brought to bear on individual deputies. As the leadership crisis continued headquarters applied an ever-growing pressure on the grass roots of the party, who were urged to drum up support for Haughey. Many deputies were influenced by these tactics.

In my constituency there was a certain amount of support for Charlie Haughey, mainly from people who believed that, as the elected leader, he was entitled to continue in that position. They were convinced that the phone tapping and bugging revelations were figments of media and of political opponents' imaginations. They believed that these allegations were being exploited for the purpose of destroying Fianna Fáil. I understood and respected their view points, but I made no secret of my own attitude or of what I proposed to do. I stressed my right to make my own decision on the matter and this was accepted by all but a tiny number of the members of the Fianna Fáil organisation in Louth.

The parliamentary party met in Leinster House on February 7, 1983 to discuss the Ben Briscoe motion. The first item on the agenda was the report of the committee, chaired by Jim Tunney, that had been set up to enquire into the phone tapping and bugging. In the report Charlie Haughey was cleared of any knowledge of the phone tapping. The MacSharry and Doherty aspects were dealt with in a relatively mild fashion, while Martin O'Donoghue was blamed for raising matters with MacSharry which had allegedly damaged the party. Three of the four members of the committee, the Party Chairman Jim Tunney, the Chief Whip Bertie Ahern and Michael O'Kennedy, had supported Haughey in the McCreevy leadership challenge. However the fourth member, David Andrews, was a supporter of George Colley, and was one of the 'Club of 22' deputies who had voted against Charlie Haughey. In a minority report, he stated that Doherty had initiated the phone tapping for party political reasons and not for considerations of national security. He also stated that Charlie Haughey, as Taoiseach with overall responsibility for Government, should have been aware of the phone tapping, a comment to which Haughey assented.

I agreed with David Andrews's minority report, but at the time my view was based on suspicion only, and we had little option but to allow both reports to stand. I knew that some deputies also agreed with the Andrews report, that others disagreed, and that some didn't wish to get involved. Had we known the truth about the phone tapping at the time it would have been a different story.

Incredibly the debate on the committee's report was kept going by one stratagem or another, and the Briscoe motion was not reached until 8 pm. For me and for many other deputies, it had been a most frustrating day – as indeed the leadership intended it to be. As the debate on the leadership finally got under way it quickly became clear that a cat and mouse strategy was the order of the day. Whenever a speaker sat down and a lull ensued, the Chairman intimated that he was bringing the debate to a close. I had intended to intervene in the debate at a late stage but I was forced to contribute earlier than I wished. I spoke in favour of the Briscoe motion, and as expected was immediately followed by front bench members supporting the party leader. The debate continued and quite a number of other deputies spoke in favour of Briscoe's motion. Charlie Haughey remained inscrutable throughout the debate.

A decision had been taken that the vote would be by secret ballot. Before the vote took place. Charlie Haughey stood up and declared that he proposed to ask the meeting to remove the party Whip from Sean Doherty and Martin O'Donoghue. I had not the slightest doubt that the withdrawal of the Whip from Doherty was a phoney exercise. My instinct was that Haughey knew all about the phone tapping and that he had persuaded Doherty to carry the blame for the time being, with a promise that he would be rehabilitated in the party at the earliest opportunity.

Pearse Wyse evidently felt as I did because he stated that Doherty should not have the Whip removed. This, apparently, strange stance for him, was made presumably because he felt Doherty was not the only one on the leadership side who should have to go. My instinctive belief became stronger as time passed. Doherty who resigned of his own volition after the meeting, as did O'Donoghue, became restive and was reputed to have made veiled threats about what action he would take if he was not quickly returned to the fold. It was clear that the day would come when the truth about the incident would be known.

Charlie Haughey won the vote, a secret ballot, by 40 votes to 33. It was quite a victory for him and it owed much to his tenacity, nerve, ability to pressurise deputies, and the manoeuvres that had ensured that his opponents did not have the opportunity to unite behind a single candidate to oppose him. My opposition had been based on the belief that Haughey's leadership had damaged and was damaging the party, and the outcome of the vote did nothing to convince me otherwise. Quite a number of deputies felt as I did. Those who supported him were jubilant. Haughey himself left the House to savour the eulogies of his supporters who had gathered to acclaim him once again. The parliamentary party meeting ended and deputies went their separate ways. Life goes on.

Over the following months the party settled down to the more routine work of an opposition party while Seán Doherty was still waiting to be re-admitted into the parliamentary party. An opportunity do so arose late in the following year, 1984, when the Coalition Government introduced a Bill dealing with nursing. I had been approached by a number of nurses in my constituency to look after their interests so since the Bill was being discussed in the Dáil on the same day of the parliamentary party meeting I was, unusually, absent. While the Bill was being debated I received a message that RTÉ wanted to speak to me about my recent appointment to the Council of State. I replied that as I couldn't leave the House I would ring back later. When I finally rang RTÉ, the reporter told me that as I was not available, and they needed the item on the Council of State quickly, they had interviewed John Kelly, a Fine Gael deputy and a constitutional lawyer. I was quite happy about this but the reporter then commented that he'd heard that Seán Doherty had been re-admitted to the parliamentary party. When I said I was unaware of this he said that this is what RTÉ had been told. Not being sure of the facts I simply told him that I'd been in the House all morning and that I didn't know what had happened at the party meeting. I'd believed that something like this would occur, yet I was surprised at the news. I left as quickly as possible to find out exactly what had happened.

As I left my office I met Pearse Wyse and asked him about Seán Doherty. He told me that when the meeting opened there were only about a dozen members present. Brian Lenihan, acting for Charlie Haughey who was abroad, had read a letter from Seán Doherty applying for re-admission and without further ado he was re-admitted. The affair had all the hallmarks of a well-planned action: the party leader abroad; the tiny number of deputies present, as was usual at the commencement of a meeting; RTÉ informed; a contentious matter resolved and all technically in accordance with the rules. I was very annoyed, not by the readmission of Doherty, but by the cavalier treatment given to a serious matter. The die was cast, however, and as I didn't care at that stage to personalise the matter, I did nothing about it.

Although some time had passed since the vote on the Briscoe motion, there was still a certain amount of bad feeling among some members, when the '77 Cumann decided to hold a dinner in the Drogheda Boxing Club with Charlie Haughey as Guest of Honour. The '77 Cumann was an excellent Cumann, the largest in Drogheda, which I had always held in very high esteem. It was highly efficient and its members, to whom I will always be grateful, had worked diligently and loyally for me since I had first stood for Dáil Éireann back in 1954. Strange circumstances, however, surrounded this function. At a previous Cumann meeting I had been approached by some senior members and informed that I was expected to buy a ticket for the event and that I would be wise to do so quickly as tickets sales were good. This was an unheard of situation. Deputies in County Louth had always been invited guests to Cumann and Comhairle Ceantair functions. A small number of the Cumann officials had strong pro-Haughey leanings and I could only interpret their action as a deliberate snub. I was in a quandary. If I decided not to attend my absence would be interpreted in a number of ways, possibly leading to some dissension locally. In the end I purchased a ticket without comment.

On the night the very large hall was packed to capacity. When C J Haughey arrived he received a good welcome from the assembled throng, while an 'Arise and Follow Charlie' tape was played over the loudspeakers. With recent events in mind I had difficulty in assessing the mood of those present. During the meal I was wondering, after the very recent Haughey victory and my opposition to him, how I would be received when my turn came to speak.

I need not have worried. When I was called upon to speak the crowd erupted, giving me a standing ovation and cheering and clapping for so long that I had to raise my hand a number of times so that I could start speaking. The people I had faithfully served for 26 years sensed that perhaps I might be under siege and they were letting all and sundry know their loyalty to me and that I was a force to be reckoned with. I was delighted. The night for me was a wonderful success.

The parliamentary party gradually settled down after the Ben Briscoe motion, with Charlie Haughey as undisputed leader. His position was strengthened by the unexpected and untimely death of George Colley in September 1983. I had been not just a supporter and admirer of George, but also a close friend. In the wake of his departure, I felt it was time to attempt a reconciliation within the party.

The leadership, as I was soon to discover, had a different view.

Twenty-Two

The Departure of Des O'Malley

One of the initiatives taken by the Fine Gael/Labour Coalition Government during 1983, was the setting up of the 'New Ireland Forum'. During his first year as Taoiseach in 1980, Haughey had had two meetings with the British Prime Minister, Margaret Thatcher, to discuss Anglo-Irish issues, including the problems in Northern Ireland. The meetings had appeared to offer the prospect of a common approach to dealing with the situation. Unfortunately the process floundered when over-ambitious statements were made, hinting at the possibility of achieving a United Ireland. The aim behind the new Forum in 1983 was to try to establish some common position on Northern Ireland policy that would be acceptable to all political parties. The various parties made submissions to the Forum, as did representatives of the churches and other major organisations.

Over the years Fianna Fáil had always been successful at bringing many different strands of opinion under its broad umbrella. As a result tensions ran high when it came to formulation of policy on Northern Ireland. They had emerged during the Arms Crisis in 1970 and they surfaced again at the Forum. The main difficulties were how to reach agreement between Fianna Fáil and the other parties, when the traditional Fianna Fáil aspiration was for a United Ireland. The solution was to acknowledge in the Forum Report that a unitary state was the particular structure that the Forum wished to see established, but to go on to refer to a federal approach and joint authority as other options to be considered. When the draft was published in May 1984, however, Haughey changed his stance. To the dismay of all the other participants involved, he maintained that only a unitary state would bring peace to Northern Ireland.

Some members of the party were unhappy that Haughey had announced his position without any consultation with the parliamentary party. Senator Eoin Ryan called for a party meeting to discuss the line taken at the Forum. At the meeting a range of views were expressed but it turned out the majority supported Haughey. He then instructed all party members to refrain from public comment on the matter. Nobody dissented and the meeting ended. I was annoyed, but not particularly surprised, when Ray MacSharry was subsequently publicly reported, emphasising the leader's approach to the issue. Fianna Fáil sources failed to comment on this breach of the leader's instruction. When Des O'Malley, however, was then quoted as being critical of what he termed the stifling of debate within the party, a surge of anti-O'Malley vibes could be felt coming from the top echelons of the party. O'Malley's stance was portrayed as an attack on the leadership and as being in direct contradiction of the leader's instructions.

At a subsequent party meeting a small number of deputies took the opportunity, for a variety of reasons, to launch a vitriolic attack on Des O'Malley. I was one of the longest-serving members of the Fianna Fáil parliamentary party, and I attended party meetings regularly. At some of these meetings there had been disagreements and tough talking, but I had never before witnessed such a display of hostility as I experienced that day. It had all the appearances of a well-planned, orchestrated attack. When I returned to my office after the meeting, I felt ashamed, not so much because of the scene I had witnessed, but because I had let O'Malley take the battering unaided.

It was now very clear that the leadership's objective was to have O'Malley expelled from the parliamentary party. His public comments were simply the tool to be used. The motive was to remove a potential rival for Haughey's leadership. I was not by any means a close personal friend of Des O'Malley, but I viewed what was being attempted as unjust and unfair and I was determined to do all I could to frustrate it. I was convinced that O'Malley's expulsion would be a blow to efforts to heal rifts within the party.

I spoke to Bobby Molloy and I suggested that both O'Malley and he should meet me in my office in Leinster House to discuss the situation. When they arrived I pointed out to Des O'Malley that it was now obvious that a prominent group within the party intended to use his public comments as an excuse to have him expelled. I told him that he had, technically, contravened the instruction given at a party meeting and I advised him to publicly accept that this was so. If he then stated that he would abide by the party decisions in future, it would put an end to efforts to undermine him. I pointed out that O'Malley's expulsion would be a serious matter for himself personally, as well as being a severe blow to the party and that he should take steps to avoid it. Molloy supported the case I made.

O'Malley replied that he was aware of what was happening but could not apologise for what he had said. He believed in it and felt he had a right to express his viewpoint. After a couple of hours' discussion we reached a stalemate with O'Malley saying that he would fight his corner.

As I had anticipated, a motion to have the Whip withdrawn from

Des O'Malley was put down for decision at the next parliamentary party meeting. When the debate started I was in a quandary about how best to proceed. If it had been a matter of discipline alone I would have dealt with it as such, but I was aware, as indeed were all other deputies willing to admit it, that this was really a matter of personal differences between Haughey and O'Malley. To avoid an expulsion the debate needed to be handled with care. My strong inclination was to go on the attack, but, while this would give me some personal satisfaction, I knew it would damage O'Malley's cause. I had to be careful with the approach I adopted, so that I didn't unintentionally say something which might stir up anti-O'Malley feelings among the members.

I decided to try to convince the meeting of the unfairness of the penalty proposed. I pointed out that while MacSharry was apparently free to express his views publicly, O'Malley was now threatened with expulsion for doing the exact same thing. Ray MacSharry quickly intervened, saying that his comments were with the full knowledge and approval of the party leader. I retorted that as Charlie Haughey had instructed all of us not to publicly comment on the Forum issue, and neither the parliamentary party, the general public, nor I, knew anything about the leader's approval of MacSharry's statements, he had no more right to contravene the instruction than had O'Malley.

As Ray MacSharry didn't reply I went on to point out that I strongly favoured a disciplined party. While deputies and senators could express views at party meetings they should not divulge these views outside. I'd acted accordingly during my long years in the Dáil, and while this didn't make me particularly popular with the media, at least it enabled me to live with myself. I conceded that Des O'Malley had made some recent statements, which in the circumstances of the prohibition he should not have done, but that the penalty proposed for this offence was too exacting. If one were to weigh in the balance Des O'Malley's long and illustrious career as a member of Fianna Fail with the named offence, the scales would come down heavily in his favour. I proposed an amendment to the motion that would mean that the Whip would be withdrawn from O'Malley until the end of the current Dáil session, conceding that a technical offence had been committed. My amendment was not allowed.

I then asked the members to think of the good of the party. I had decided against listing the various statements other deputies had made in the past which had injured the party and been ignored by the leadership. I knew this would be a contentious issue so I simply said that I was fighting to retain party unity by keeping within the fold a man we could ill-afford to lose. Party unity had been improving in recent months, but a majority vote in favour of O'Malley's expulsion would severely damage it. The damage would not only be within the parliamentary party, but throughout the organisation nationwide, making it more difficult for the party to achieve an overall majority at the next election.

This I said was not a leadership issue, although some deputies, for their own reasons, wished to pretend it was. I made a strong plea to Charlie Haughey to exercise clemency. He replied that it was not a matter for him personally but for the party, and I knew then what I had subconsciously felt all along – that O'Malley's fate was sealed. We both knew Haughey held the upper hand. At that stage I began to regret that I hadn't taken a really tough line on the issue, but, of course, I had no reason to believe that this approach would have succeeded either. To be frank, my experience told me that from the outset O'Malley hadn't a chance.

The vote was taken, with 56 favouring the motion, and 16 deputies, including myself, voting against. Never in my long career in Dáil Eireann, have I seen such a proud and pleased group leave the party rooms as those 15 other deputies. An outside observer would have been forgiven for thinking they had won the vote. They were convinced that they had done the right thing by voting against O'Malley's expulsion. Each of them was aware, as they cast their votes, in an open ballot which they knew they would lose, that though this was not ostensibly a leadership contest, their future prospects would be very poor indeed under the current leadership. I had the greatest respect for the 15 other deputies, particularly for the younger deputies, who had the courage of their convictions. As for myself I was moving towards the close of my career, and I had simply my own self-respect to concern me.

After the vote was taken we all left the room and I had no further discussion with Des O'Malley on the subject. When the Dáil next convened O'Malley no longer sat on the Fianna Fáil benches.

The final parting of the ways between Fianna Fáil and Des O'Malley took place early the following year. O'Malley, then an Independent deputy, failed to support a Fianna Fáil motion in the Dáil. Haughey then called a meeting of the National Executive, which took place on February 26, 1985, seeking O'Malley's expulsion from the party. O'Malley asked for a secret ballot on the issue, but Haughey again insisted on an open vote. By 73 votes to 9 the decision was taken for Des O'Malley to be expelled from the party. As I had expected the unity of the party was severely damaged and the prospects of Fianna Fáil ever gaining an overall majority under Charlie Haughey ended.

It was only a few months later that party unity was tested once again when, on November 15, 1985, Garrett Fitzgerald and Margaret

Thatcher signed 'The Anglo-Irish Agreement' at Hillsborough, on behalf of the Irish and British governments. The Agreement was well received by the Irish people as it recognised the Irish Government's right to be involved in Northern Ireland's affairs. This was something I had suggested in my Dáil speech during the Arms Crisis in 1970 and referred to again in 1975 at the Council of Europe. Now ten years later I felt that the Anglo-Irish Agreement was an endorsement of my views, and I sincerely welcomed it.

The Fianna Fáil front bench had decided to get together to watch the proceedings on television, to study the Agreement's content and to decide on an attitude towards it. Meanwhile that same night I was attending a Fianna Fáil function in Drogheda, with Bertie Ahern as guest of honour. When Bertie arrived I asked what decision had been taken by the front bench and was told that they proposed to oppose the Agreement. I argued that that decision, even from a purely political point of view, was wrong. The general reaction to the Agreement was favourable and many supporters present that night endorsed my view. Bertie did not agree.

Shortly after the meal ended Bertie left the room and was absent for an unusual length of time. When he returned he looked worried and downcast. I suspected that he'd telephoned Dublin for a report on Haughey's television defence of the front bench decision. I thought he'd probably found out that it had not gone well, and had received little support. It may be that he later informed the party leader of my own views, because, unusually, Charlie Haughey, who was preparing a speech for the Dáil on the subject, invited me to his office and asked my opinion. I advised against continuing to reject the Agreement outright, and I gave my views on what I thought he might say. He used some of the points to amend his speech, but he qualified them to such an extent that he neutralised them. When he asked what I thought of his speech now I said it might satisfy a very green element in the party, but otherwise was not effective. He asked me, 'what the blankety-blank I wanted', and I told him I would think it over and let him know the following morning.

I drafted a short statement commenting that while there were aspects of the Agreement which were unacceptable to us, nevertheless anything worthwhile emanating from it would have our full support. I gave it to Haughey, who announced it, as his approach, at a parliamentary party meeting that morning. A deputy sitting beside me asked why he hadn't said this first, as it would have saved a lot of criticism of the party. I was glad that the statement was well received, just as the Agreement itself, had also got wide support at home and abroad. I understand that Haughey went on to repeat the statement at a Caírde Fail dinner, giving the impression that this was the real Fianna Fáil attitude, which had been misunderstood at first.

At the parliamentary party meeting itself, a number of deputies and senators had argued that the Agreement had merit and should be accepted. The majority, however, followed the leader's stance and opposed it, usually citing constitutional issues. Shortly afterwards, on November 20, one of the young deputies, Mary Harney, issued a statement supporting the Agreement. She voted for it the following week in the Dáil and was expelled from the Fianna Fáil parliamentary party. Des O'Malley, as an Independent deputy also voted for the Agreement and it was welcomed publicly by the former Taoiseach, Jack Lynch.

The debate over the Anglo-Irish Agreement had further damaged unity within the party and when Des O'Malley announced the formation of a new party, the Progressive Democrats, the following month, there was further upheaval. Mary Harney joined him immediately and it soon became known that Pearse Wyse, a long-time and highly respected Fianna Fáil deputy, was also considering his resignation. Haughey asked Bobby Molloy to reason with Wyse, which he did but to no avail. Wyse left the party to join the Progressive Democrats.

Bobby Molloy was also becoming more and more disillusioned with Haughey's leadership and was considering leaving. I discussed his position with him on a number of occasions, urging him to remain in Fianna Fáil. He was a young man and I was convinced that he had a bright future ahead of him. I was surprised and disappointed when shortly afterwards, I heard on the radio that he was also joining the PDs, as they had become known.

O'Malley, along with Harney, Wyse, and Molloy were now gone, but their views and mine on the issue of the Anglo-Irish Agreement were finally accepted by the Government in 1987. When questioned on the change in attitude they referred to it as an International Agreement.

As 1986 progressed party energies began to focus on preparations for the election, due in 1987. The period since the 1982 election had brought many changes in the condition of the country. Unemployment figures had gone up, emigration was once again a major problem and government finances were in a serious condition. It remained to be seen whether the dramatic changes within our party would have any effect on our prospects for returning to Government.

For my part, at no time did I ever consider leaving Fianna Fáil. I knew, of course, that for other reasons my role in the forthcoming election would be a new one – the passage of time called for a fresh decision to be made about my future.

Twenty-Three

As I Saw It

After the November 1982 election I had decided that if the new Fine Gael/Labour Coalition Government lasted the normal three or four-year term I wouldn't go forward for re-election. I delayed informing Charlie Haughey of my decision, as I was concerned that an early announcement could reduce my effectiveness, both as a deputy and at parliamentary party meetings. I also thought that a premature announcement could lead to dissension in my constituency. Having made my decision, I felt very uneasy each time a government crisis loomed which might cause the Government to fall and trigger off a new election.

When the 1986 Dáil session opened I had been a member of the Dáil for almost 30 years and decided that this was the time to announce my decision to bow out of active politics. At the earliest opportunity I informed Charlie Haughey of my intention to retire. He reacted in his usual enigmatic manner, showing neither disappointment nor elation about my decision, only requesting that I defer my announcement for a number of months. This I agreed to do.

I waited until Autumn 1986 and then began making preparations for my retirement. I decided to make the announcement to the Comhairle Dáil Ceantar, the governing body in the constituency, as I wanted to give them time to prepare for the election due in 1987. I prepared a circular requesting a full attendance, as the meeting would be an important one. I also prepared a letter of thanks to all the party members in the constituency, which was to be sent to the secretary of each Cumann after my announcement. One copy of this letter was sent early by mistake, and news of my retirement broke prematurely.

Some of the local media expressed surprise that I should retire, when in their view, my re-election was assured, but for me 1987 was the right time to go. The Coalition Government finally collapsed in disorder, the tide was flowing with Fianna Fáil and the prospects for the party candidates in the constituency were good. I could hand over responsibility for the future with an easy mind.

While I was initially unhappy that my retirement leaked out, I later realised that I hadn't taken sufficient account of the impact it would have on my many friends and supporters in the party, who now had some opportunity to prepare for the Comhairle meeting. I was overwhelmed by the strength of the emotions expressed on the occasion. Being human I was pleased with the tributes paid to me, not only by the organisation, but also by the media and the many friends who wrote to me.

I had enjoyed my work as a TD. It suited my temperament, as I had an inbred sympathy for people in trouble. Very long working hours made it a strenuous and sometimes stressful life but, thank God, my health remained good and my mental outlook hopeful and optimistic, vital elements in the make-up of any public representative.

Kitty, my wife, had also been a tower of strength to me throughout our married life and more especially during my 30 years in Dáil Éireann. As a result of my regular absences from home, she almost single-handedly managed household affairs, looked after our family, met constituents who called to see me and answered telephone calls, when many years after I was first elected we had a telephone. She also had to cope with, reassure, advise and console a husband constantly in the public eye, with the many vicissitudes such entails, and for all I am deeply grateful.

I also had the support of a tremendous organisation, the members of which kept my spirits high when the going was tough. The efforts they made at elections and on other occasions were of the highest order. Their fervour and dedication never ceased to amaze our political opponents, and I am sure on occasion, must have very nearly broken their hearts.

Some members were initially surprised when I also made it clear that I would not take an active role in the local organisation in the future. While I would help where I could on a personal basis, I felt that I had been the focus of the organisation in Louth for a long time. It was now right that the younger Deputies, Seamus Kirk, who had been elected in 1982, and the newly elected Dermot Ahern, should have the opportunity to develop the organisation as they thought best.

For 30 years the Dáil had been a kind of home from home to me, yet I left it for the last time, without any great feeling of sadness. The friends with whom I had been closely associated in my early Dáil days, Paddy Lalor, George Colley, Tom Fitzpatrick and Jim Gibbons, were no longer there. The volatile nature of Dáil membership is not particularly conducive to deep friendships and while it is possible to have a high regard for many deputies, that is not quite the same thing. Of the 78 Fianna Fáil deputies elected to Dáil Eireann in 1957, only the party leader, Charlie Haughey, and myself remained members with continuous service 30 years later. Death and each election had taken their toll and the deputies who had been my first colleagues were gradually being replaced by a younger generation. I was becoming an *'Oisin i ndiaidh na Féinne'*.

Leaving the Dáil on my own initiative could be done with no regrets.

Epilogue

In my close on 30 years in the Dáil, I served as a TD for a time under Éamon de Valera and his successor, Seán Lemass, but the two figures who dominated the public eye during my time there were Jack Lynch and Charlie Haughey.

Lynch, I remember as being very much like his public image; a courteous quiet man but with an inner steel when it came to defending his basic values. As I have noted there was more than one occasion when I had good reason to appreciate his willingness to defend what he believed to be right, especially during the postal strike in 1979.

It is because of this experience of working closely with Jack Lynch for many years that I do not believe the claims that he knew about the attempted importation of arms earlier than he stated. Evidence shows that whenever Jack Lynch came across activities that looked towards violence as a solution to the Northern problem, whether it be military training or the movement of arms, he acted at once to have them stopped. The very fact that he sacked two powerful Ministers goes a long way to illustrate Lynch's courage and resolve, especially when you remember that both Ministers had ambitions to succeed to the party leadership after what they assumed would be a short tenure on Lynch's part.

I will always consider the way he was undermined and forced from office as one of the darker chapters in Fianna Fáil's history.

I believe that, despite his ability to have others act as his frontmen, C J Haughey was the principal architect of Lynch's downfall. Ironically in playing that role Haughey planted the seeds of his ultimate political failure. While refusing his predecessor even a limited loyalty he was prepared to accept nothing less than absolute allegiance from his own followers. It is perhaps one of the great ironies of Irish politics that having pushed out the people he considered to be his main enemies Haughey later had to turn around and coalesce with them, in order to ensure his political survival. I was always opposed to coalitions because I believed that the groups involved found it difficult to agree on positive actions. I feel that subsequent revelations made by both Garret Fitzgerald and Dick Spring about their time in power together justifies this stance. I regret that what was, in effect, a split in Fianna Fáil brought about by an obdurate leadership, could have condemned the country to a coalition government for the foreseeable future.

My decision to vote for George Colley after the resignation of Seán Lemass rather than Jack Lynch was influenced by my personal friendship with George and the arguments of Frank Aiken. It had nothing to do with my doubting the direction Fianna Fáil might take under the Corkman. My reason for voting for Colley in the Haughey and Colley leadership contest was different.

The Fianna Fáil I joined was the radical political movement that became the champion of the small man in the Thirties. To me, Haughey represented something quite different. Big business will always have great influence in society and, because it creates the wealth necessary to make many other things possible, that is accepted. That influence, however, must not be unbridled or it will lead to inequalities and unrest. Government must act as a moderator, a counter to what the British Prime Minister, Ted Heath, once described as the unacceptable face of capitalism. In that way the battle between Haughey and Colley was one for the very soul of the party. It started a debate within the movement that continues until the present day.

We now live in the age of the Celtic Tiger and, as one who has lived through the hard times, the material wealth now evident in the country is gratifying to see. However, it must be remembered that in the areas of the world where he prowls the tiger is considered to be a very selfish and vicious beast by those who encounter him.

* * * *

Politics is often described as the art of the compromise. Since few people get all they hoped for from its practitioners it is inevitable that members of the public sometimes take a cynical view of politics and politicians. Indeed, seeing Ian Paisley on the steps of government buildings, talking about reaching an agreement with the Nationalist community in the North and establishing friendly relations with Dublin I couldn't help feeling somewhat sad. If Paisley, and those who reflect his extremism on the other side, could have had the imagination to be better politicians many years ago we might have come to this compromise much sooner.

In Northern Ireland, during the seventies and eighties, the worldwide publicity generated by the Civil Rights Movement, combined with the outstanding diplomatic efforts of both Jack Lynch and Paddy Hillery, had resulted in changing a system that was riddled with injustices. I feel that people who had a much narrower view of Ireland's future then hijacked this peaceful revolution. The irony is that three decades later the rhetoric of the leaders calling for a United Ireland, through peaceful means, is so similar to the policy Jack Lynch followed in his time that it would be amusing if it were not so tragic.

The French Revolution has been described as being like the falling of snow on blossom because the work of the early reformers, who were winning improvements from the *Ancien Régime* in a gradual and peaceful manner, was overrun by a winter of terrible violence. In Northern Ireland the admission that the bombs and the bullets that marked the onset of the Troubles achieved nothing, other than driving the two traditions further apart, is of little consolation to those who have suffered on both sides.

* * * *

Another issue that I feel it is essential to comment on are the tribunals that have been set up in recent years to investigate the misuse of large sums of money by institutions and by a wide variety of people, including politicians. Disclosures at these tribunals have, rightly, shocked the nation. Institutions and many of the individuals involved, hitherto regarded as pillars of society, were seen to have feet of clay. The revelations have created a new situation for Fianna Fáil with the party as a whole condemned by association. The impression is that every member of the parliamentary party knew what was going on but did nothing about it. This is far from the truth.

I spent, well nigh, 30 years in Dáil Éireann before retiring in 1987. Since then it has been said to me on several occasions, in reference to the revelations, that I must be delighted to be away from it all. My reply is that during my years in Dáil Éireann I met with many deputies from all walks of life. The large majority of them were decent, hard-working, upright people, who devoted themselves unsparingly to the welfare of their constituents and the good of their country. I was privileged to serve with them.

It was also said to me that as I had been a member of Charlie Haughey's Cabinet I must have known that he could not maintain his lifestyle on a Taoiseach's salary. The fact is that I knew nothing of Charlie Haughey's lifestyle. I was not one of his confidants. At his request I met him at his home in Kinsealy once, for less than half an hour. My only involvement with Charlie Haughey was, firstly, as a government colleague and, later, when he was Taoiseach. My knowledge of the origins of his wealth was no more than that of any member of the public.

Ministers are very busy people and their main concern, generally speaking, is with affairs of State. They meet with their colleagues once or twice a week at government buildings. Sometimes they meet at meal times and very occasionally at public functions. Other than that, except where a Minister has close personal friends in Cabinet, as I had in Paddy Lalor and George Colley, Ministers often know little or nothing about their colleagues' private lives.

On the political side when Charlie Haughey was elected party leader and Taoiseach I endeavoured to work, as best I could, within the new system. However, the memory of the unacceptable treatment meted out to Jack Lynch remained with me. Later on, because of the autocratic manner in which the party was being run, I was convinced that only a new leader could unite the party and restore it to its original culture – and I acted accordingly.

For some years the Fianna Fáil party passed through a turbulent period, with leadership problems, internal strife, deputies leaving to form a new party and divisions such as I had never experienced before. Nevertheless my faith in the party never wavered. Leaders might come and leaders might go, but the party was capable of surviving its ups and downs – as long as sufficient members continued to have faith in it and to support the fundamental principles on which the party was founded.

I am proud of my party's achievements over the years. Perhaps in retrospect, I am proudest of all, that with Jack Lynch, Paddy Hillery, George Colley, Paddy Lalor, and others, we as a government, laid down and gained acceptance of a policy for the reunification of the country – our primary objective – by peaceful and democratic means only.

* * * *

It is the lot of all human beings to be influenced by the people, events and philosophies they encounter over the years. In a lifetime of more than eight decades, I can hardly claim to have been immune to such influences. It was my good fortune to have the opportunity of playing my part in so many of the events that shaped the Ireland of today. This is my account of that era – as I saw it.

The All-Ireland Dream

Seamus McRory

PB €14.99 0-86327-936-8

THE
ALL- IRELAND
DREAM

OVER 25 INTERVIEWS WITH GAA GREATS

SEAMUS McRORY

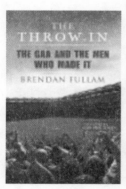

Features over 25 in-depth interviews with GAA all-stars. From famous footballers and hurlers, such as Brian Corcoran and Johnny Dooley, to leading GAA officials, team managers and match referees, best-selling author Seamus McRory unfolds six decades of Gaelic Games' achievement.

Delve into the lives of the players as you read interviews with the likes of James McCartan, Pat Henderson, Joe McKenna, and Frank McGuigan. Read the views of eminent referees Dickie Murphy and John Bannon. Find out what former GAA President, Peter Quinn, thinks will happen in the challenging times ahead.

The All-Ireland Dream will inspire the next generation of 'GAA Greats'.

The Throw-In

Brendan Fullam

HB €19.99 0-86327-925-2

The Gaelic Athletic Association has developed into a magnificent organisation since its foundation in 1884.

Meet the idealists and visionaries of the infant days of the Association – its founders, patrons and dedicated officials. Get to know the GAA's presidents as the lives and times of all thirty-four of them are explored in intimate detail.

Join in the debate on team selections by well-known personalities, including Jack Lynch, Tommy Doyle and Sean Óg O'Ceallachain. Celebrate the Camogie Centenary and discover the neglected heroes of the hurling and football fields.

Relive moments that have thrilled thousands down the decades and remember the games and names that the passage of time has failed to dim.

Available from all good bookshops nationwide.